Praise for
Everything / Nothing / Someone

* *New York Times* Editor's Choice * *Publishers Weekly* Best Nonfiction 2023 *
* *Kirkus* Best Nonfiction 2023 * Jennette McCurdy Book Club Pick *

"Remarkable . . . A timeless tale of surviving emotional neglect and mental illness; but it is also the story of a singular household filled with complex and exceptional artists, and the author's experience of inheriting their prodigious legacy. . . . Raw, filled with sorrow, dark humor and sharp observation."   —*New York Times Book Review*

"I don't know which is more stunning: the triumph of this life, or the triumph of this beautiful book. Or perhaps they are one and the same. Out of the ashes of a childhood that may have appeared shiny on its surface but was unnerving and profoundly lonely, Alice Carrière has made art. *Everything/Nothing/Someone* is a master class in memoir."   —Dani Shapiro, author of the *New York Times* bestseller *Inheritance*

"Spare and direct, with flashes of Didionesque elegance . . . The writing of this book and the presentation of Carrière's life is brutal and honest and funny and shocking. . . . One of the most compelling first-person memoirs I've read in a long time."   —Bret Easton Ellis, *Bret Easton Ellis Podcast*

"Extraordinary."   —Sarah Jessica Parker

"The writing is pure elegance."   —Lisa Taddeo

"Propulsive, intense, moving, and breathtakingly honest, this searing memoir about family ties, trampled boundaries, and mental illness is completely unforgettable. What a writer!"   —Molly Shannon, author of the *New York Times* bestseller *Hello, Molly!*

"Mind-blowing!"   —Lena Dunham

"I read this brilliant book in one mad gulp. The prose is like a fever dream; Alice Carrière is an amazing writer. What a story—from start to finish."
—Kate Christensen,
PEN/Faulkner award-winning author of *The Great Man*

"Stunning . . . What begins as a memoir about suffering and disconnection ultimately ends with forgiveness and gratitude."   —*The Observer* (UK)

"Extraordinary, relatable, beautiful . . . The do-or-die question of memoir—do we care?—is answered in the form of a direct pipeline to the reader's heart."   —*Minneapolis Star Tribune*

"A story of immense bravery and resilience. It is clear, too, that this book was written by an exceptional human being, one with a remarkable capacity for forgiveness and a keen ability to see 'love hidden in the heart of our failings and misfortunes.'"   —*Washington Post*

"Creatively exceptional . . . This isn't only about Carrière's life. It's also about how people make art and build family, how philosophy . . . intersects with lived experience, and how people try and fail to connect."
—*Booklist* (starred review)

"Carrière's surgically precise prose compresses her broken-glass experiences into hard diamond truths about family trauma and the mental health industry. This brutal, illuminating account reads like a contemporary *Girl, Interrupted*."   —*Publishers Weekly* (starred review)

"A spellbinding memoir."   —*Kirkus* (starred review)

"*Everything/Nothing/Someone* will stay in your mind for a long time."
—*Real Simple*

"Wild, dark, riveting . . . *Everything/Nothing/Someone* is held together, even elevated, by the force of Carrière's honesty, which lives in her prose."
—*Chapter 16*

Everything / Nothing / Someone

Alice Carrière

Spiegel
and Grau

For Gregory

S&G

Spiegel & Grau, New York
www.spiegelandgrau.com

Interior design by Meighan Cavanaugh

Library of Congress Cataloging-in-Publication Data Available Upon Request

ISBN 978-1-954118-55-3 (TP)
ISBN 978-1-954118-30-0 (ebook)

Printed in the United States of America

First Paperback Edition 2024
10 9 8 7 6 5 4 3 2 1

Wo aber Gefahr ist, wächst das Rettende auch. /
Where danger is, grows that which saves also.

—Hölderlin

To be mad is to be enraged is to be insane is to
be uncontrolled is to commit violent action is
to be fashionable, as of wind or as of sea.

—Jennifer Bartlett, *History of the Universe*

I / Everything

1.

My mother's disembodied voice came through the intercom. "Alice. Alice."

Or maybe it was "Alice! Alice!"

Or maybe it was "Alice? Alice?"

If I couldn't get to the phone fast enough, she'd hang up and then I couldn't call her back because she kept her phone on privacy mode. She could reach me, but I couldn't reach her. I had to go looking for her to find out what she wanted. By the time I found her she didn't seem to care why she had called me in the first place. Maybe my mother was just a voice in my head. Maybe I was just a figment of her imagination.

She had put her bed in the third-floor pool room, which had a fireplace and views of her lush garden. During the day she was below me, painting in one of her two downstairs studios, and at night she was above me in the pool room with her bottle of white wine and her books. My bedroom was below the pool room, on the second floor. The pool held ninety tons of water and I could feel it all balancing over my head. As I lay in bed at night, I pictured the ceiling giving way. I wondered at the shape that water would take once it was cut loose from its parameters, violently free.

The intercom connected us within the massive house in New York City. Our address was 134 Charles Street, between Greenwich and Washington Streets, in the West Village. We never got the numbers put on the door, so there was just a torn piece of paper with *134* written on it taped to the inside of the glass. It was a seventeen-thousand-square-foot, three-story building with a concrete facade, large windows, and steel doors. The building used to be a factory for manufacturing train parts back in the days when trains ran along the west side of the island.

On the ground floor was an office and a gigantic studio, which led, via a spiral staircase, to an even bigger basement studio, where my mother painted every day from 6 a.m. until 7 p.m., with a two-hour nap in the middle of the day. Between the office and the upper studio was a small room where my father lived after my mother kicked him out of her bed and before she kicked him out of the house. It was also where my uncle Roy came to die, where Max hemorrhaged, and Michael wept. It was where people came to lock themselves in and fall apart.

The building had huge windows that let the world see us as we moved through the house. Once, for one of her lavish parties, my mother had the staff light hundreds of votive candles and line them along the windows. In the middle of the party, firemen in full gear stormed into the house thinking it was burning down. A neighbor had misinterpreted the chic flicker of tiny candles as a deadly blaze, or perhaps they had seen something in us, identified a threat, that we couldn't see ourselves.

On the second floor was my bedroom; a second room, which I called "my study"; Nanny's room; the library with a fireplace and rolling ladders that extended to the ceiling for access to the walls of books; the kitchen where Katy the cook prepared our meals; and the living room with another fireplace and a wall of windows that looked out onto a garden. Nanny was Eileen Denys Maynard, who went by Denys but was only ever called Nanny. She existed to everyone like a paper doll Mary Poppins, two-dimensional, her life beginning and ending as the British governess paid to raise me. To me, she was a mother, but one who could be fired and disappear at any moment.

The garden on the second floor had fruit trees and a koi pond and a spiral staircase covered in roses that ascended to another garden with a grape arbor and apple trees. My mother liked to be surrounded by things that were growing because she always felt she was killing things, that if she touched something, it would die. There was a tool shed, like on a farm—I'd never been to a farm but I imagined that's what a farm was like—but right on top of the building in the middle of Manhattan. I liked to go in there and smell the fecund fustiness of the shed. The bags of fertilizer, rusting tools, and drying twigs created a tranquilizing fog that curled itself between me and the city below. Our world had all the disparate components of the world from which we were disconnected—steel and trees, fire and water, soil and decomposition.

There were no locks on the doors inside the house. The doors were just sheets of opaque glass in steel frames. Not even the bathroom doors had locks. Nanny once walked in on me masturbating and said, "Oh dear, I forgot you are a woman now," and walked out. Nanny once walked in on me cutting myself and cried. No locks meant I couldn't say, "KEEP OUT!" When I was six, I put a NO SMOKING sign on my door. It didn't work. My parents were both chain-smokers and their smoke entered the room before they did, making my eyes water and my throat itch. Only mythic beings could do that—make their presence known inside another person's body. The boundaries were porous.

In this house one could not tell the difference between fantasy and reality, art and object, parent and child. In this house, I couldn't tell what I was to my mother. In this house, I couldn't tell if I was my father's daughter, wife, or mother.

The bathroom attached to my bedroom had two entrances, one from the hallway and one from my room. When my mother had parties and I was in my room, people sometimes didn't notice the door connecting to my bedroom and didn't close it, so I could hear them pee. Sometimes I could even see them if the mirrored door reflected into my bedroom. I liked to watch them and I liked the moment when they realized they had been seen. There would be a fat pause as they tried to remember what sounds they had made or what parts of them had been exposed. They would clear their throat before they zipped or yanked up their pants, before fabric fell back over knees. In this house, our most secret selves and our most private moments were meant to be spectated and thought about. The toilet flushed with an intensity that made me jump every time. The taps of the sink and bathtub and shower were marked with *C* and *F*, for *chaud* and *froid*—the French words for "hot" and "cold." People unfamiliar with the house often scalded themselves when they washed their hands. The house forced you to move differently. It could be a bewildering, even harmful place if you didn't know its rules.

It was as if I lived inside my mother's mind. Everything had been designed especially for her and her alone. The space was built to accommodate the particularities and peculiarities of her gestures and habits. The house had many horizontal surfaces—daybeds, kitchen counters, spacious hearths, hardwood floors on which she could assume her typical recumbent pose: on her side, arm cocked to prop up her head while smoking or reading or talking on the phone. She spread herself out on these domestic plateaus like Manet's *Olympia*, and life lived itself around her. She had transformed this place from a factory into a fortress, an irresistible nexus of strangeness, luxury, and niche functionality—the architecture of my mother's desires. Everything around us had her in it. She designed her own jewelry (a gemologist who rode a unicycle and had worked with the Hope Diamond was her collaborator), the pieces so elaborate that they tested the limits of engineering. She designed her own very uncomfortable furniture. She designed and commissioned our drinking glasses, handblown cylinders so light you could hardly tell there was anything in your hand. The concept behind them was to create something as close to nothing as possible but still be functional. I hated them because I couldn't stop breaking them. And I had to use them because they were part of the fundamental routine of my life. Which meant destroying them would also have to be a fundamental routine of my life. Even the most utilitarian aspects of our lives were impossible to negotiate—conceptualized beyond utility, aestheticized beyond the physics of living.

Nothing on the walls of my room was my own, nothing had been selected by me. There were no posters or drawings, only my mother's art or her friends' art. Every year my mother redesigned my room as a surprise for my birthday. She hung things up or took them down, added or took away, rearranged and reconfigured until the room was new and unrecognizable. Every year I would identify the changes from a master list and note what had been taken away or added. This new room had new rules, demanded new ways of living. This was the new place I would be doing my homework, the new direction I slept, the new view I had when I opened my eyes, the new me, curated by my mother. I felt the excess of it—the new teddy bear, rocking chair, computer, vanity mirror, canopy bed, and glow-in-the-dark constellations stuck to the ceiling in the correct configuration by my mother's studio assistants. It set me trembling with excitement but also panic, the trepidation of meeting the girl this unfamiliar room belonged to.

Roaming through the house was the purebred Welsh terrier, Charlie of Charles Street, my mother had bought me. She had sent him away to be trained at a fancy pet boarding school, where he was abused, and he returned to us a broken animal with a behavioral repertoire of biting, cowering behind the toilet, and eating his own excrement. I learned quickly that I could not touch or go near him while he ate or he would turn on me, snarling, and try to bite me. I'd encounter him in the hallway shitting on the floor and I'd edge by him as he growled, knowing if I tried to interfere with him feasting on his feces he'd attack. I tried to be affectionate with him, but he seemed consumed by the imaginary war that waged inside of him.

The house was full of people. There was a cook, a housekeeper, a house manager, a gardener, a fish man who looked after the koi pond, a studio manager, the studio manager's assistant, three studio assistants, and a studio assistant intern who cleaned the brushes. They were like family, especially the studio assistants. They worked with my mother in her most intimate space—her studio. They knew her way of thinking, discussed math, patterns, what came next in a series of paintings. Their jobs had no clear parameters. They worked in the studio but they also decorated the house for Christmas, organized my birthday parties, played with me. When my uncle was dying in the downstairs bedroom, Nancy, one of the assistants, got him his marijuana. Ricky, the studio assistant intern, sat with him as he was dying. These people existed for my mother. To keep things moving, to keep things clean, to keep me tended to, to keep paint fresh and canvases stretched and the whole operation going with my mother at the center, head down, brush up, painting.

I would stand in her studio and look up at the massive canvases: a wall of fire devouring a tartan square, playing cards, a skeleton; the shape of a house made up of thousands of small dots; a man holding an axe. She had a real human skeleton in the studio named Lucy. I would hold Lucy's excarnated hand, caressing the bumps and curves of her fingers in a morbid mother-and-child tableau. I wondered at the fact that my mother could casually own a human skeleton. Just because she wanted it, she could summon a whole dead human to hang out in the studio, to be named and petted and painted. Later, when my friend's father, a war photographer, was crushed by the second tower on September 11, my mother was given the film from his camera, and she rendered his final moments in paint, huge and bright. My mother was powerful. She could take over someone's remains, own the imprint they had left on the world, the imprint the world had left on them, and make that imprint even bigger, immortal. When my mother became the only Westerner commissioned to paint a temple ceiling in Japan, she let me put paint on the soles of my feet and walk across a square of paper. The idea that my feet would be walking across a ceiling in a temple in Japan made me feel like my mother could perform magic. She could make me everlasting; the feet that would only be tiny for a fraction of time, those feet would run forever across a ceiling where prayers were being chanted. I looked at the square of paper after the painting was done and saw for a brief moment how my mother had seen me, that my mother had seen me.

I spent most of my time in 134 Charles Street alone in my room listening to audiobooks. I didn't have many friends. I didn't know how to behave around children. I listened to audiobooks all the time. I listened to them to go to sleep at night, while I showered, while I did my homework, while I played in my room, on my way to school. The words slid down my ears and lit me up, helped me recognize where everyone else ended and I began. Stories taught me the right words for things; if I had the right word for things, everything could feel okay. I populated my life with the Watsons in 1963, with Marty and Shiloh, with Louis the swan, with Jonas and his memories. When I listened, I recognized my friends, I recognized myself. I had mastery over these spaces, these rooms built out of language. I could invite words in and I could say, "KEEP OUT!" I knew these worlds and I knew their rhythms and rules. I knew how Ron Rifkin pronounced certain words, where he paused to breathe, the exact inflection that came before the big reveal, and even though I knew to expect it, it thrilled me every time. I could say, "Aw, man!" in unison with LeVar Burton. These were disembodied voices too, but they didn't hang up if I couldn't get there fast enough; they let me turn them on and off again whenever I wanted. They could reach me, and I could reach them.

When I wasn't listening to audiobooks, I thought about myself in the third person. Walking down the street to school I would think, "She is walking down the street. It is raining. The rain falls on her jacket." I turned myself into words and my life into a story. Years later, when I didn't recognize my own face in the mirror, when my body didn't feel like my own, I would again recite myself to myself, narrating myself into existence, trying to locate myself in my story.

The characters in the story of 134 Charles Street were rich, brilliant, loud, drunk, high, beautiful, careless, reckless, genius, gluttonous, well-dressed. Anna Wintour dropped off clothes, Steve Martin joked at the table, Wynton Marsalis played trumpet in the first-floor studio, Joan Didion sipped vodka-on-the-rocks in the garden, Al Gore won votes in our living room after bomb-sniffing dogs determined it was free of explosives, Merce Cunningham shuffled gracefully through the upper studio, Susan Sarandon and Julia Roberts compared colonoscopy stories over brunch at the dining room table. Starting at the age of seven, it was my job to tell the story of 134 Charles Street. "Would you like a tour?" I would ask in my Bonpoint dress to every guest who arrived at the extravagant parties my mother threw. I brought them through the studios, the gardens, and the pool room, naming the artists and designers for them. I was good at talking about where and how we lived; I just had no idea who I was talking about.

I first cut when I was seven. My mother would throw pool parties for my entire class of twenty kids, all of whom made merciless fun of me in school and out. I only ever hung out with adults. I'd stay late after school to visit with my teachers, asking them questions about their lives. I was excellent at anticipating what adults wanted from me, but I just couldn't read my classmates. Every year, they would descend on my house, invading my fortress. One year I walked into my room to get away from them and everything that belonged on my shelves was on the floor, much of it broken. We had just gotten Charlie and all my stuffed animals had been crammed into his crate. I couldn't see the floor. I felt woozy and faint. Adrenaline burned the underside of my skin, heating up the surface of me until it pulsed. I held my breath and felt an immense pressure against my entire body and an unfolding outward from deep within, as if I could be crushed and explode at the same time. I was angry, I was sad, I was terrified at how anger and sadness felt inside me. I needed to get the feelings out. I found the Swiss Army knife my father had given me. I pried open the biggest blade and pressed the edge of it against my palm. I pressed and dragged until I saw blood. Instantly my heartbeat receded from my ears, tucked itself calmly back into my rib cage, and my mind folded itself into a neat origami brain—clean, calm lines. The wild pitching was replaced by a thick stillness, the laceration a hot horizon, steadying and orienting me. It had come to me so easily, so naturally, and it had worked. I didn't know how I had known to cut myself to feel better; I had never heard about self-harm. With a tiny, shiny blade I learned I could unlock a doorway that led to a place that was entirely my own, even if I could only stay there for a moment within those seconds of pain. I didn't yet understand that the rage and sorrow I felt were not from mean kids. The feelings emerged from deeper deposits, cavernous compartments where the disembodied voices of my parents echoed, telling me things I shouldn't know, chanting the desires and fears that ruled them, until I couldn't tell the difference between my voice and theirs. Each cut organized into legible symbols the confusion of cravings—my father's, my mother's, my own—that made me feel like too much and eventually nothing. As a teenager, when I started cutting regularly, it felt like a passion, like a calling. Me upstairs, crosshatching my skin with a razor blade, my mother downstairs, crosshatching canvases with oil paint, each of us telling our story.

IT WAS HARD TO KNOW what was true in my house. There were no absolute truths because there were endless ways to say something, innumerable angles from which to see, so many media with which to transform things. At any moment something could be what it was and also the exact opposite. 134 Charles Street was a place of abundance and of absence. The kitchen had a pantry that was stocked with extra everything. Four bags of Cape Cod Potato Chips next to five bottles of maple syrup next to four boxes of Walker's Shortbread. I'd stand in the laundry room and stare at the repeating orange jugs of Tide detergent that stretched out along the shelves, a promise that things never ended. I didn't recognize this muchness for the extraordinary privilege it was. I didn't realize not everyone else had what we had, or that what we had was not an inherent quality of who we were. The excess felt like an exoskeleton, an impermeable shell that was naturally part of us. It never occurred to me to feel grateful, just like I wasn't grateful for the skin stretching across my bones.

My mother was, in her chronic extravagance, somehow always almost broke. Once, she came into my room, sat on my bed, stared over my head, and told me she had made two million dollars. Months later she came into my room, stared at her lit cigarette, and told me we were broke. She was a woman who didn't know her own social security number, how much money she had in the bank, the grand total of all the bills for all her extravagances. She didn't know how to manage the resources that, in the '70s, '80s, and '90s swelled and swelled and would later, from her profligacy, drain away. She only knew how to paint. She worked constantly, unflaggingly, and that meant that at any moment we could have everything or we could have nothing. Everything could change at any moment. Money, a parent, a mind, could all disappear.

I wasn't taught anything about real life. I knew the locations of Fra Angelico frescoes, I could recite all the lyrics to Bertolt Brecht's *The Threepenny Opera* in German, I could name all the famous examples of Gothic architecture. At fifteen, I still didn't know how to use a tampon because no one thought to tell me and I hadn't thought to ask. There were no lessons or tips or admonishments. My bed was made for me every morning, a towel was whisked away and washed every time I used one, my underwear was ironed. I floated around 134 Charles Street and didn't leave a trace. Not in creases in my clothes, nor on the walls or floors of my room, where even my mess couldn't stick. Later, I would do everything I could to make something stick to me, to the walls of my body and the sloping, slanting floors of my mind, until I finally understood the place that could contain me was the page.

Once, at my mother's Christmas tree decorating party, when I was old enough for the subsequent reaction to be inappropriate, embarrassing, strange, I dropped an ornament and it broke. I stared down at it, paralyzed. The only thing I could think of to say was, "What do I do?" My mother's assistant and a family friend were standing next to me. Their eyes widened with confused alarm. There was a pause, a heavy silence saturated by the colors of the lights and the density of my ignorance. "You get a broom and clean it up," one of them said. I could hear the amazement glazing her voice. My mind was blank. Destruction came easy, but what to do after, how to clean it up and move on, was a confounding proposition. In a house with no locks, in a family with no rules, in a mind with no limits, it was in the moment of demolition that I felt most at home.

The house that had been a structure for putting things together turned into the place in which we slowly came apart. In her work, my mother was obsessed with the archetypal house image—a square with a triangle on top. The most elementary, identifiable shape that indicated so much more: house, home, family, history. My mother rendered this silhouette in ink, in pastel, in Testors paint, in charcoal, in oils. It was big, it was small, it was crosshatched or composed of dots. It was chopped in half, it was dissolved, it was splintered. It was repeated over and over, as if she were trying to learn the meaning of the word, decipher its secrets.

My mother's muchness was matched by a grandiose but remote generosity. Our house became a repository for people fallen on hard times. Whether dying of AIDS, escaping an abusive parent or partner, facing poverty, or descending the spiral of manic depression, people would show up at our house and stay. I would be excited and curious about each new addition to the household and would focus all my thoughts and feelings on them, growing to love them as I walked by their rooms while they slept or wept. I liked to sit and talk to these people about their pain and their fears, nodding my head and thinking how big and unwieldy life could feel. I loved these people who seemed so lost, and I hoped our house could keep them safe. My mother cared from far away. She was not the person to bring the soup; she paid someone to bring the soup. But that was her way of showing that she wanted you to have soup. Later, when I would require ministration, my mother would lavish this care-by-proxy onto me in the form of psychiatrists and their pills, with the instruction to take them unquestioningly. Later, in the moments when I felt like I was disappearing, I wanted my mother to talk to me, to sit with me, to touch me. I craved a warmth that existed so deep inside her that it couldn't reach me. It couldn't even reach her. I wanted her to say, "Alice?

Alice?" and mean it, unspooling the question mark until it made four walls and a triangle roof where she would finally invite me in. I wanted her busy hands that built everything that surrounded me to help me prop up the walls of myself. Maybe she thought 134 Charles Street would magically protect us, that nothing could get to us. Except she didn't realize that the thing that wanted me dead was already inside the house.

2.

My mother, Jennifer Bartlett, broke onto the New York art scene in the 1970s. She was born in 1941 in Long Beach, California, to a bitter, beautiful, emotionally closed off mother, whose career in fashion illustration had been thwarted by my mother's arrival, and a charming alcoholic pipeline contractor with a secret second family. At five, she stood on the beach and declared to the expanse that she would be a great artist. She had always wanted to get away and she succeeded, graduating from Mills College then moving east to get her MFA at Yale. She married a handsome psychiatry student and then divorced him to move to New York City and pursue her career. She took a teaching gig at the School of Visual Arts and rented a loft on Greene Street in SoHo, joining a social milieu that came to include the artists Jonathan Borofsky, Joel Shapiro, Richard Serra, Barry Le Va, Alex Katz, Brice Marden, Lynda Benglis, Susan Rothenberg, Elizabeth Murray, Chuck Close, and Jasper Johns. "I was just crazy about New York," she said. "I remember the first time I got there, being knocked down by a big, fat woman when I was trying to hail a taxi. For some reason, this appealed to me enormously." She was catapulted to art world fame in 1976 with a piece called *Rhapsody*. In the *New York Times*, the art critic John Russell called it "the most ambitious single work of art to have come my way since I moved to New York." The piece, he said, "enlarges our notions of time, of memory, of change, and of painting itself." It was over 150 feet long and composed of 987 one-foot-by-one-foot steel plates with a baked enamel grid silk-screened onto them, a medium she had invented, inspired by New York subway signs. *Rhapsody* was enormous—in size and ambition. When it later hung in the Museum of Modern Art atrium, it took up all three walls. She wanted to make a piece that "had everything in it."

After hitting it big, Jennifer Bartlett bought her first mink coat, slapped on giant sunglasses and lipstick that was always crooked, sprayed on too heavily the Fracas de Robert Piguet perfume she ordered directly from Paris, and was dubbed "the Joan Collins of SoHo" by *New York* magazine. A 1985 twelve-page profile in the *New Yorker*, appropriately titled "Getting Everything In," described her "disconcertingly direct manner, her helmet of close-cropped dark hair, and her habit of cracking jokes at her own expense" and wondered how California could have "produced an artist of her energy, analytic rigor, and undissembled ambition." She had become, at that time, "one of the most widely exhibited artists of her generation." Her best friend, the artist Elizabeth Murray, described her as "sort of a brat. She was outspoken, and she seemed very sure of herself, and she made people angry—especially men." Another friend described her as "a monster pain." An article written by Joan Juliet Buck in *Vanity Fair* declared that "there is no actress glamorous enough to play Jennifer Bartlett. She believes in hot lunches, good clothes, and champagne. And she never stops working."

She was beautiful in a smudged way, crooked bottom teeth behind imperfect lipstick, short dark hair, and crystalline blue eyes that had an unexpected softness to them. She brought her own atmosphere with her wherever she went—a cloud of perfume, a cloud of smoke, a cloud of utter fucklessness. She had a loudness that came not just from the amplitude of sound waves, but from an orogenic pressure that brought the hilt of her desires—for something to stop or continue, to be given or leave her in peace—thrusting up through the moment, separating what was not about her (not much) and what was about her (much more). She was the center of attention all the time, but the way she tugged on the spotlight seemed protective, as if she were trying to conceal herself with the glare. There was a vulnerability about her that revealed itself precisely in the moments most marked by crassness, by will, by stubbornness; a clumsiness to her attentional gluttony. She was extremely guarded. There was no one she opened up to. And she couldn't figure out affection. I received the occasional awkward pat, as if she were checking to see that all parts of me were still there, adjusting or confirming me, but never reaching me. When we did hug, she would cough out a laugh as our bodies touched, or a sarcastic "oh" would loop out of her, and I felt it, an overstuffed pillow between us, blocking the contact, the connection. She had zero ability to speak about emotions and often bit off the moment with the glib announcement that she "felt like working" or "felt like not feeling," amputating the sentiment at the joint. The *New Yorker* quoted her as saying she "developed an infinite capacity for work and none for reflection." She worked all the time, and it was all she wanted to do.

I watched my mother as she lived her life around me, passing by on her way down to the studio or up to her bedroom and down again in her fog of perfume and smoke to work or attend a party. I read her traces like letters. I knew this story; I was familiar with the narrative of her goings-away. She was downstairs or upstairs doing and thinking about special, mysterious things. Maybe, if I became special and mysterious too, she would turn her eyes to me. But later, when the mysteries of my own mind proved nearly lethal, when I became special with madness, she would avoid my gaze even more.

MY FATHER WAS A European sex symbol. Mathieu Carrière had been working in film and television since he was thirteen years old, acting in English, French, German, Italian, and Spanish with Orson Welles, Isabelle Huppert, Brigitte Bardot, Marlon Brando, Romy Schneider, and Antonio Banderas. After a brief career as a teenage equestrian vaulting champion, he left Lübeck, a small town forty-five minutes outside Hamburg, Germany, in 1969 to live in Paris, performing in drag in cabarets, bedding Princess Caroline of Monaco, attending philosophy classes at the Sorbonne, and becoming the protégé of the famous philosopher Gilles Deleuze. He tripped on acid in front of Visconti and Alain Delon at Domaine de Monthyon. He and Andy Warhol drew different shaped penises on the backs of Polaroids at Angelina's in Paris. "Some are curved," said Andy, "and maybe some are even like spirals."

My father spoke six languages, wrote a book about the poet Heinrich von Kleist, and was awarded the Légion d'Honneur, the highest French order of merit. He was six-foot-one and thin, had wavy light-brown hair that would turn white at forty, penetrating blue eyes, and puffy lips that gave the impression of sensuality and innocence. He was never still, always smoking, drinking, playing speed chess, inhaling cocaine, exhaling outrageous stories or wild theories. His body couldn't handle inertia; he rolled his thumb over his fingers over and over, as if compulsively checking that they were still attached to his body. He was loud, explosive, disruptive. He left people jarred and exhilarated, offended and compelled. He asked personal, invasive questions, and people would respond by telling him the worst things that had ever happened to them, things they had never told anyone before.

My parents met at a dinner party in New York in 1980, when my mother was thirty-nine and my father was thirty. He made her smoked salmon sandwiches and piled them onto her plate. She lit a Marlboro Red and inhaled as she ate.

"Shouldn't you do one at a time?" my father asked.

"I like to smoke and eat at the same time," my mother replied, pungent oil and thick smoke on her lips.

At dinner, she was seated next to another man named Matthew. My father fixed his attention on her and asked, loudly from across the table, "Which Matthew do you want?"

"You," she announced, and brought him back to her SoHo loft.

After my mother's success with *Rhapsody*, there was only one goal left to achieve. As the psychiatric files from my later hospitalization explained: *Alice was born to a mother with two driving ambitions: to be a successful artist and to have a child.* After years of trying to get pregnant without success and a failed adoption attempt, my mother learned, at forty-three, she was pregnant.

As the doctor performed the cesarean, my father played a word game with my mother.

"Name a French writer who has the same name as a piece of meat," he said.

"Colette," said my mother.

"Not bad, but that's côtelette," he said.

"Chateaubriand," the surgeon said and pulled me out, as if I were the answer to every riddle.

We spent the first four years of my life in Paris, with many trips across the Atlantic on the Concorde. My mother would hold her Abyssinian cat, Kanga, on her lap and feed her caviar. The apartment was a spacious penthouse on Rue Vavin, with terraces and a skylighted studio where my mother painted. A spiral staircase led up to my parents' bedroom. It was steep with huge gaps, making it impossible for me to access their room, but I didn't live there anyway. Nanny and I lived in a small apartment next to theirs. I spent my days with Nanny. She took me to the Jardin du Luxembourg, where she'd watch me ride the carousel. We pushed wooden boats across the pond in the center of the park and named the ducks that swam there. We watched the old men smoke cigars and play boules, listening to the tock of the metal balls and their rough laughter. She brought me to La Coupole, where I sat at the bar, my legs swinging, and pulled cold, booger-like snails out of their tiny black helixed homes with a pin and ate them. One day, my father brought home a crab as big as my head and put it in our bathtub as a joke. I was terrified of crabs and wet my pants because I refused to pee next to that monster that waved its claws and made skittering noises as it tried to escape.

While Nanny and I went about our routines, in our little apart-ment, with our little delights and disappointments, my father and mother tried to exist together. My father watched her paint and direct her assistants to build a giant replica of a house, cut it in half, and then put it back together again. He was in awe of her. It was entirely her world, he'd later say, occasionally visited by him and me. Everything she did, she did alone. He watched her neutralize every-thing with work—her feelings, her environment, her moods. My father, busy playing speed chess and doing cocaine, would disappear for days, returning home irritable and wired. He wrote, produced, and directed a film about a German pianist addicted to cocaine and gam-bling and married to a successful architect. In the movie, called *Fool's Mate*, the wife, named "Alice," kicks him out to protect their daugh-ter, "Isabelle" (my middle name), and he confesses to a murder he didn't commit to get out of his debts. He told me later he made the movie so the ending wouldn't happen in real life, a creative prophy-laxis, bending life into art to bend life. I played his daughter, Nanny played the nanny, and in the role of the main character's mistress my father cast the woman he had been having an affair with. My mother designed the costumes, which meant she had to dress the woman my father was fucking. When my mother found out, they sat at Le Select, the bar around the corner from the apartment, and weighed their options. My mother decided they should stay together and never mention it again.

3.

We moved to New York City and into 134 Charles Street in September 1990, when I was five years old. My father spent his days writing screenplays and playing chess in Washington Square Park, making friends with his opponents—the drunks, hustlers, and unhoused who spent most of their lives curled up on the benches or hunched over the concrete chess tables. My mother's crowd found him very cute, and her friends joked that she had married him because he was so photogenic.

My mother started therapy with Dr. Viola Bernard. She drank too much, had relationship problems, and had a troubling memory about walking in on her father fucking a family friend. Under Dr. Bernard's care—intense psychotherapy sessions and hypnosis—my mother began to be flooded with what Dr. Bernard told her were repressed memories, horrific scenes of ritualized abuse and murder of children at the hands of a couple, Bertie and Russell, who were family friends from her youth. Dr. Bernard encouraged her to "remember," disclose as much as she could, and write about it in journals. My mother, haunted, hunted for clues in her past. She hired a private detective who couldn't find anything. She tracked down Bertie and Russell's phone number and confronted them over the phone. She was convinced that her parents had been complicit and confronted her mother, Joanne, who told her it was all nonsense. She believed her younger sibling, Jessica, had been raped by Bertie and Russell as an infant. She asked Jessica, a trans woman, if her gender dysphoria could have been a result of the abuse she believed they had both endured. Jessica said no but remembered having sleepovers at Bertie and Russell's and that there was not an extra bed for her, so she had slept in their bed. She also remembered their mother telling her that she could never go over there again. Something could have been happening, but no one could confirm any of my mother's claims. My mother told her friends what she had discovered in therapy. They recalled her matter-of-factly describing child rape and murder in a flat affect as she sipped glass after glass of white wine. When speaking to me years later, my godmother Paula would wonder, "If all these children were going missing, where were the news articles? Where were the missing persons reports?" "How could they have been so well-organized and keep it so secret?" another friend wondered. "It didn't seem possible or plausible. But she really believed it."

I learned my mother's story when I was eleven. I was spying on her for my father. She had filed for divorce when I was six, starting a custody battle that would last six years. When we were all in the middle of it, my father told me to look for a list of witnesses that my mother might call to testify. I looked in her closet and found a journal. I read an entry about my mother giving my father a blow job and that, in the middle of the act, she'd had a "flashback" to being on a boat with Bertie and Russell. Russell had pushed her head under the water as she threw up and he said, "You're feeding the fishes." The sides of my mouth twitched into the inappropriate smile I made when I felt the barbed worm of unease twist around inside me. When my mother came up from the studio to have her lunch, I told her what I had found. We sat in my bedroom, and she told me how a married couple who were friends of her parents had used her in a sex cult. They had raped her and her one-and-a-half-year-old brother. They took them on trips on their boat, where they had orgies with other children. They used the Black children of maids who worked in the neighborhood in ritualized sex games. They murdered a seven-year-old Black boy, who they called "Monkey Boy," through erotic asphyxiation and made my mother bury the body on the beach at night, telling her that if she ever told anyone she would be thrown into prison for life.

She told me this story in a very straightforward way and then went off to take her nap. She told me the story as if I already knew it, as if we'd been through all of this already, and I sat and listened as if it were one of my audiobooks. She didn't tell me how she felt about any of it or ask how I might feel about it. She didn't cry and her voice didn't strain against any feelings I could discern. I sat and stared at her, thrilled that she was sitting in my room talking to me. She told me that the series she had painted called "Earth Paintings"—some of which were hanging in our house—was about the abuse. My mother left me in my room thinking about my father getting a blow job and how to spell erotic asphyxiation.

I stood in front of one of the paintings. My mother had done several versions of each image—in oils on a large canvas, on a medium canvas, in gouache on paper, in pastels, in ink, until there were 108 of them. Over and over and over, she painted and drew and smeared and shaped and formed and brought to life these memories that had been brought to life inside of her. For days and weeks and months, she dragged her terrors into the world for everyone to see and froze them there forever. Maybe she was frozen in them too. I stared at the painting showing "Monkey Boy" being buried on the beach. I was suddenly able to see into my mother's mind. I could be there with her on the beach, being forced to bury a body. I could be her. I stood in front of that painting and imagined all the feelings she must have felt. I understood the power of not feeling, too. Of being able to tell your story with paint or with words and then just going to sleep.

I WOULD LATER LEARN that my mother was most likely a victim of the Satanic Panic, a moral hysteria that swept the nation in the '80s and '90s. Unsubstantiated claims of children being used in Satanic rituals involving sex and murder were leveled against daycare workers and parents. Patients in psychotherapy were persuaded by overzealous clinicians that they had repressed memories of unspeakable abuse involving incest, pedophilia, and murder, and needed to uncover them. The science of recovered memory therapy would be debunked but the damage remained—families torn apart by accusations, patients tormented by the continued belief in these persuasive inventions or the awareness of their fiction. My mother's memories were likely false, just stories. But "just stories" were powerful. Just stories led her far, far away from people, and killed off something inside her.

My father was negotiating his own indoctrination. For ten years, as the protégé of French philosopher Gilles Deleuze, he had been involved in the most anthropologically anarchistic, mind-boggling philosophical theories he had ever encountered in his life. It was not only a philosophy, he would explain, it was a militant activist move-ment to change the world based on a theory of desire. The only thing that existed was the constant production of desire, which was over-flowing, and state and capitalism and laws were all ways to tame it and put it into oppressive structures. Deleuze and his students believed they were radical revolutionaries. In 1977, a group of influ-ential French intellectuals penned an open letter to French Parliament calling for the decriminalization of sex between adults and minors. Among them was Gilles Deleuze. An excerpt from my father's jour-nals, written when I was three, captured the type of thinking the

movement fostered: *There is a possibility of a non-abusive, not traumatiz-*
ing sexuality between children and grown-ups. Nakedness and tenderness and
relaxation with the body of the other person is possible. My daughter does not
excite me. I think the fear of the people who make the rules is that their own
repressed desires could come up, which makes them see that area as an inappro-
priate field between a child and an adult. Maybe it's their way of keeping
their own incestuous desires in check. My father's flirtation with this ide-
ology would soon encounter the full force of the American puritanism
he reviled, and his attempts, in the face of this convergence, to shore
up his identity with these theories would leave me ever more confused
and abstracted.

My mother, in the care of Dr. Bernard, saw transgression everywhere. She became terrified of my father's behavior around me. One
night, drunk, she came into my room and saw my father in bed with
me under a blanket, reading me a book. Screaming, she ripped the
blanket off and hauled him out of the room. The next day she banished
him downstairs, to the small first-floor room between the office and
the studios. The next night, I woke up and sneaked down the stairs
to visit my father. I stood under the glowing exit sign, a remnant from
when the building was a warehouse, which hung above the large steel
door that separated upstairs from downstairs. The house was always
kept very cold and I was chilly in my nightgown. I felt for the doorknob
in the dark. The frigidness felt magical, the frosty bite on my palm
marking the breaching of another world. I held my breath and turned
the knob. As if my hand had exerted some powerful sorcery, alarms
began screeching all through the house, convulsing the cold air around
me. I felt the screaming in my body, the noise grabbing me by the
arms and shaking me, trying to tell me something I wasn't listening
to. I stood at the threshold of my mother's and father's worlds, a limen
loaded with alarms, and shook with fear and confusion.

A few months later, my mother began the divorce proceedings that
would last six years. Those years would be crowded with lawyers and

witnesses and judges and forensic psychologists. My mother told me nothing about the trial. My father told me everything—what he was accused of, how everyone was out to get us, what to say to the judge. I stared at the stenographer in the judge's chambers while I recited what my father had told me, her face wooden, the chittering of her machine seeming to emanate from inside her, like she was a wind-up toy. I would keep the judge's decree in a manila envelope for decades, and it grew yellow and faded as I read it over and over, trying to figure out what was true.

My mother's lawyers charged my father with "a variety of inappropriate conduct," which included: climbing into my crib at night, lying on the sofa with his hand in my underpants, taking me swimming in the ocean beyond my depth and without a life jacket, putting me on a horse without a helmet, giving me a cartoon book with "inappropriate" images like "a man masturbating, a woman engaged in a series of salacious movements," keeping porn in his room, kissing me on the lips when we said goodbye, feeding me with his fingers as if I were an infant, exchanging chewing gum mouth to mouth, taking my underwear with him when he traveled, showing me films he had been in that were inappropriate for a young child, giving me knives and cigarette lighters as gifts, letting me, at seven, give him subcutaneous injections for a medical condition he had, and leaving me alone on Manhattan street corners while he went to buy cigarettes and a newspaper. Some of the charges I remembered and some I didn't. I remembered all the times—when I was five, six, and seven—when I stood awkwardly with a stranger who had been dispatched with my care while my father made a phone call or strode into a deli. I remembered that little gummy nugget being pushed into my mouth by his tongue, receiving it slick from his saliva, bursting with our liquids as I started to chew. I remembered bending over his stomach, sliding a needle into his flesh, holding my breath as I slowly depressed the syringe and injected him, the bruises that rose to the surface the next day. I remembered watching him pack the little square of my underwear printed with the days of the week or cat faces into his suitcase. I did not remember his hands down my pants. "No charges of sexual abuse were made," read the documents, but people started to view my father with suspicion, and reprobation and rumors clung like barnacles to our lives. A story began to circulate that my father had said that a daughter's first sexual experience should be with her father. According to my father, he had been at a dinner party speaking to an anthropologist friend of his who was telling him about an academic paper that described mothers in Japan giving blow jobs to their sons before exams. My father jokingly exclaimed, "Incest is best," which Nanny overheard and told my mother. From father to Nanny to mother to family friends, this story reached me as the edict "A daughter's first sexual experience should be with her father." It was something I would have lodged in my head for decades. My father fought the allegations. Some of them were misunderstandings or overreactions, and some were intentional exaggerations and fabrications by lawyers. The porn magazines that had been found by the housekeeper and reported to my mother were brought into court. The judge went through each one, concluding at the end of his inspection that since they were all images of middle-aged women (my father had a penchant for older ladies) they were okay but should not have been kept in the house. A forensic psychologist had to phone a colleague in Europe to confirm that Europeans did in fact kiss on the lips and sometimes took baths with their kids. But my father was coming apart under the constant scrutiny and condemnation.

My visits with my father—to the apartment he had rented nearby or to Europe every alternating vacation and half of every summer—were monitored by court-appointed supervisors. Nanny was the first court-appointed supervisor. Then came my babysitter Pem, who looked after me on Nanny's days off. Then came Pem's cousin. Then my mother's nineteen-year-old studio assistant whom no one knew very well. Then my third-grade assistant teacher who was allergic to all fruits and vegetables and who screamed at me for making faces when I was tonguing a loose tooth. The supervisors were the embodiment of that alarm system between my mother and father's worlds—constant reminders that we were not a normal family, that there was something wrong.

I didn't think anything was wrong with my father or how we were together. When he was with me, he told me stories all the time—stories he made up, stories from the books he was reading, stories from Greek mythology, stories from philosophy, stories from psychology, stories from history (of art, architecture, humankind). He seemed to know everything and wanted to share it with me. He played games with me constantly, something my mother refused to do because she was, according to her, "too competitive." He challenged me to come up with words in different languages with as many meanings as possible, to solve riddles, to say a sentence with the emphasis each time on a different word to change the meaning. He tipped matchsticks onto the table and told me to make a house by moving only one matchstick. He wanted to know everything about everyone, and I watched him ask strangers who lit his cigarette about their childhood, invite cab drivers and waiters to dinner, drill into the world and soak himself, and me, with what came rushing out. Along with his games and stories, my father told me everything about the trial. He told me often about American prudishness and my mother projecting her past onto him. I watched his face scrunch and slacken as he told me all the ways he was being accused and attacked, his features like an EKG, recording the electrical impulses of distortion that formed the rhythm of our lives. His eyes would fill with tears as he lit another cigarette and ran his thumb over his fingers. My mother told me nothing, asked me no questions.

My allegiance was to my father. I would follow my mother around the house as she poured her coffee or wine, as she worked in the garden, as she looked for a book in the library, and bombard her with questions and accusations. "Why do you hate Dad? Why do you want to take me away from him? Fuck your American prudishness," I'd say to her back.

"It's complicated," she'd say. "You sound like your father."

"Good," I'd say. I didn't understand that she was terrified, afraid to do the wrong thing, say the wrong thing, touch me the wrong way. So she just didn't. She withdrew into the places over which she had mastery, exiling herself to the worlds she reigned over with confidence—her studio and her bedroom. Downstairs in her studio, if she made a mistake she could just paint over it. And upstairs there was no such thing as a wrong book read or a wrong cigarette smoked. But her child was an entirely different medium; her child was a photogram—the interplay of object, light, and time resulting in an irreversible exposure. The things she believed had been done to her had marked her irrevocably, and she was sure that she would somehow, through proximity, mar me as permanently.

As the custody case continued, as I was brought to forensic psychologists and met with the judge, and had it all explained to me by my father, I became desperate. When I was seven, and my mother and I were visiting family friends at their house in Connecticut; I started shouting at her in their kitchen, telling her all the ways she was destroying my father's and my life. She stood, arms at her sides, helpless. Interpreting her helplessness as indifference, I grabbed a knife from the knife block on the kitchen counter. "If you don't let me have more time with Dad I'll kill myself," I screamed. She moved toward me, trying to take the knife away. I ran. I ran through the opulent rooms, the cream carpets so thick they muted the sounds of our movements, threatening to stab myself as my mother's friends looked on. My mother ran after me, begging me to put the knife down. Finally, she was pursuing me. And all it took was a knife held against my body.

Over my father's objections, I was sent to be observed by forensic psychologists who watched me play with anatomically correct dolls, took notes, and then wrote up reports about me. I was sent to a child psychologist for treatment. After my first session with Dr. Shore, I told my mother and father that the doctor had hit me. My father was furious. My mother didn't believe me and bribed me with an electric toothbrush to go back. I went back. And since I was back, I figured nothing bad had really happened, maybe nothing had happened, because I wouldn't be back there if it had. I was learning to doubt myself. The unbelievable story of being hit by my child psychologist felt so real—I could recall his arm whizzing through the air, the full dimensions of my smallness as he towered over me—but there would always be a part of me that wondered if I had fabricated the memory from the raw material of my father's recalcitrance. I had no idea what was true.

My father kept journals where he wrote down everything that happened every day. During disagreements with me he would take one out, flip to a page, and read out loud what had really happened. "No, you did not ask me to watch a movie in the afternoon," he would say, holding the pages open and gesturing to that day's entry. I'd squint my eyes and try to decipher his writing, which was sometimes in German, sometimes in English, sometimes in French. I'd search for the words to match the version of reality I had in my head and, not finding them, I'd doubt myself.

Nanny also kept journals about everything that happened when I was with my father. Her journals told the story of a seven-year-old who stayed up until midnight, drank beer, never took a bath (*not for a week straight*), and was at the mercy of her father's erratic moods and mercurial family. *I wish I could tell M what a blank blank human he is*, she wrote. *I have never disliked someone so much or had such little regard for them. Yet I have to deal with him. In my heart I am glad he is hurt because he has so little thought for anyone else, from his mother to the people he works with, unless it's to his advantage. Poor Alice. I can see her getting hurt and so cross. It is frightful to think one person can make life so difficult for so many people, yet we do nothing. That is the worst part for me. The fact M gets away with it. Such ego. I am so angry I cannot sleep.* Everyone told a different version of what happened, what I needed, and who I was. Everyone seemed like a credible narrator, but how could so many things be true at the same time? I was at the center of so many stories, piles of documents that would only grow larger—notebooks and court judgments and psychiatric files and eventually even a psychological case study— that claimed to tell me who I was, but in whose pages I disappeared.

There were moments that threatened my allegiance to my father. My mother took me to Japan when I was seven. She had been commissioned by the Homan-ji Temple, in Chōshi-shi, Japan, to design and paint their ceiling, and she brought me with her for the unveiling. I accompanied her everywhere she went, she in her blue and white yukata—a cotton summer kimono—and me in my white one with red cranes on it. We sat next to each other at the elaborate breakfasts the hotel served every morning—low tables piled with endless kinds of fish, raw and roasted whole, blue and white china, black lacquered bowls holding soup, large, rough-hewn bowls that looked like a giant had scooped them straight out of black rock. She took me to a hot spring near a famous noodle shop. We sat in the steaming water as people threw leftover noodles into the adjacent stream, the white squiggles of noodle a pop-art augmentation of the current's ripples. We got lost in a forest together before eventually emerging onto a mountain road and hitchhiking back to the hotel. I watched her closely as she navigated this foreign world with confidence, as she invited me to explore it with her. Far away from the site of our turmoil, in a place neither of us had ever been, wearing matching clothes, it was as if I were seeing her for the first time. Then my father arrived. His lawyer had called him and told him that my mother couldn't just unilaterally make decisions for me and my father should respond, so he bought a ticket and followed us to Japan. The monks had prepared a special ceremony for my mother, and my father insisted on being there. The monks chanted and scattered leaf-shaped pieces of thick paper painted in gold as we knelt on the floor. I watched my mother move through the ceremony. She knew when to bow and when to smile, when to speak and when to be quiet. I had never seen her follow rules and pay attention to the other people around her. There was a stillness and an ease in her that amazed and perplexed me as I watched her accept a string of carved prayer beads from a monk. She seemed content and competent, and I felt myself admiring her. Then something hit my leg. My father had started rolling Mentos across the floor to me while the monks chanted. We were kneeling in a line so he had to bend forward and roll the candy past my mother and her esteemed guests. I was very embarrassed. My insides seized every time I saw those fat white discs spinning toward me. I didn't want people to think that I condoned this game or that I was bored, but I was afraid that my father would be even more disruptive if I didn't try to catch the mints. I let them come to rest in the crescent of my palm, putting them in a little pile, each time hoping it would be the last. I could see the glances, near-bursting with acid disapproval, that my mother and the other guests were directing at my father. I felt very old and tired, as if my father were my ungovernable child. In that moment, I wanted to follow the rules. I wanted to separate myself from him, make it clear that his desires were not mine.

My father had rented an apartment near 134 Charles Street so he could be with me when he was in the United States. He got me a black hooded rat to keep at his place. The white spots reminded me of the reflection of clouds in water, so I named it Claude after Monet. We thought it was a fat male but Claude turned out to be a pregnant female and soon we had nine rats. I would put a rat in my sleeve and let it crawl up my arm, around my shoulders, and back out through my other sleeve. Nanny was alarmed when she watched me change clothes and saw bright red rat scratches all over my torso. One day, I was sitting on the sofa watching TV in my father's apartment with my rats crawling all around me. My father came and sat down. We watched some TV. I decided to put the rats back into their cage. I could only find eight of them. Edgar, named after Degas, wasn't there. I crowbarred my father off the sofa and yanked up the pillow he had been sitting on. Edgar lay on the sofa. He did not move. He had his mouth open, not wide, not like he was screaming, but like he was trying to interrupt someone who wouldn't stop talking. I screamed and started crying. I scooped Edgar off the sofa and he lay in my hand—he fit perfectly in my palm. He was warm—not just alive-warm, but over-warm from the weight of the pillow and of my father. I wept.

My father, not wanting to tell me my pet was dead, took Edgar from my hand and told me he would be fine. He held Edgar in his left palm and with his right pointer finger began massaging Edgar's chest. He said he could get Edgar's heart to start beating again by forcing the blood through it. I watched. Edgar did not move. My father told me now all we needed to do was put him in the freezer and he'd be fine in a few hours. He took Edgar into the kitchen, wrapped him in tinfoil, and put him in the freezer, next to the Pop-Tarts. I had never had a Pop-Tart before; my mother didn't let me eat food like that, but my father did and I knew it was what normal kids ate. We waited on the sofa for Edgar to come back to life.

A few hours later, I reached into the freezer, took Edgar out, carefully placed him on the counter, and slowly unwrapped him. Edgar did not move. He was frozen. I started crying. My father said now we just had to put Edgar on the heater and he would be alive again. He threw away the tin foil and wrapped Edgar in a clean towel and put him on the heater. We sat on the sofa and waited for Edgar to come back to life.

Later that night, I unwrapped Edgar and held him in my hands. He felt very warm, very alive. I knew that it had worked. He wasn't moving yet but I knew that he would. I put him in my pocket and could feel his warmth against my leg. I carried him around in my pocket, waiting.

Edgar did not come back to life. Over the course of that day, my father had scrubbed at the boundaries between life and death, between his power and the rules of existence, until the only things left were the force of my yearning and a warm rat carcass.

The adults around me, I would later learn, were bracing themselves for how I would turn out. My mother's staff would whisper predictions to one another. I was a hyper-talkative kid and had inherited my mother's loud voice, her stubborn will, and her need to occupy to capacity any room she was in. When words failed me, head swimming and heart pounding, I threw powerful tantrums, stomach on floor, limbs flailing. If my underwear creased under my tights, or my socks folded in my shoes, or the bows on my dresses were not tied breathlessly tight, I wept and screamed. Starting at seven years old I said that the only feelings I could feel were "guilt, regret, and nervous excitement." I didn't know the word "anxiety" so I called it "nervous excitement." My anxiety left me painfully indecisive. Every morning before school, my mother and I picked out my outfit for the day. I'd stand in my room, sweater sets and wool slacks, jeans and a flannel shirt spread out around me, struggling for air as I held a cardigan up to my body, weeping until I was an hour and a half late for school. Every day after school, at the corner deli, I'd hunch over the freezer and stare despairingly down at the frost-flecked Sundae Crunch Bars, the patriotic-hued Rocket Pops, the sophisticated mini-tubs of Häagen-Dazs, the frigid blast of air making my tears sting. I could not choose. I invented rituals and rules to feel like I had some control over my "nervous excitement" and my life. I'd gather my stuffed animals and pretend to remove stones from their stomachs, lining them up along the windowsills of my room in various stages of recovery after I had removed from them that hard lump of nervous excitement that I felt in my own gut. I hated going to bed. In order to calm down enough for sleep, I organized my stuffed animals in an arc around me. There were strict rules governing their arrangement, and every time one tipped over, I had to get up—disrupting and collapsing the entire structure—to make it inviolable again. Sometimes I had to do it many times a night, but it had to be done. Many nights, I wet my bed.

Nanny was with me all the time. My parents had hired her three months before I was born because of her "straightforwardness" and her ability to handle "unconventional problems." She was the one who tried to console me when the bows on my dresses weren't tight enough, when my socks or underwear bunched, when I was confronted with a decision. Despite her dyslexia, she read to me at night. She sat with me while I did my homework because I couldn't concentrate when I was on my own. She had her sister, Thelma, send me audiobooks from England: *The Peppermint Pig*, *The Animals of Farthing Wood*, *The Wolves of Willoughby Chase*. The narrators had the same accent as Nanny, and I sometimes felt like they were all related, that this was my family. Nanny was family but she was also not family. Sometimes I felt that division imposed by my family, and sometimes I felt it coming from her. Every Christmas, while we opened presents, Nanny would spend the morning cleaning the kitchen. That wasn't her job, and it didn't need to be done, but she did it. I would run from tree to sink, tugging at her apron, trying to get her to come and be with us. But she refused. Each time I ran back and forth it felt like I was trying to sew us together. She told me later that she had always wanted to do more, to protect me better, but she had been afraid. She was scared she would be fired and then there would be no one to protect me.

As Nanny witnessed, my mother worked in her studio and my father worked overseas. When he was away he sent me faxes—from the Lalitha Mahal Palace Hotel in Mysore, India, Gran Hotel Havana in Barcelona, the Hilton Luxembourg, the Vollererhof Kurhotel near

Salzburg—telling me everything he did and everything he saw, with drawings of creatures doing human things: an elephant on roller skates, a pig learning vowels sitting on a tortoise, a stork carrying a postcard, a rat with a paintbrush. He told me all about the movie or play or TV show he was in and the screenplays he was working on, that he looked forward to talking to me about movies and poetry and his screenplays because I was "so sharp and good with characters and plot." He wrote: *How I love your name, Alice, Alice, like a door to another, new world. You have helped me understand the world a little better. The world has become more beautiful because of you.* He was with me even when he couldn't be, and he made me feel seen and wanted in a way my mother didn't. I was a door to another, new world that only we inhabited. When he returned, it felt like all the pieces of me would rattle apart from the momentum of my excitement. I stared out the window and waited for him, trying to picture him first in the airplane, then in the taxi, then walking down the street. From the library windows of 134 Charles Street, I scanned the street below for his waves of white hair to come floating into view and hover below me as he rang the doorbell.

One evening, when I was seven and it was time for his visit to end, we stood in the foyer of 134 Charles Street saying goodbye. My father stood over me and looked down at me. His white hair made him look like one of those deep-sea jellyfish that possess the ability to glow, to make themselves alive with light in the pitch-black depths. He was crying and the tears and the fading light smeared his features into a disarray of shadow and pain. He stood over me and said, "Lick the tears from my eyes."

I hesitated. A low, humming current started to run through me, little flutters that left me queasy. It felt important, what was being asked of me. It felt strange but I trusted it was necessary. I stuck out my tongue and stood on my tiptoes. His skin was so thin and I could feel it crimp as I applied pressure with my tongue and dragged it up, following the path of his tears to their source. I smelled the stale cigarette smoke in his hair. I stopped when I felt the soft, flat triangle that meant I had reached the outskirts of his eyeball. I didn't want to hurt his eye so I withdrew my tongue. I had taken something of my father's into me, something intimate—his liquids and his lonely need. In the foyer, between the two sets of steel doors that kept the outside out and the inside in, the boundaries were blurring, smudged into confusion by a salty little tear. My father smiled through his tears, told me he loved me, and left. I stood alone in the foyer, tasting salt.

4.

I spent every alternating vacation and half of each summer with my father in Europe, accompanied by a court-appointed supervisor— first Nanny, then the revolving door of random chaperones, then my father's steady girlfriend. My father and I traveled to many places; film shoots took him all over the world. In Tunisia, when I was twelve, he told me stories about the Tuareg and the Berber people as we rode on camelback through the Sahara. We walked along the beach and ate the bright orange sex organs of the sea urchin, which young men sold out of plastic crates for one dinar. They cut the creature open with a pair of blunt scissors and handed me a spoon and a wedge of lemon. I ate eighteen in a row and felt sick. We drove out into the Sahara and stopped at a shack where an old man served us mint tea with pine nuts in it and, according to my father, offered to sell us his daughter. We walked through the souk and drank more mint tea in rooms piled high with carpets and kilims. In Madrid we bought two kittens off the street, which my father convinced the director to adopt when we left. In a small town outside Berlin, my father bought me a wild boar, which I named Obelix, and which also required rehoming when we left. In St. Tropez I sipped Bellinis and read Agatha Christie novels. In Rome I stood in front of the *Dying Gaul*, wanting to run my fingers across the weeping lip of his marble wound. We lay splayed on the stone floor of the Sistine Chapel and stared up at a white-bearded god who touched his animating forefinger to a muscled mortal, until security guards told us to leave. I'd accompany him on his movie sets or wait backstage at his plays, watching him fall onto a floor lined with blazing candles or sword fight his lover's husband. I was confronted with newness constantly, my only routine the instructions I knew so well—to buckle my seat belt and stow my tray table, or to be quiet when the director yelled "Action!" Traveling with my father was an adventure, but in that adventure was, like degrading dynamite, an explosive instability. He was impatient and had a temper. I'd watch him closely as we stood in line to walk through the metal detectors or waited for our bags at baggage claim, trying to identify the fizz of imminent rage that popped off him like bubbles off soda right before he exploded. He'd throw his bag down or abandon half our luggage and me and storm off. In those moments I felt accountable; I needed to get the situation under control. I would stammer apologies, swiveling back and forth between him and everyone who saw what was happening, drag our suitcases off the baggage carousel, and run after him, humiliation and panic rippling through me.

Each trip to Europe, we'd visit my grandparents, who lived at Weberkoppel 70 in Lübeck. My grandfather, or "Opa," Dr. Bern Carrière, was a handsome, clinically depressed psychiatrist whose mother, according to my father, had had one of the first "successful" lobotomies in Germany. Opa smoked a pipe and brought the dictionary to the dinner table. He played solitaire and saw his patients, some from a local jail, in his office in the house. My grandmother, or "Oma," Jutta Mühling Carrière, was a self-proclaimed "radical" with a passion for literature, politics, and conflict, who had, as my father described it, "a Jekyll and Hyde personality" marked by a foundational rage I was too little to recognize. I never fully understood the depths of her wrath until I heard about a letter my father had discovered. It was written by Oma in 1968, addressed to my father and his younger sister, Mareike. There was one word that my father couldn't make out: "If at the time the _____ had existed this whole horror wouldn't have happened." Mareike deciphered the word. It was *pill*. If the birth control pill had existed, she would never have gotten pregnant with my father, she would never have married Bern, and she would have been a free woman. But that was not what had happened.

My father was born in Hannover, Germany in 1950. He spent the first ten years of his life in mental institutions, where his father worked and where doctors and patients lived together. The patients had jobs, which included looking after the doctors' children. Frau Feit, who only had one tooth, had been committed after she had tried to burn her two children alive in a psychotic episode. When Till, my father's one-and-a-half-year-old brother, was left in her care, she would sit by the window, with newspaper spread at her feet, and hold him naked over the pages as he shit and pissed. After six hours, she would fold the newspaper and throw it away. My father's babysitter was named Herr Lachs—Mr. Salmon. Herr Lachs had a hole in his forehead—an old war wound—which he could put a ping-pong ball into. He would put my father in the basket on the front of his bicycle and ride through the village. Children would run after them, taunting Herr Lachs with a chant made mean only by the repetition of his strange name, and Herr Lachs would take out his knife and throw it at them. When Oma asked if Herr Lachs would throw a knife at Mathieu if he teased him about his name, Herr Lachs said, "No, Frau Jutta. He reminds me too much of my corporal." Their other babysitter was a man who said that God was transforming him into a woman so He could have a child with him. He took my father downstairs to the coal cellar and fondled him. My father couldn't tell who was sick and who was sane; he just knew if they were nice to him or not. After spending his early years living side by side with mental patients, nothing in human nature would ever be strange to him.

The family later moved to Lübeck and into Weberkoppel 70, which became its own holding cell for damaged people slipping in and out of fantasy, denial, love, and rage. Jutta chased her children—Mathieu, Till, and now a daughter, Mareike—around the garden, hitting them with a carpet beater until they were bloody. My father, the eldest, tried to protect his younger siblings. Forced to accept the authority of his violent mother, he would fight against authority of any kind for the rest of his life.

Bern suffered his entire life from depression, which he treated himself, and when my father heard Bach coming from his closed office, he knew his father was having one of his episodes and that he'd soon have to talk him down from suicide.

"But I love you," my father said to his father, who hung limply in the doorway of his office, the air itching with violins.

"I hate you," my father screamed into his mother's face, thrusting out his ten-year-old chest as his little sister hid under the table and his little brother balled himself up in the corner, their hands clamped over the fresh burns from Jutta's hot iron.

By the time I was born, Weberkoppel 70 was a house of old things—old food, old people, old ghosts—revivified by smells: Nivea Creme on Oma's face, smoke from Opa's pipe, mildew in the kitchen, mold on the cheese, rotting compost and swan shit in the garden. That spiky bouquet—sprays of despair and hard buds of anger— released its fragrance as we moved among one another, among the things of Weberkoppel 70. These things were different from the things in 134 Charles Street. These things were crammed with feeling, brimming with the traces of people—whether dead or leftover from death. Each artifact oozed an essence that kept us in a chronic state of remembering that could sometimes replace living. At one end of the living room, across from her doll collection, Oma had built a shrine to her dead son. On December 19, 1979, when Till was twenty-six, Opa, Oma, and Mareike went to Oma's father's birthday party in a town two hours away. Till stayed behind. He had long suffered from mental illness marked by mood swings and psychosis, and that night, took the phone off the hook and made a cocktail of LSD, which he had with him, and sleeping pills, which he took from the chest of medicines that Opa had in his office. He wrote a note that said: "Here is the money I owe you. Thank you for lending it to me," and slipped seventy Deutsche marks into the envelope. He got hungry and wandered into the kitchen, where he passed out and choked on his own vomit. When the family returned and saw him lying there, blue and dead, Oma grabbed a knife from the kitchen counter and cut his throat, trying to get the vomit out. She would never forgive Opa for making her be the one to slit her son's throat, for giving up on their death-blue son. Mareike called my father, who was in Berlin, and he jumped in the car and drove as fast as he could. When he arrived, Opa was silent in his office, not moving, not talking. Oma was in a fury that never went away. Later, as they drove to the morgue, Oma screamed at Opa that he was driving too slowly. As if there were still time, as if the power of her mind and need could reanimate her son.

After Till's death, Oma commissioned one of my grandfather's psychiatric patients to make a doll that was an exact replica of five-year-old Till. This doll sat at the center of the shrine, below a large oil painting she had also commissioned of Till the year he died. Oma's kitchen, the place where Till died, was also a shrine to him. It was organized but famously filthy, as if the accumulation of all that had happened in that kitchen, the rage and sadness, like the grease and grit, could never be washed away. My head level with the counter, I could see the contours of sticky residue, rust like dried blood on the curves of the dish rack, the ring of scuzz in the sink, the cobwebs in the corners of the window. No one was allowed to use the kitchen except Oma. She screamed at anyone who rinsed a dish or changed out an old sponge for a new one. Till had lived in the attic, and Oma had also kept that room exactly as it was the night he died. His pipe lay on its side still full of half-smoked tobacco. His bed was not made and his pillow still had an indent in it.

Every Christmas I was there, we visited Till's grave. Oma brought buckets and brushes to clean the gravestone and candles and flowers to lay on it. No one touched. No one spoke. Oma filled the silence with the slurping sound she made whenever she exerted herself—a grating inhale followed by a wet hissing that puffed her cheeks out. She must have made that noise when she was chasing her children around the garden, when she beat and burned them. She must have made that noise when the inexperienced doctor ripped the head off her about-to-be-born baby as it was sliding out of her, another dead child. That disgusting and scary sound pinned me down and jammed my face into the tender, rotting center of all her heartbreak.

Underneath Till's attic reliquary was where I slept—in my aunt Mareike's old room, which had also been kept exactly as she had left it, half-used lipsticks and her stash of '70s *Penthouse* magazines still in her closet. The ceiling, covered in '60s-style wallpaper with giant swirls of color like the inside of a lava lamp, slanted so steeply that I could wedge my body between the ceiling and the bed, my nose squished by the ceiling-wall. On the slanting walls hung black-and-white posters of the famous mime, Marcel Marceau, his face painted white, his mouth a slash of black, too narrow for words. He terrified me and sent me looking for Nanny at night. Oma made Nanny sleep in the basement. In the journals Nanny kept, she described the sleeping arrangement: *I feel as if I have been completely neutralized as an observer in one very clever move by Mathieu and Jutta. My bedroom is about as far away from Alice and Mathieu as possible—downstairs in the cellar tucked away at the far end of the house. I did not know this room existed. Jutta said Mathieu came up with this idea.* To get to Nanny, I would have to sneak through the house in complete darkness, feeling my way past Opa's room, past Oma's room, down the stairs, through the hallway, to the basement door. I moved slowly. The darkness felt like flesh, an invisible body bear-hugging me, and with each step I tried to pry myself loose. The basement stairs were steep and narrow and my heart thudded as I made my way down. Sometimes I got too scared and froze, too frightened to move forward and too frightened to go back to my creepy room. Eventually I would admit defeat and slip past Oma and Opa and Marcel and back into my bed.

Nanny spent her days in Lübeck witnessing and documenting. She would silently sit at the round dining table in her long wool skirt and collared sweater, salting half a tomato, and observe: *Big argument at the table. Jutta, Mathieu, Bern all in German. Oh how I wish I could tell the lot to get lost. Good grief, four more weeks. What have I done to deserve this? What are Bern's thoughts as a doctor? He is a good one and respected but he sure has trouble with his own family.* The next night she wrote: *Oh what a life! Supper was eaten in silence. It's like walking on eggshells. Everyone has their own ideas as to how Alice is to act. Alice is being good and knows things are tense.*

Oma was often angry. She was angry at my father for not playing with me, for playing with me too much, at me for having eaten a yogurt, for refusing to eat a yogurt, at Nanny for not making the bed, for making the bed wrong, at Opa for talking when she wanted to talk, for not talking when she wanted to talk to him.

The next day Nanny wrote: *God the games people play. Mathieu and Jutta are control freaks. Mathieu is giving Alice such terrible ideas of ways of getting through life. I forgot one gem. Mathieu said to Alice when everyone returned at 6 p.m., "I've been with you six hours, give me a break." This is the kind of thing that makes me want to laugh at this man who pictures himself as such a wonderful father. He is only happy when he is drawing Alice into his world but when she wants to stay there he gets tired. He treats Alice like an adult and the next time like a spoiled brat then expects her to be quiet when he wants to do something. Mathieu kept saying "I know you are jealous" to Alice when at dinner last night he was speaking to a 13-year-old and her mother.*

My father could be very charming, but Nanny was immune. *M is playing the game*, she wrote. *But I still think he is acting. After all he grew up around Drs and knows their games of the mind.* Sometimes, she would be pushed too far. *I ended up having words with Mathieu*, she wrote. *Real words. He said I am the cause of him being ruined. That I am a spy for the court. He said he would tell me why I had ruined him but not in front of his daughter. I said "Why not? You have told her everything else."*

She described my own exchange of words with my father: *Alice is really getting angry with Mathieu and telling him why he does not protect her like a father should.* Finally, she reached a breaking point: *They are all such egos!!! I feel so degraded. How does one deal with it? As I look at them I see a bunch of egotistic, selfish, dirty muddle lot.* She could witness, but she could not intervene. She saw herself in a war, a constant battle she had to fight alone, for me. *I will be surprised if I can keep quiet much longer*, she wrote. *I keep being corrected in what I say and do. Talk about undermining a person. I keep thinking of being a POW and that I am stronger than my captors and after all in just over 3 weeks I will be free to fight another day on my ground.*

She was fiercely protective of me. The pen nearly broke through the notebook paper when she wrote: *ALICE MUST NOT BE MADE RESPONSIBLE FOR HER FATHER'S ACTIONS.* She defended me against Oma's accusations that I was spoiled. Nanny understood me and saw how my pain was often misunderstood as petulance. *Alice gave me her hand as if to make me know I am there for her*, she wrote. *Alice came to me and gave me a big hug while we were sweeping in the garden.*

Nanny was dyslexic and didn't like to write, but she was diligent about writing in her tiny, palm-sized notebooks. There was an urgency to her chronicle, as if words were the only way she knew to put up a fight. When I discovered her journals almost thirty years later, I would recognize that urgency, how things only became real when they were turned into language, how that language was often the only thing left when that reality fell apart.

FOR ALL THE CHAOS, there were things I loved about being in Lübeck. Weberkoppel 70 had its own special rules and rhythms. The day began with a breakfast of Müsli. I'd spend the morning running through the garden, swimming naked in the lake, or reading in the hammock. The big meal of the day was lunch. Oma would make potato pancakes with sour cream and apple sauce made from the apples that grew in the garden, which I helped her pick. She had a collection of plates with scenes painted on them: a farmer in a field, a woman stepping out of a wagon. I stood at the table picking each one up and examining it, trying to decide which would be mine for the meal. In the afternoon, I'd sit with Opa in his office, adorned with his spicy pipe smoke, and play solitaire or read Asterix and Obelix comics. For our supper, Oma scraped the mold off blocks of cheese and put them on a lazy Susan along with sliced tomatoes, a tube of liverwurst, a tub of quark, a tub of schmaltz, a tub of margarine, and some hard-boiled eggs. I liked to squeeze the liverwurst out onto a hot piece of toast and wait for the deep, rich aroma of the liver, activated by the heat, to hit my nose. Sometimes she made Rote Grütze for dessert, a kind of gelatinous cherry pudding, bright red with the consistency of mucus. I poured thick vanilla cream on top. Oma was proud of her cooking and proud that even her little American granddaughter asked for second helpings. Sometimes she treated me to Labskaus—the sailor's fare that was a hash of beets, beef, and potato, served with rolled herring—and laughed and patted my arm as I shoveled it into my mouth. As a concession to my Americanness, Oma kept a box of Corn Flakes in the cupboard. She offered it to me once, at the beginning of every trip, and reveled in my refusal as I reached instead for the Müsli. She kept the same box of Corn Flakes for twenty years. The day would end with Oma playing dice and drinking Schnapps as I sat next to her on a dirty beanbag watching *Mr. Bean*, which she had recorded for me on VHS.

The house had a sprawling garden that led down to Lake Wakenitz. In the winters, I'd walk on the lake's frozen crust. My grandparents' dogs would pull me on a sled so fast I could barely open my eyes for the cold wind. Neighbors set up tables on the ice and ladled hot wine with apple and cinnamon into cups. In the summer, I'd ride my bicycle down the country paths, pulling over to rescue slugs that had crept out after it rained. My father and I went frog catching in the ponds and brought them back to the garden so they could eat all the pests. We built a treehouse with a zip line. Every other year on August 14, my birthday, we had a giant bonfire in the garden. Oma spent all year collecting twigs and sticks and limbs and branches, stacking them on a stone circle at the bottom of the garden until the pile towered above me and I got to light it, running around the base, coaxing it into a mountain of flames. We had a big party around the bonfire and Oma made sausages and potato salad and plum cake and invited all the neighbors. We played charades in English and German. The swans, threatening and beautiful, would walk up from the lake into the garden. The party sparked a thrill and an unease inside me. I loved being surrounded by the eager, curious children who appeared every summer in my life as if they had been waiting for me all year. They treated me better than my peers in America. They didn't make fun of me, they were interested in me. They asked me genuine questions, and when I didn't understand a word they used, we'd embark on a collaborative journey to decipher each other. I looked forward to the mystifying moments with these kids, when we hunted for the right words. Each year I returned with my German a little better, bringing an offering of more shared words, lexical contributions that, like a bonfire, could blaze into understanding.

In the summers my father and I would take a rowboat out onto the lake and spend the day exploring, swimming, picking up the neighborhood kids, or just rowing back and forth. He would tell me stories—about history, things he made up, about his life. He told me about the poet who went mad and locked himself in a tower. He told me about the royal who bathed in the blood of children to stay young. He told me about the Borgias and Romulus and Remus and Gilles de Rais. I felt happiest when I was listening to my father's stories. One day when I was ten, my father was rowing us across the lake and telling me the story of the book he was reading called *Smilla's Sense of Snow*, and I was trying to figure out how it would end. He rowed us around the lake as I invented endings. After a while I'd exhausted my imagination. I felt good. The sun was hot and I trailed my fingers in the cool water. There was a huge old boat that had been abandoned in the tangled reeds. My father pulled our boat up next to it and we climbed aboard. I spent hours climbing all over it, looking out the windows and piecing together a mysterious history to this deserted vessel—pirates, soldiers, runaway children. As we rowed back, my father said, "I stuck my toe up your mother's cunt."

My mind felt like it was being pried open, hinging wide as the image of my father's toe up my mother's cunt stuffed itself inside me. I wanted to have the right words for this, to respond in a way that proved I was the perfect confidante. I looked at the skin of the lake and pictured all the information shut into it. All the lost rings and dead dogs and secret things done and seen and felt, sealed under the placid surface. My father was now telling me that one of his girlfriends had been "frigid," that she could only orgasm with a shower head, not through sex. It was my responsibility to take in these stories, swirl them around in my brain until a thought or an opinion formed at the edges that I could scrape out and offer as proof that I could think about and understand anything, whether it was a murdered boy or the sexual hang-ups of the people close to me.

"That's interesting," I said. "Then what happened?"

I was the receptacle for my parents' stories. My mother would eventually burn the journals that captured her memories of abuse, as if their physical incineration would wipe away the consequences too. But I would keep those stories alive, in my mind and in my body. Her silence was like a fire, too. A roaring, violent thing that spread through my life as my father's burning wall of information raced toward me from the other side. I tried to do my own documenting, tried to put down into words what I felt before it blew away. In August 1996, when I had just celebrated my eleventh birthday in Lübeck, I wrote in the journal I had gotten as a present from Oma: *Nothing sick happened today.* I never specified what I meant by "sick" or how I felt about it. The next day I wrote: *I guess it's good that nothing sexy happened. Although when I was massaging my Papa's shoulder I felt like more than his daughter, if you know what I mean!* When I discovered that entry twenty years later, I wondered about the exclamation point. Had I been shocked or amused or curious? At eleven, I had already become a dispassionate documentarian of my life.

My father had started letting me know I had "a great ass." I started calling him by his first name. It wasn't a fully thought-out alteration, but I needed to create distance between us, to add delineation to spaces that had none. Replacing "Papa" with his given name felt right, but it also left me feeling unmoored. I was no longer the daughter to his "Papa," I was something else, or I was a little bit of many things.

I had always been *more than* just me. To my mother, I was a symbol, proof that she could create anything she wanted to, against odds, against expectation, against nature. To my father, I was the mother who didn't regret him, the wife who hadn't left him, the collaborator who would never outgrow him.

That same year, my half-sister, Elena, was born. My father had been dating her mother, Bettina, throughout the divorce, and they lived together in my father's Hamburg apartment. After Elena was born, Bettina took over from Nanny as the court-appointed supervisor. With Nanny gone there was no expectation of order or routine, no tether to my mother's world, and I set about trying to situate myself alone in my father's newly reconfigured one. Bettina was a beautiful, big-assed blond with soft skin and a soft voice. She was tender and affectionate, and I liked her. I was excited to have a sister. I'd bounce Elena on my lap as I watched German MTV in the living room. I'd heft her onto my hip and take her for walks in the neighborhood. I fed her her first oyster, played her her first Beatles song. I loved my sister and I loved taking care of her. It also made me feel tied to my father in a way I couldn't articulate. When Elena was six months old, and I was eleven and a half, I picked her up from her crib and held her in my arms. I lifted my shirt as I had seen Bettina do and tried to get Elena to attach to my tiny nipple. She refused. I tried again and again and each time she turned her head away from me. She started to cry. I felt angry that Elena wanted someone other than me, that Bettina could give her something I couldn't.

Bettina was effortlessly maternal most of the time, but she vibrated at a high frequency, and my father was not an easy man to live with. They started having trouble almost immediately, and I would sit them down across from me in the living room and conduct couples therapy, asking them to list their grievances as I sat with my hands clasped, mimicking the therapists I'd been to. My father seemed to love these sessions and took them very seriously. He'd lean forward, nodding at everything I said.

"What are you feeling right now?" I'd ask Bettina, who looked uncomfortable.

I liked being at the center of their relationship, and I felt competent and useful.

The evening following a particularly stressful session, she and my father were having a fight as I sat on my father's lap. I couldn't understand what they were saying because they were speaking very fast and in German, but I could feel him getting angrier and angrier underneath me. I watched Bettina as she talked, then yelled, at him over my head. I felt invisible but I also felt powerful, nestled in between them, at the heart of their discord, observing. I felt lulled by the indecipherable acrimony happening all around me, and then suddenly I was cold and wet. Bettina had thrown a glass of white wine in my face. It was meant for my father, but it had hit me. My father threw me off his lap and screamed at Bettina. I stood to the side, licking drops of pinot grigio off my nose, wondering how I would address this in our next session.

That same summer, my father was on a reality show where *Promis*, the German word for "famous people," helped build houses for charity. He took me to the set. The celebrities mostly posed with power tools, smiling and laughing through their endearing incompetence. My father always wanted to put me in front of the camera. I assumed everyone would be captivated by a non-famous eleven-year-old saying not very exciting things in English on German reality TV. I thought hard about hilarious and clever things I could say. They filmed my father and me sawing something with a giant saw. My little body rocked back and forth and I yelled in German, "Better than sex!" They filmed us hammering some nails into a wall and I shouted, "Better than sex!" They filmed us digging a hole and I sang out, "Better than sex," and winked. In the backyard of the celebrity construction site there was a pit full of mud and water. My father took off his clothes and got in. I took off my clothes, leaving on my kitten-print underpants. We were very hilarious and spontaneous and wild for sitting in this hole of cold muddy water on TV. To break the silence that had settled over us I yelled, "Better than sex!" My father laughed.

5.

I was split between two kinds of lawlessness: there were no rules in my father's house because they didn't apply to us and were meant to be broken anyway; there were no rules in my mother's house because it never occurred to her to make them. Back in New York, I would sit at the butcher block table in the kitchen while Nanny made me breakfast and told me stories. Nanny loved to talk about her past. She was born in 1926 in New Cross, on the outskirts of London. Her family lost all their money when her uncle embezzled from the family business, and they had to move into a small apartment above a shop that sold linoleum and nails. She'd lived through WWII, recalling the sounds of the doodlebugs whirring through the air, and fought off a would-be rapist. Her aunt killed herself right in front of her. ("She asked me for a glass of water and I gave it to her. Then she took all her pills and dropped dead.") Nanny was dyslexic and not as pretty as her sister, and no one had thought she would make anything of herself, but other people's incredulity made her even more determined. She went to governess school, got her certificate, and left

England. By the time she retired, she had lived in Montreal, Telluride, Paris, and New York, had traveled the world and met all sorts of glamorous people.

As she stirred my Cream of Wheat in a pot or heated my clothes up in the oven on cold days, she told me about the families she had worked for. She told me about the Johnsons and how the father left the mother for another man. She told me about her time working for Edward Litchfield, the chancellor of the University of Pittsburgh, and how the entire family, including their two little boys, died in a plane crash over Lake Michigan.

"I was devastated," Nanny said. "But the rest of the family acted like I was irrelevant, like I hadn't loved those boys since they were born."

Nanny walked me to and from St. Luke's School, five minutes away. There were twenty kids in my grade and I tried to fit in with them. JP was my best friend and my first great love. We'd met when we were three at Tadpoles swimming class, would end up going to the same elementary and middle school, the same high school, and I would be the last person with him the night he died from brain cancer at twenty-seven. Everybody liked JP. He was a tap dancing prodigy who studied under Savion Glover. He was kind and funny and had the coolest flattop we'd ever seen with his initials shaved onto the back of his head with a crown on top. I'd go over to his house and we'd watch Michael Jackson videos and eat frozen mint Milanos and coffee ice cream. We'd play *Street Fighter* on his Nintendo and then play it for real out in his hallway. I was very interested in sex, and when we had sleepovers, I'd make JP take off his clothes and I'd lie on top of him.

All the other kids at school made fun of me. They made fun of the continental way I pronounced certain words. They made fun of my strange haircut—short like a boy's, like my mother's. They made fun of how much I raised my hand in English class and my long and rambling comments. They made fun of my outfits. My mother dressed me, and I went to elementary school in wool sweater sets and pearls. They made fun of my school lunches, prepared by our cook, Katy— smoked salmon with crackers, fiddlehead ferns when in season, bouillabaisse. The other kids' lunches were full of all the foods I had seen on TV—humanoid-shaped squeeze bottles filled with fluorescent liquid, cookies shaped like kangaroos that were dipped into icing, fruity drinks with tiny colorful globules floating around in them, soft gummies that exploded with tropical ooze, perfect circles of lunch meat and cubes of cheese in plastic compartments. I bought these snacks at the corner deli after school and forced myself to try them. I hated them and I hated that I had failed to tap into that common joy. I didn't get it. The other kids knew a lot about the popular music of the time. Green Day's *Dookie* had just come out, and everyone had a copy. I bought one and held it in my hands, staring at the colorful album art that reminded me of a Hieronymus Bosch painting I had seen. I forced myself to listen to it over and over, trying to love it. I had not been exposed to much music. My mother didn't listen to music, only audiobooks. From six in the morning until seven at night, my mother listened to audiobooks while she worked. When I walked by the upper studio on my way to school, I heard, over the audiobook I was listening to on my Walkman, Trollope or Dickens booming from Bose speakers. Words surrounded me, pursued me, as if I were a part of them they had lost and needed to reclaim.

I listened to my mother's audiobooks when I worked with her in her studio. She helped me with my creative school projects. I would meet her in her studio and we'd lay out all my supplies. She painted as I hunched over my replica of the Sahara Desert. Little wooden Bedouins crouched around a fire I had created out of tendrils of colorful blown glass my mother had leftover from a piece. We constructed a life-size Egyptian teenager named Nofret, complete with toys and games and a scroll covered in hieroglyphics. We didn't talk, we worked, the words of nineteenth-century novelists filling our heads.

My mother and I were a good team in those moments. I'd have an idea that impressed her, and she'd help me make it come alive. I worked hard on my projects—I loved learning and I was good in school—and my mother seemed to respect that. When we worked side by side, when our focus was trained on turning what was inside of us into something that would exist, beautifully, on the outside, I felt connected to her. Art and invention brought us together, bridged the gap between us.

She took me to Tuscany when I was twelve and we visited a tiny, ramshackle church, where inside, totally unguarded, was a Fra Angelico fresco. Even at twelve I knew how special it was to be so close and alone with something so spectacular.

"Isn't it extraordinary?" my mother said, her voice softer and quieter than I had ever heard it.

"Yes," I said, as awestruck at my mother's reverence as I was at the fresco.

I was close with my mother's sister, Julie, whose graphic design office was on the first floor of 134 Charles Street. I'd come home every day from school and go directly to Julie's office, where she would talk to me, show me the projects she was working on, and draw funny faces on the pads of my toes. Julie loved musicals from the 1950s and '60s, and she gave me a box of DVDs of *South Pacific*, *Gigi*, *Guys and Dolls*, *Singin' in the Rain*, *My Fair Lady*. I'd learn the songs and belt them out in her office. Every New Year's Eve I'd go to her apartment, where she and my uncle, Takaaki, would hide a new pair of pajamas and I'd have to find it. Julie and Takaaki seemed to really like each other. I would watch them move around their small apartment and study their interactions—how they made each other laugh or touched each other on the back or elbow. I had not seen anything like that up close, their easy intimacy a momentary correction to the vocabulary of love I was learning.

When I was twelve, my mother's younger brother, Roy, moved in to 134 Charles Street. He had lost all his money because of his gambling addiction and had been diagnosed with cancer. He was six two, almost bald, and very skinny. He moved into the room on the first floor that had been my father's room.

I first learned about Roy's existence one Christmas morning when I was nine. Under the tree, I found a Ziploc bag with *To Alice, From Roy* written on it in Sharpie marker. Inside the bag were pins with strange symbols, fabric badges with writing in different languages, and a man's watch with no wristband.

"Mom," I called across the room to my mother as she unwrapped a set of overly designed Moss oven mitts.

"What?" she answered, not looking up, unwinding a swathe of tulle that had wrapped itself around her arm.

"There's a Ziploc bag that says it's for me from Roy and it's got all this random stuff in it," I said.

"That's from your uncle Roy." She paused, distracted by a gigantic origami swan. "He probably won them from gambling."

"Why?"

"He's addicted to gambling. He lives in Las Vegas and works at Kentucky Fried Chicken."

She said all this without once looking up.

I sifted through the contents of the bag. My mother had never told me about Roy. I had never met him and had also never heard of him but he knew me and had thought of me enough to send me his hard-won treasures.

I liked Roy a lot. We played Scrabble almost every night after dinner. We sat in the library, on the green leather sofas, and slapped words onto the board. He was very serious about it. He never gave me hints and he always won. He helped me study for my tests, making up tricks and strategies to help me remember information. He gave me money for good grades and put it in funny greeting cards that he signed "Uncle Wiggly," which was a character from my favorite board game. We played the "gotcha last" game, where we teased each other or made puns and whoever said "gotcha last" first, won. One time, after he had won the gotcha last game, he typed up a very official-sounding letter that began with *To Whom it May Concern* and was signed *The Gotcha Last Board of Administrators*, informing me, in businesslike language, that I had to be his maid for a week.

Nanny, my mother, and I had always eaten our meals together, me reading aloud my school projects—the fourth-grade speech I had written in favor of legalizing gay marriage (which I was prohibited from reading at school assembly), the creation myth I had written where the sky made love to the sea (returned to me with a smiley face and a request from the teacher to please write another one that was "more appropriate" but declared "great and totally acceptable" by my mother). Now Roy was part of this routine, sitting across from me at the table and critiquing my projects like I was a grown-up. Then his dying began, and tracking its progress became my new routine. His vitality fell off him hard and slick and fast. He lost more and more weight. His limbs seemed longer for the weight they had lost, but unwieldy in their lightness. His weakness turned every movement into a different movement because he was too weak to carry it through. As the months went by, he grew sullen and stopped looking me in the eye, but I couldn't stop watching.

My babysitter, Pem, took me to the movies to see *Home Alone*. One of the previews was for *Edward Scissorhands* and it terrified me so much that for years after, I couldn't watch previews. I had to sit outside the theater doors and someone had to come and get me when the previews were over and tell me that it was okay to come in. Now, with Roy in the house—in the kitchen or climbing slowly up the stairs or in his room with the door open—always dying, I was being forced to watch those horrifying previews over and over. Every day when I entered or left the house, I would pass by his open door and see him sitting on the edge of his bed staring into space. Even if I looked away, the smoke from the weed he used to manage his symptoms slipped inside me. When I retreated to my room, I'd hear him shuffling around at night in the kitchen. I couldn't escape him and I couldn't just wait outside the door for it to be over because no one knew when it would end and no one told me anything anyway.

It was hard to know what to do for him. I made him macaroni and cheese from a box once and brought it to him in his room. I felt as if I wasn't supposed to see what was going on in there. There was only one window, which was closed, so the room was filled with cigarette smoke. The walls were yellow from it, the same yellow as his jaundiced skin. There was a twin bed, a La-Z-Boy, a TV, and a bookshelf. On the bookshelf were a lot of books and a bowl filled with packs and packs of American Spirit cigarettes. He liked adventure novels. On the covers were cowboys with huge hats. Suns were always blood red and skies were bruisy.

Roy was sitting in the La-Z-Boy, smoking an American Spirit and watching a boxing match on TV. I put the tray on his lap. I glanced at his face. He had lost so much weight that the skin just dangled, exhausted. It made me forget I was looking at a face.

"Thanks," he said, not moving his eyes from the screen.

"You're welcome," I said.

I stopped myself from saying the only thing that came to mind: "I'm sorry I'm not dying."

At this stage of his decline, there was no more Scrabble, no more quizzing, no more book report debates. I was a girl growing up, but I couldn't help feeling like I was supposed to accompany Roy, that in my youth and my health, I was betraying him.

6.

I was growing up. I put on makeup, I wore a leopard-print bra whose straps revealed themselves under my tank top. My hair had grown out from the short, fluffy helmet I had in middle school into shoulder-length ringlets. I was fourteen and in my freshman year of high school at the Dalton School on the Upper East Side. I was excited to be there and very friendly. I approached everyone with a huge smile and asked them how they were. One girl told me, "When I first met you I thought you were mentally challenged. But you're just really friendly." I was desperate for attention and friendship, but I was clumsy and confused about who I was. I still needed my mother to dress me. I couldn't decide if I liked something unless she told me it was good. Every day still began with the fraught hour it took for us to plan an outfit, which ended with me in tears.

Dalton was populated by the kids of the ultra-rich—fifteen-year-olds dressed head to toe in Chanel, or in a jersey from the football team owned by their parents, touting last names that appeared on hospital buildings and museum wings. These kids had the regular traits of youthful immaturity carved away from them by the shining edge of money, and Dalton felt like a sovereign nation ruled by small grown-ups. There were strict sartorial, linguistic, and aesthetic rules. All the girls owned the same Longchamp purse. They straightened their hair and wore pajama bottoms to school. The rumor was that most girls' parents gifted them a nose job the summer before freshman year. I watched and listened, adopting their "like"s and "literally"s, hoping to sneak into their ranks, even though I showed up one day wearing the same skirt as my history teacher. I wasn't bullied like I had been in middle school, but I didn't fit in.

Halfway through my freshman year, my father came to visit from Hamburg, where he was now living full-time in order to maintain his career and be closer to Elena. I was excited to see him. He had always been the person I could talk to about my thoughts and feelings. I could ask him anything, and he would answer me honestly. "Have you ever felt like killing yourself?" I asked him. We'd have long conversations about Till, about madness, loneliness, otherness. He spoke about sadness and compulsion in ways I could understand, and ways that made me feel understood.

But this night was different. Sitting at the table at a Chinese restaurant, I was tense and couldn't look him in the eye. I felt uncomfortable, and that discomfort confused and scared me.

"So what's going on in your life?" he asked.

"Nothing much. You know. A lot of work. The usual," I said.

"No, I don't know. I'm not really allowed to be too involved in your life," he said, his words echinated with contempt.

I jiggled my leg and he ran his thumb over his fingers, over and over.

I stared hard at the menu, studying the names of entrees, trying to soothe the nameless unease that was rising inside me. I could feel my father across the table, buzzing along with the fluorescent lights. I put the menu down.

"I hate making decisions," I said.

"I know," he said.

I felt attacked by his knowledge of me. Every awareness he had of any of the things that made me Me felt like a violation instead of the comfort it had previously been.

We finally finished dinner and my father hailed a cab. Inside, I was pressed up against the door and he had his arm around me. His long legs were spread and he was slid down the seat halfway. Our bodies were as close together as they could be. I felt the tight fist of heart in my chest, clenching as if it were trying to retreat from being inside me, who was inside his embrace inside this taxi inside the night. I wanted to run. I realized I was clutching the door handle.

"You two newlyweds?" the cab driver asked.

I turned my head to look at the reflection of this stranger's eyes in the rearview mirror.

My father laughed.

"No, I'm her father."

I looked away from the mirror to avoid the driver's eyes.

"I would never hold my daughter like that," he said.

My father laughed again. His fingers stroked my forehead. I felt their caress in my guts, turning my organs in a nauseating plowing. My face got hot and my chest smoldered. I opened the window. My father's hands, placed just so, could change entirely who I was, turning me from daughter to newlywed.

That summer my mother took me to Iceland for four weeks. We lay on the lava fields, our bodies leaving deep imprints in the thick moss that covered them. We set up a tent on a black sand beach and wild ponies nosed their way inside. The wind was so strong that it flattened the tent on top of us and we rolled out of it laughing. We ate Arctic char and bread as we both drew the landscape. I felt calm and happy as we sat side by side in a lava field, passing pastels back and forth as the landscape we were both sharing in formed under our fingers. We rode on Ski-Doos up a glacier, the fog getting so thick we couldn't see our hands in front of our faces. Over dinner every night, we talked. She told me how she felt like an "alien." How she felt a distance between her and everyone else, like she was watching them from behind a pane of glass and didn't understand the rules that everyone else was following. I told her I knew exactly what she meant, how unfamiliar even the most familiar things could feel. As we spoke, I hoped I wasn't included in the "everyone else," that I got to be on her side of the glass. I ate slowly and ordered two desserts, trying to stretch the evening as long as I could. As we deboned our fish in the endless Arctic day, our alienation brought us momentarily together.

We visited a man who read tarot cards at the base of a glacier. He performed our readings separately. After studying my cards, he asked me if I had been sexually abused.

"I don't know," I said. "I've wondered that."

Afterwards, my mother and I went to eat fish stew. I told her what the man had asked me.

"Do you think I was sexually abused? Do you think Dad did that?"

"I don't know," she said. "Maybe."

"Maybe what I feel is just because of what you went through. Maybe I've confused your experiences with mine," I said.

"I don't know. Maybe," she said and ate her stew.

I realized I was jealous of my mother's abuse. I was jealous of her for having it as an excuse for everything. She couldn't give me affection or talk about feelings because pedophile Satanists had ruined her. She drank because she had witnessed murder and endured torture. I couldn't have her, because the abuse had taken most of her away, and what remained belonged to her work.

. . .

BY MY SOPHOMORE YEAR AT Dalton I had developed an unexpected popularity for two reasons: I was skinny and I had gotten pretty, which offset my weirdness. I started performing in the school plays and made a best friend. Effie was a talented actor originally from Switzerland, who lived in the worst projects in all of New York. She was at Dalton on a scholarship. Effie and I would go to the Angelika Film Center and watch indie films, then roam the streets for hours discussing the plays we would write, composing Dada poetry from words on signs and billboards, and planning the naked photo shoot we were going to have with the fifty-year-old photographer Effie was corresponding with. Effie had struggled in ways that were both familiar and unfamiliar to me, and she had a reckless, radiant resilience. She had a dark sense of humor and could make anything funny, but would fall into steely seriousness if I mentioned thoughts of self-harm or waxed too romantic about suicide. Despite our different backgrounds, it felt like we shared the same rare disease, one that made us uniquely sensitive to the world.

Along with a best friend, I had a boyfriend. Nate and I started dating when I was fifteen and he was eighteen. We were both part of the theater crowd, and Nate would be voted most handsome in his senior yearbook. I was excited to be dating him. He and his friends seemed to possess the correct ratio of quirk and competence, unlike me. I was too loud, too talkative, too hyper, and tried too hard. When someone asked me how I was, I answered: "There is a smattering of novelty in my life." I used increasingly big words, some of which I didn't entirely know the meaning of, in casual conversation. I was terrified that unless I applied myself to the moment like thick oil paint with a palette knife, I would go unnoticed and unloved.

Nate noticed and then loved me. Things were going well with him, but I found myself unable to look at or touch his penis. Panic creaked inside me whenever I thought of trying to make my way around his genitals. Nate was patient with me. He surprised me with a giant, phallic candy cane, as thick as my forearm, in my locker to lighten the mood. Sometimes when Nate and I were making out I would hallucinate my father's face onto his. I would push through it, not wanting to have to explain why I had stopped. Every time we had sex, I felt angry and guilty afterwards. "Wow, your ass is incredible," said Nate. Yes, I thought, my father thinks so too.

As I was squirming inside the expectations of a cool group of teenagers and my handsome boyfriend, Roy was still at home dying. One night, Nate and I were in my bedroom having sex. I heard Roy's slippers shuffling around in the kitchen. It was dark in my bedroom, and dark everywhere else in the house, but the shuffling sound of Roy's slippers was like a searchlight slipping its glare all over me, lighting up the scene. Nate paused and said, "Shit, we should stop." He started to move off me, but I gripped his back and pressed him back down onto my body.

"No, it's fine, keep going," I said.

"But it's weird," he said. "He'll hear us."

"It's okay," I said. "He always walks around at night. It's okay."

The shuffling continued, and I tried to drown out the friction of Roy's footfalls with the friction of Nate's body on mine.

"Keep going," I insisted.

We kept going. The sound of Roy's slippers faded as he retreated downstairs.

As my relationship with Nate progressed, I spent time with his family. His parents seemed to adore each other, and he had a smart, pretty sister who was two years younger than me. I was fascinated by them. His parents loved art and also knew what a retirement account was; they read interesting books and also their children's report cards. I was especially struck by the way they loved one another—Dad, Mom, brother, sister, talking to each other, showing affection, with a

clarity of emotion that confounded me to my core. My confusion
translated to rage and paranoia. I became fiercely jealous of his sister.
When Nate took me to a circus and bought me a T-shirt, I became
enraged when he bought one for his sister too. I loved them, I envied
them, I hated them, I wanted to be wrapped up in them, I wanted to
tear them apart. Their uncomplicated love didn't seem possible or
real, but more like a delusion that Nate needed to be cured of. My
efforts to make him see his family as I saw mine failed, and, after
sixteen months of dating, Nate broke up with me in my junior year.
He was the first person to calmly admit they suspected I was "crazy."
As if that word were air, I rushed up to the surface to breathe it in,
huge gulps of "crazy" that found me sitting at my desk trying to focus
on homework, pulling out my hair, cutting my thighs. My grades
dropped. Teachers commented that I had been the star of the class and
now they weren't even sure I was paying attention.

When I asked my mother to get me a therapist, she asked me no
questions, but had her assistant make me an appointment with a
woman uptown. I was also sent to a psychiatrist who diagnosed me
with depression and put me on the antidepressant Paxil. Numbness
thickened over me like scar tissue, pangs of anxiety, irritability, and
hyperactivity breaking through. My therapy sessions felt like English
assignments, opportunities to construct perfect stories about myself
and wait for praise.

My mother never asked me how I was feeling or about the medication I was put on. We did get drunk together at parties and talk about
books we were reading and gossip we had heard. Loaded up on red
wine and hors d'oeuvres, we'd lie on the sofas in the living room and
make each other roar with laughter as fancy people milled around us.
I still gave the tour of the house as I had done as a child, now in a red
Miu Miu dress my mother had bought me in Italy, leading actors,
writers, politicians, models, and rock stars around the studios, the
gardens, the pool. My mother and I were a good team at those parties.

She liked that I looked good and talked well. At that moment—when my damage was still inconspicuous—I was what she needed me to be. But that moment would soon be over.

Every year we'd go to Joan Didion's Easter party at her Upper East Side apartment. The year I was sixteen, we were seated in the living room, along with Patti Smith, the artist Brice Marden, and his wife, Helen. Helen was talking about superstitions. A lone word glowed in my brain: *imbrued*. I wanted to use that word because it was special and difficult. I wanted to impress these people. I started to say:

"It's interesting how these superstitions are imbrued with—"

"I think it's *imbued*," my mother said, cutting me off.

I felt destabilized, wobbly, as if that *r* were structural and removing it would topple me. To steady myself, I pictured the dictionary I had been studying that week. I could see that *r* curving over the *u*. I felt its growl under my tongue, between that plosive and that rounded vowel. I knew it was there but my accomplished, brilliant mother was telling me I was wrong. I tried not to panic as Patti Smith and Joan Didion stared at us.

"Well, *imbrued* is also a word, and it means saturated with blood, so I mean it more as a metaphor," I said cautiously.

"I think she's right," said Patti.

I wanted to hug her. I opened my mouth to continue my thought, but my mother was telling a story. As we left, my mother grabbed an unopened bottle of white wine and told me to stick it in my purse. She didn't have room for it in her tiny clutch. We were going home in a car service. There was plenty of good wine at home. Why did she need to steal this bottle? But there was something in her gesture I recognized—an urgency, a thrill, a way to seize control. I had taken to carrying a razor blade around in my purse. Even if I wasn't going to use it, I liked knowing it was there. I understood why she was taking the wine, but I couldn't tell her that I did. In sharing this transgression, I chose to believe we were communicating.

. . .

I LEFT MY MOTHER and a dying Roy and went to visit my father and his family. In Lübeck, I spent a lot of time in Till's attic bedroom. I would sit there for hours and stare at the dead insects, the only sign that time was passing. On his desk were papers covered in his neat, loopy handwriting, and I would pore over them, convinced they contained valuable information that only I could understand. I liked to put his pipe to my lips and suck, plugging myself into him, into a cosmic source that only we could tap into, the ancient grit lining my tongue. Oma had always told me that Till and I would have loved each other, that we were very similar. We would have made each other laugh. We would have understood each other. I pictured him deciding whether or not to live anymore. My father told me that Till had believed it was simple. "If fifty-one percent of your life is bad," Till had said, "and forty-nine percent is good, then you have your answer. It all depends on that one percent."

My father was in his second custody battle. Bettina had married a Venetian and taken Elena to live in Venice. During that time—the summers I was fifteen, sixteen, and seventeen—my father and I drank and talked a lot, filling ourselves to bursting with booze, words, grandiose ideas, trying to still that hyper bird that lived in our chests, a thrashing bundle of unease. My father surrounded himself with a coterie of hard-partying, morally suspect middle-aged men who took an interest in me. Tim was a tabloid journalist who wrote for the *Bild Zeitung*, the most widely distributed publication in Germany. He was small and compact with a pointy nose, wore shiny shirts with the top four buttons undone, loved heavy metal music, and wrote dark, angsty poetry that he read aloud to me. My father introduced me to Tim when I was fifteen and he was thirty. He was instantly attracted to me and my father seemed proud of that. Whenever I came to Hamburg,

Tim would take me to heavy metal clubs. We'd drink Jägermeister, and he would back me into dark corners and kiss me. Then we talked about death and pain. Tim loved to hear me talk about all the ways I hurt and hurt myself.

"I don't like you as much when you're not in pain," he told me. I stood in those dark bars tasting the brown, herbaceous syrup and watched Tim as he shimmied around the dance floor, getting closer and closer, a smirk on his face. I was not attracted to Tim, but I found his interest in me compelling. It felt important to be liked by this man, however uninteresting and gross I found him. I was taller than him and would slip out of my heels so our mouths could meet. I wondered if my father knew about this, if he had matched me up with Tim to be pushed into corners and kissed. When Tim's eyes dug into mine, when his hands dug into my waist as he ground his pelvis against me, I felt like I was doing a good job. When he read me his terrible poetry, I knew I was in the right place at the right time doing the right thing. When I told him about cutting myself, he held my wrist and traced the scars with his finger, sometimes kissing them. My pain had a reason, and the reason was to entertain this man. His face softened and his body gyrated with desire, and in this dark club, where the Beatles played their first show, I found merit and meaning.

My father invited Jürgen Schmidt over to the Hamburg apartment, telling me, with great drama, that Jürgen had been the top mobster in Hamburg and the most successful and famous pimp. I couldn't wait to meet him. Pimp meant power. It meant deciding who was worth what. Jürgen Schmidt had a mustache and wore aviators and a fedora. The first few buttons of his shirt were undone and curls of chest hair wandered up to his neck. My father introduced me to him like he was throwing open the door to a room of secret splendor.

"Well, what would you charge for her?" my father asked.

I felt suspended over a deep pit in the pause before Jürgen's final valuation. What if he didn't assess me high enough? What number meant I was valuable? How would I ever know if I was worth anything? Jürgen gave a number. My father seemed satisfied, and we all laughed. We played darts in the living room. My father had told me Jürgen never took off his sunglasses so I hopped around him and draped myself on him and flirted and tried to get him to take them off. If I succeeded, it would mean I was incredibly sexy, irresistible, and valuable, and that would make my father proud.

We went to parties thrown by Udo Müller. Udo was an infamous denizen of Hamburg nightlife, renowned for his debauchery. He was in his fifties, with a dark tan, conspicuous veneers, and a glistening pompadour. One night, I was seated on a sofa with Udo, my father, and a handsome thirty-three-year-old actor named Johann. Johann was on my left and my father was on my right. We were smoking a joint. I never liked weed but I liked the idea of smoking it in a club with a handsome thirty-three-year-old actor and my father. I liked showing my father that I was a wild, untamable, riveting creature. I danced and I drank and I flirted with Johann, who wrapped his fist up in my long hair and kissed me. At 3 a.m. my father told me it was time to go. I pouted and refused. He grabbed my ponytail and yanked. I laughed and hid under the table. He pretended to drag me away by my hair, both of us laughing. I refused to leave. He threw his hands up and said to Udo and Johann, without looking at me, "Fine. Get her home safely, boys," and left. I spent the rest of the night making out with Johann on the sofa until Udo said it was time to go. He had located a pretty brunette sex worker and she, Udo, Johann, and I got into a taxi. I assumed they were taking me home. We drove along the water and the taxi stopped in front of a house, not mine, in a part of Hamburg I was not familiar with. It seemed that none of the adults had any money. The driver started yelling and Udo yelled back. I found some cash at the bottom of my purse and paid the driver, pushing the men out of the cab as they cursed at the driver over their shoulders. We were at Udo's apartment, and once inside the girl went to cry on the couch. The men got beers. I knelt next to her and comforted her in broken German. Udo and Johann stood behind us watching and drinking. Udo held out his hand, palm up. The girl got up, still crying, put her hand in his, and followed him to the back of the apartment. My father had told me that Udo had a special penis pump that he used when he had taken too much cocaine and couldn't get erect. I felt bad about what awaited her. Johann went to the bathroom. I took the opportunity to arrange myself, leaning into the doorway of the balcony, jutting out my hip, and tilting my head sideways. Johann came back into the room and said, "Who are you posing for?" He wrapped his arms across my breasts from behind.

"No one," I said coyly.

Johann led me into a bedroom. I lay down on the bed and faced away from him. My heart was racing, my breath catching in my throat. It felt like something was slipping away from me, fast. I gripped the sheet, pulling it up from the mattress. I heard Johann's belt buckle thud to the floor. He got into bed and put his body against mine. He was soft and warm, and his softness and warmth draped me in a grotesque humidity. I lay completely still and pretended to be asleep, trying to smooth my breath over the wild hopping of my heart. "Are you asleep?" he asked. I didn't answer. He rubbed himself against my back and sighed. And then he was still. I waited until I heard him snoring and then got out of the bed and locked myself in the bathroom. I sat on the floor, with my back against the door, waiting for the suffocating heat from Johann's body to dissipate off my skin. I stared at my phone and called my friend JP, who was in New York.

"I'm stuck in a bathroom and I don't know where I am," I told him, breathlessly. "I don't know what to do. I need to get out of here."

JP told me to call my father. We hung up and I stared at my phone. I called my father but he didn't answer. I managed to reach my German uncle who said he would pick me up. I didn't know the address so I walked outside and started reading street signs. I walked alone through the still, early morning streets. As I waited on the corner for my uncle to arrive, I stared at the river, blurred into inflexibility by the gray dawn—a steel ingot. I stared at my hands, leaden at the end of my arms. I closed my eyes and saw the image of me dancing in a club for my father and his friends. It had been fun, hadn't it? Finally my uncle pulled up and I got into his car. We drove to his house and I went to bed. When I woke up I called my father. He screamed at me that he had been calling every hospital in Hamburg. Johann had called him frantic because I was gone, informing my father that he had put me to sleep on the sofa and covered me with a blanket. I needed to apologize to Udo and Johann, my father said. When I got home my father dialed Udo's number and handed me the phone. I mumbled an apology and thanked Johann for taking care of me.

THAT WINTER, my father threw a New Year's Eve party in the Hamburg apartment. In every room I entered, my father's friends reached out to me, hands on my thighs, in my hair, up my skirt. Was this what my father wished he could do? I walked into my bedroom, and Karl approached me. Karl was a photographer in his forties with long, wavy hair, a pointy chin covered in blond stubble, thin, curling lips, and intense blue eyes. He brought his body close to mine and gripped my arms. His tongue in my mouth felt mushy and too wet. He was vigorous with it. His facial hair was tough and spiky in my mouth. The combination reminded me of a sea urchin—the glistening pile of soggy sex organs bordered by spikes. He removed his face from mine, peered down at me, and walked out. I spent the rest of the night positioning myself in his sight line. He and my father left to go to a club. It got late and I wanted to go to sleep. I got into bed and wrote in my journal, which had streaks of dried blood on the pages: *Dad's drunk. More ambiguous than when Mom is. Which is worse? Dad is so plastered. He tried something with me. I don't want to start out this year as an old-man-teasing sex object.* I didn't offer any more information about what I meant when I said that my father had "tried something"— whether the attempt was sexual or confrontational. *Maybe this is not a good world for me. Why do I feel so guilty?* I turned off the light and was beginning to fall asleep when my father's friend Detlev crawled into bed with me. I got up and left the room. I tried the doorknob of the guest room but it was locked. I went into the room I used to share with my sister before Bettina had taken her to Venice. People were having sex in it. I interrupted them long enough to remove one of the mattresses, and put it on the floor in the hallway. I managed to doze for a few hours.

The next afternoon Karl called to chastise me for kissing him. He warned me that he was far too old and though he knew it would be difficult for me, we couldn't do that again, much as he wanted to have sex with me. His voice had a placating, conciliatory tone that made me doubt my memory. Did these men know me, know my desires, better than I did? I apologized to Karl.

On the plane back to New York, I was reading *Crime and Punishment*, and a handsome, blond man in the seat next to me asked how I liked it. He introduced himself as thirty-three-year-old Captain Will Price. He taught literature at West Point military academy. I told him I was reading the book for my Russian literature class, and that I was sixteen. He told me that he had been a virgin until he was twenty-three because of God and that now, at thirty-three, he was determined to be a virgin again. We made out as the plane landed and it felt like something right out of a romantic comedy. Back in New York, we made a date to go out for sushi. He ordered two sakes and sneaked me one because I was underage. I brought him back to 134 Charles Street. The house was dark and still. I brought him into my room and closed the door. We kissed deeply and his hands made their way to my body. I knelt on my bed and he bent over me to meet my mouth. He still had his coat on and I held on to his lapels. He pulled away from me to look around, at the crossword puzzles I had taped to the walls, at the stuffed animal on my bed, at my backpack on the floor, at the teenage mess. I sucked him back into our kissing. I felt his crotch and he was hard. The next time he pulled away his face was bright red. His eyes darted around the room.

"Don't worry, my mom's asleep," I said. I wasn't worried. I suspected that if she walked in on us, she'd simply apologize and close the door.

He started stammering. He never said out loud that he was alarmed that he was about to fuck a teenager, or that he was scared my mother would walk in, mid-felony, or that he feared a wrathful god might deny him heaven. Instead, he muttered an apology and ran out of the room. I froze, kneeling in the center of my bed, wondering what I'd done wrong.

The summer I turned seventeen, my father and I were at the Kempinski Hotel in Berlin. When he wasn't on set, we spent our days by the pool, swimming, reading, and eating french fries. I read books in the steam room until the pages grew wet and glued together. We talked about movies and books, and he asked me for my opinions about the screenplay he was writing. We were sitting at a table near the pool, wet from swimming, our bathrobes open. My cuts itched under my swimsuit. I smelled french fries and chlorine. We had our notebooks open on the table. Water from my hair dripped onto the page, making the ink spidery and diluted. We were talking about filmmaking.

"It's always been my dream," said my father, "to make a movie that stars a father and daughter in the roles of the lovers and have a sex scene between them. It's never been done. It would be the first. It would be revolutionary. We would star in it."

We spoke all the time about art, about pushing the boundaries of art, about collaborating. And I loved it. Today's idea was that we fake-fuck on camera. Or maybe it was real fucking? I wasn't completely sure. I gripped the french fry in my hand, my body bracing for the impact as this image was dropped into me. But this suggestion of onscreen incest sank, its detonation muffled, as if I were an endless, bottomless body of water. The new banality of these comments made them more dangerous. They could sneak into my psyche, disguised as any other thought or feeling, and pollute the entire ecosystem.

Back in Hamburg, we decided we needed to do something transgressive before I turned eighteen and became an adult. "We should do naked photos while you're still a Lolita," my father suggested. This made a great deal of sense to me. I would only be a "Lolita" for one more year. I felt a nameless loss and wondered what time was taking from me. Karl the photographer came over. My father and I decided on an Amazon queen theme, based on Heinrich von Kleist's play *Penthesilea.* My father sat in the corner working the tip of a long stick into a point with a knife. This would be my spear. He gave me a small piece of gray cloth to wear around my hips tied with some rope. The three of us drove out into a forest, where my father had arranged for a horse. I jammed my bare foot into my father's cupped hands, pushing against them to hoist myself up onto the horse. I had never ridden a horse naked before and the vigorousness of the bouncing of my breasts surprised and amused me. I rode bareback and without underwear, for historical accuracy, and the thin, pilled pad I sat on rubbed against my vulva. The sensation of rubbing and motion and the rhythmic force and release of pressure against my crotch brought me from arousal to pain and back again, sensations that were not the same, but also sometimes the same.

I felt powerful. I felt exposed and exalted as the two men watched and directed me, my body telling a story. But underneath was a shivering disquiet, as if at any moment I could be thrown from this system, this fantasy these men had created, and break into meaningless, invisible pieces.

7.

I was trying to fulfill the basic milestones that were expected of me.
My peers had been studying with private SAT tutors since freshman year. I had barely opened any of the big, glossy prep books. When
I took the test, one of the questions in the verbal comprehension
section was about my mother. There was a paragraph that discussed
her being commissioned to design a garden for Battery Park City. I
gaped and looked around, bursting to tell someone. But everyone's
head was down, struggling to answer questions about my mother,
about our life. I filled in the bubbles on the test sheet, hoping I had
gotten the answers right.

My mother took me to visit colleges. I had wanted to take a gap
year, but she disapproved of that idea. We drove to Yale and Middlebury
and Vassar. She was a terrible driver, both aggressive and unsure, and
I pushed my legs against the well of the car and my hands against the
dashboard as she weaved back and forth, trying to change lanes. As
we waited for AAA in the dark (she had driven up onto a curb and
broken an axel), eating chocolate and trying to decide my future, I

watched my mother's profile, studying the woman whose desires for me, whose desire for me, preoccupied and perplexed me. She took me shopping at Bed Bath & and Beyond for college supplies, and we deliberated over bedsheet patterns. It felt good to join her in picturing my future, to know that we both held in our minds an image of me walking across a quad or finally making my own bed with the plaid comforter we picked out. In the end, I applied just to Vassar because it was the only place I wanted to go. I lied to the college counselor, saying I had absolutely sent in the recommended number of reach, target, and safety-school applications. I made Till the subject of my college admissions essay. I was accepted.

I ARRIVED AT VASSAR COLLEGE in August 2003. I felt good. People seemed to like me, boys especially. I had long, over-excited talks with new friends who would appear at night and pull me from my bed for adventures. We walked the campus in our nightclothes—me in a pink satin slip with a tuxedo blazer thrown over it. I met interesting people from places I'd never been—like Bulgaria and Pennsylvania. We developed absurd inside jokes. I wasn't cutting. During orientation week I wrote in my journal: *Here I am at Vassar. I'm smiling as I write this. I'm hesitant to say it's been great. It's hard to believe I'm here all on my own. I feel so comfortable.* I bought my books. I wrote my schedule in my new planner. I convinced my roommate, a cheery, cherubic Texan, to put a poster of the porn star Jenna Jameson on our door. Classes began. I loved my Gothic literature class, and outlined hypothetical essays before they were even assigned. I even liked the cafeteria food. I went to parties, developed crushes. But my gossamered euphoria was fragile. I was afraid it would tear, and I wrote in my journal: *I don't want this to go downhill. I'm not quite sure how to pace myself to make sure that doesn't happen. I have to write. I have to have something to show for myself.* Over the following weeks I continued to raise my hand in class and swish into parties in my vintage dresses, trying to perform who I thought I was, but with each verbose answer or too-loud laugh, I felt more and more distant from myself and from everyone around me. I started to panic. I couldn't tell if there was a nascent someone huddled within the grandiose construct I had managed to assemble out of the loudest, brightest bits of my parents. As if the dial were being slowly turned on a radio, the lively tempo of my college life dissolved into static. I slept longer and later. I barely made it to class, and when I did I couldn't focus. I stopped doing homework.

I covered my minuscule dorm room with mess. I didn't wash my clothes. The unisex bathroom down the hall felt too far to walk to, so I urinated in mugs and emptied them out of the window at night. My roommate had started sleeping over in her friend's room, so I had more room for my mess to spread. On the ledge at the head of the bottom bunk, where I slept, were cups of old coffee, mugs of old tea, bowls of old ramen noodles. They sat there for weeks. I watched the mold change colors and grow and take on different textures. I coffined myself in the bottom bunk, zipped up in a sleeping bag I had bought so I wouldn't have to wash my sheets, asleep more hours than I was awake, surrounded by decay. Blood stains streaked my pillow. I wandered around campus in a somnambulant haze, wearing a bathrobe, blood soaking through the terry cloth, drinking vodka from a mug. I was cutting every day, numbering each cut with a pen, trying to impose meaning and order as my reason dissolved, as I dissolved. I wrote in my journal that *I have a fantasy of making a smooth cut along the outside of my body, up the side, under the arm, over it, around the neck, down the arm, under, down the other side, under my foot, end. Cut in half.* One month shy of the end of my first, and only, semester at Vassar, I brought myself to the campus medical services building and showed them my arms and legs. They locked me in the medical center—my every movement supervised—and called my mother. The next day, a friend of my mother's helped me pack my things and drove me back to 134 Charles Street.

Being back at home, I was able to pee in a bathroom and dress myself, but I felt like I was watching myself from far away. I resumed sessions with my therapist and continued taking the antidepressant my psychiatrist prescribed. A month after I returned from Vassar, Roy was taken to hospice to finish dying. I visited him only once, with my mother. As we got into the car, I handed her stories I had written over the last few years—about a man who builds a house just to burn it down, a funeral where the next of kin are required to eat the deceased, a doctor who performs an autopsy on the man he murdered.

"What's this?" she asked.

"They're stories I wrote," I said. "I want Roy to read them."

"Oh, he can't read anymore," she said, and handed them back.

On each side of the long hospice hallway were open doors, one after another, and in each room someone was dying. I felt like I was seeing something I shouldn't be seeing, something obscene and private. Every body in every bed made that pyramid where the sheet tented over the toes. The same shape over and over and over, in every room, all the way down the hallway, as if someone had pressed the wrong button and multiplied reality. We were there to find that one shape, to find the right name on the whiteboard next to each doorway. I watched as a nurse erased and rewrote a different name on someone's door.

Roy lay in his room with his door open, making strange, ugly noises. We sat in chairs next to him listening to his mystic growls and alien wheezes.

A rabbi came up to us.

"How do you know Roy? What faith was he?" he asked my mother.

"He wasn't religious," I said.

"Was he like a father to you?" he asked me.

I didn't know what to say because it didn't feel like I knew what that meant.

"I don't want to talk about him like he's not here," said my mother.

The rabbi asked me to help him clean up a small conference room. I followed him. I carried a plastic platter of stale, neon-orange cubes of cheddar cheese and tipped it into a garbage can. I asked the rabbi if there was more cleaning to do, but he said, "No, go and be with your family." I had no idea what me doing that would look like, how it would feel. I wanted to throw more things in garbage cans, scrunch up trash, wipe dust off tabletops. I wanted to keep moving.

A week later, my mother told me Roy was dead.

"I wasn't there when he died," she said. "I went to make a phone call and he died."

I didn't know what to say. I watched her face for signs of how one responded to this kind of thing. I wondered if I would see her cry for the first time. I didn't. I went with my aunt and my mother to the funeral home. I brought my journal with me because this was novel and this was information, and collecting that information seemed imperative. The funeral director led us into a thickly carpeted office with no windows. All around us were shelves with urns for sale and little peaked cards with prices written on them. I walked around the room writing down how much each urn cost.

We took the elevator to the third floor.

"In the last room to your left," said the funeral director.

The room was huge and fat with carpet. There was a long rectangular table against the back wall and on it was the corpse of Roy, his head sticking out from an enormous blue plastic bag. I didn't understand what I was looking at. I felt dizzy and far away. My mother and Julie left the room. I walked over to the corpse. I couldn't figure out if it was real, if I was real. I watched myself put out my hand and touch the forehead of the corpse. The forehead was so cold. The room was warm so I didn't understand why the head was cold. I felt the frigid ball of flesh under my hand. I was trying to understand, as the head cooled my fingertips, where the edges were, where he ended and I began. I imagined myself as a projection, the final image his brain had sparked before it had sputtered out. I felt like a dream being dreamed by the people around me, a reverie fading as it was dragged into wakefulness. I walked out into the hallway where my mother and aunt sat in high-backed, upholstered chairs, and was surprised when they looked up at me, that they could still see me. The funeral director appeared and led us into an elevator, down a hallway, and then into a small windowless room. The man stood in the doorway and said, "You can have a moment in here." He closed the door behind him. There was a water cooler in the room with tiny cone-shaped paper cups. Someone filled one for me and put it in my hand. The water was very cold and the cup was very thin. It felt like there was nothing separating the water from me, and that at any moment the water would lose its shape and just spill all over me. At any moment things would lose their shape and spill all over onto everything.

II / Nothing

1.

I moved blankly through unstructured days. I looked up stripping jobs in the city. I researched writing letters to death-row convicts. I sat in my room, wondering if lonely men waiting to die, in a club or in prison, could give me purpose. I didn't have the follow-through for either activity. Some nights I drank myself to sleep, other nights I cut myself to sleep. During the day, I sat in my room, trying to write and listening to Nanny talk to herself in the kitchen. Nanny, now seventy-seven, had retired, and my mother had invited her to live with us for the remainder of her life. Nanny was lonely, and her disembodied voice sneaked her loneliness into me, past my door with no lock, until I was crowded with both of our alienation, jam-packed with an emptiness that would grow bigger than I could have ever imagined.

I was trying to be normal, and what normal looked like was hanging out with a guy with a soul patch and taking a giant hit from a bong, which I'd never done. I inhaled deeply and held my breath for as long as I could. As I exhaled, I felt the smoke take everything I was with it. I heard myself say "whoa, whoa, whoa" over and over. I couldn't stop saying "whoa," as if the sound would somehow adhere me to the body I was now far, far away from. I crawled to the bathroom, locked myself inside, and lay on the floor. I stared at the warning on the side of a bottle of Clorox spray that lay under the sink a few inches away from my face. I tried to read the words over and over again but I had no idea what *contact with eyes* or *call poison control* meant, and the less sense they made the more panicked I became. My body boomed with heartbeats, an empty, shuddering shell on the floor of a bathroom. I touched my face, my arm, trying to convince myself that the membrane between inside and outside was still intact. The feeling of my skin on me made me sick and I began to vomit. I flushed the toilet, and it started to overflow. I slid slowly across the floor as the water inched toward me. When it finally reached me, I opened the door, ran through the living room, and out the front door. I ran barefoot through the streets, the guy with the soul patch running after me. A cop car drove by and I flagged it down. Soul Patch told them I had smoked weed and needed to go to the emergency room, could they take me? The cops told him that they could take me but they'd also have to arrest me. Take a cab, I was advised. Soul Patch hailed a cab as I sat in the fetal position on the curb. I was sent home from St. Vincent's Hospital with a piece of paper telling me about panic attacks, but I knew it was something more. I went to sleep that night hoping unconsciousness would reverse the horrifying depletion that had taken place. But I awoke the next morning and fell, breathless, into a room I could barely recognize, a body I could barely feel, and a mind I could barely follow into perception. The unmistakable arrhythmia of the "disconnect," as I had begun to call it, that had been disrupting my life, was now louder, more insistent, a second heart that beat along with my original heart, out of time, out of body.

. . .

THREE MONTHS AFTER ROY DIED, my mother was diagnosed with cervical cancer. I went with her and Julie to Sloan Kettering Cancer Center for her hysterectomy. As they prepped my mother for surgery, she looked scared. It was hard to identify; the expression was not at home on her face. I didn't like her looking like that.

While we were waiting, I got hungry. I always got hungry in the middle of crises. (On September 11, when Dalton went into lockdown after the second plane hit the Twin Towers, I went straight to the deserted cafeteria and devoured two plates of lo mein.) I now went to the hospital cafeteria and ate as much as I possibly could. I went back upstairs, and we were told we could go and see my mother. She had her eyes closed and was making noises.

I touched her. She was hot and soft, like melting wax.

The next day we visited again. I stared as the doctor checked the wound, even though he told me not to look. It was huge, the size of my hand, and deep. She contracted a MRSA infection and the wound would not close. Weeks passed and it still did not close, a mouth hanging open in the middle of her, as if frozen in shock or yawning in boredom. A team of surgeons prescribed and scraped and cut away but the infection would not abate. They sent her home with a wound VAC, a large suction cup that fit over the wound and was attached to tubes. The tubes extended from the vacuum device attached to her stomach, over her shoulders, and down into a canister she wore as a backpack, sucking and drawing the infected sludge out of the wound. She had to wear the wound VAC all the time. A sound like gravel under car tires filled up the space as the red-brown goo sailed across her chest, over her shoulders, and disappeared into the black-hole backpack. I could see her insides on the outside, the boundary between internal and external eroding. The more I saw of her, the less I understood. She was remote in her indomitability and she was remote in her frailty.

As she recovered up in the pool room bedroom, I didn't do anything for her. If she wanted to see me or needed something, I refused
to go upstairs to her. I would not bring up her glasses, I would not
come and talk to her. It felt too far away and too high up. But really
I was confused. This was not how the story was supposed to go. And
that felt scary. My mother was not supposed to be one of those sick
strays who came here to die. She was not the person who lay in her
room, in the dark, in weakness and uncertainty. She was the woman
who ordered up other people's skeletons, who rendered the world and
herself gigantic and powerful, who was the exception to every rule.

As my mother convalesced, I was having a hard time finding and
then holding on to myself. I tried to describe to my therapist the
feeling that I wasn't real, that I didn't exist. She didn't understand
what I was talking about. She seemed to have been caught off guard
by my cutting and now by my burgeoning unreality. I tried over and
over to explain what I was experiencing. I couldn't look in the mirror
because I didn't recognize my own face. I didn't know who or what I
was. I couldn't remember being a person. I had memories but I felt
no connection to them. I looked at my hands and I didn't understand
that they were mine. Sometimes they felt very small and sometimes
they felt very large. When I spoke, I didn't know where the sound was
coming from, who or what was making it. Everything was too bright,
very far away, and unfamiliar. Time stopped being linear, and instead
curled in on itself in a lethal looping. Each moment was the first
moment in the history of the universe, when things were just taking
shape, though never forming something solid. At the same time there
was a constant sense of déjà vu, as if everything that was happening
had already happened. I felt far, far away. The thing that I was had
crawled into the very back of my brain and was huddled there, squinting through a peephole at an unrecognizable world.

To get back to myself I was self-harming all the time. The self-harm
did what nothing else could. The way I cut varied. Sometimes, I

sucked in air and sliced at my flesh as quickly as possible, separating as much skin as possible, going as deep as I could. Sometimes, I drew the blade across my skin slowly, daring myself, seeing how much pain I could endure. It was a conversation. I asked my body a question and a red mouth opened on my flesh, answering me. If the answer wasn't loud enough, if I needed more pain, I would heat the blade of my Swiss Army knife with a lighter until it glowed red and press it sideways against my flesh, take a sharp breath, and listen to the skin crackle. After a few seconds I removed the blade and, hit with the rush of endorphins, felt wrapped in warm velvet. My mind and body unkinked and slackened. The burning lit up every neuron, set them singing in a barbershop harmony that revealed every pitch of injury—the shivering falsetto of pain, the rich bass of analgesia. The skin bubbled up and I popped the burn blisters and watched the liquid emerge. Sometimes I sampled the fluid issuing from my injured body as if it were a precious antidote. I loved those wounds, I revered them. My scarified body was a monument I was continually erecting for the confounding, darkly divine-seeming mind that felt so powerful, so alien. The scab that formed on top of the cut was the scarlet dome of a cathedral, the white scar lines left behind carvings on the facade. After each cut, after each burn, I was returned to my body, I touched the walls of myself again. It was also a way to mark time. Day one was when I hurt myself, and each successive day after, I healed. I knew then that I at least had the body of a human. I was alive and I could still move from the present into the future, whether I wanted to or not.

In March 2004, I was in the shower cutting, watching the water turn red, watching the blood streak down my legs like a second set of veins. I had dismantled a shaving razor and was using that keen, slim metal to slice up my thighs. On contact with the water, the blood, diluted, grew limpid, lighter, creating swift runnels of bloody water down my body. It stung when the water pelted the wounds. I sat on the floor of the shower and stared out at the world. I had been given a name, I had memorized all the semantic information having to do with Alice Carrière, but I was someone, something else. I was crying. Not from the physical pain, which no longer registered as pain, but from that collapsing feeling, so empty inside that the swollen world crashed in on me like a waterlogged ceiling. The weeping echoed in the bathroom, spread out over it, bounced off the walls and back at me. It was not me making that noise; the room was screaming at me, hollering warnings of what could happen if I kept this up—or what might happen if I didn't. I realized I couldn't stop cutting. The razor flitted back and forth across my skin. It felt like it was part of my hand, a disloyal extremity, a mutinous appendage. Somehow I managed to lay it on the rim of the bathtub next to the shower. The shower had steamed up the room, giving all my movements a dreamlike quality, as if I were a creature emerging from the mist. The water was so hot it had turned my skin pink, with streaks of deep red where I had opened myself up. I turned off the shower and dried myself, avoiding the cuts, and put on some clothes. I called my therapist and said:

"I think I need to go somewhere."

She told me to go to Lenox Hill Hospital.

I should let my mother know, I thought. On the phone the red light next to "bedroom" glowed: privacy mode on. I called my mother's secretary downstairs.

"I'm going to check myself into a psych hospital," I said.

"You should let your mother know," she said.

The secretary told me that my mother was in her room with two socialite friends. I felt like someone else had made the phone call to my therapist, someone else had made the choice to commit me. I needed to run. I grabbed cash, a change of shirt, a bottle of Chanel No. 14 perfume, and a toothbrush, and shoved them into my purse. I pitched out of my room, and there they were, standing in the kitchen. My mother's secretary must have gone upstairs and told them what I had said. All three of them were staring at me, silent as the sucking tubes of the wound VAC growled. I met my mother's eyes. I ran.

Outside, I didn't know which way to go because I didn't know why I was running. I ran down the street. The two socialites ran after me. One of them screamed at her chauffeur to stop me. He revved the engine and followed me. They caught up to me and cornered me. They were holding out their slender arms, their skin pale and smooth and glowing. Their hairstyles were the same—smooth and voluminous and shiny and curled at the ends, like fancy, looping calligraphy. Even the way their hair fell across their shoulders as they shifted back and forth, caging me with their arms, had a serenity, a calmness to it. They were ill-suited for these crazed postures, this urgent locomotion. Their eyes were not meant to be wild. I looked at them looking at me. They looked afraid, and I was the one making them afraid, and that scared me.

"It's Sally," said Sally. "Don't you remember all those clothes I gave you?"

"I know who you are. I'm not that far gone," I said. My brain stilled as it tried to figure out why it was being asked about borrowed clothes. In that moment of stillness, the soft, pastel urgency of these two women, trying to help my sick mother by trying to help her sick daughter, drained me of fight and I agreed to walk back to the house.

Back in the kitchen, my mother looked terrified, weighed down by those sucking tubes and her weakness. I went into my room, opened the tiny drawer where I kept my cutting kit—a shiny black LeSportsac pouch full of Swiss Army knives my father had given me, the sharp inserts of box cutters from my mother's studio, and the slivers of metal I had pried loose from shaving razors—brought it out into the kitchen and silently dropped it into my mother's hands. My gesture, pouring the sharp edges I used to flay myself into her soft, warm palm, contained a rage of such density that I flattened under it. I felt small and ashamed, and the force of regret knocked the breath out of me. I wanted to hug her and I wanted us to cry together. But I said nothing.

I went with my mother to Lenox Hill Hospital. She was silent as I filled out the forms. She said nothing as we rode the elevator to the eighth floor, the psych ward. We were buzzed in. A tech went through my bag, flipping through the pages of Sylvia Plath's *The Bell Jar* and Ken Kesey's *One Flew Over the Cuckoo's Nest* that I had brought with me, searching for razor blades I may have stashed inside. I felt oddly excited. A strange elation tickled the base of my spine as they stared at me, rifled through my belongings, tried to figure me out. This place was new. This place was unusual. To be a person in this place was new and unusual. This could be me. I could tape this identity over the busted-out hole of me.

"How do you know I haven't hidden something in my shampoo bottle?" I asked.

The tech eyed me with boredom and contempt.

"We don't," he said. "Did you?"

"No," I said.

He confiscated my shampoo bottle.

My mother left, and I was alone, eight floors up among strangers.

I was brought down a hall and into the second room on the left. An old woman was bent over one of the beds, her torso and face pressed into the mattress and her ass in the air.

"This is your roommate," said the nurse. "Elaine, this is your new roommate."

Elaine was making noises. Groans and mutters.

"I must have gained weight, these bloomers are killing me," she said into the mattress. "Everything is torturous."

Good word, I thought.

I wandered out into the main room that had tables and chairs, a broken rowing machine, and a tiny TV hanging from the ceiling. I started introducing myself to the people I would spend the next week with.

Evelyn had dissociative identity disorder—the new name for multiple personality disorder.

"I have ten different personalities with no dominant alter," she explained to me. Some were male and some were female, some were gay and some were straight, one was a baby.

"It's like cold water turning into hot water," she said about switching between alternate personalities.

Her scalp showed through her dry strawberry-blond hair, which was falling out because of her medication.

Ray always had rubber gloves hanging from his back pants pocket.

"What's your hobby?" he asked me and then answered his own question. "Ice skating. I read the obits voraciously. I just said ice skating to be sociable."

Rachel had survived Auschwitz. She was very old and her body was slight and gnarled. I felt drawn to nurture her as if she were an infant. I rubbed her back and spoke to her in hushed German. She rocked back and forth as much as her frail body allowed and murmured, "I hallucine. I hallucine." Marlene, who had also survived Auschwitz, walked over. Rachel looked up at her and asked if I had been in Auschwitz with them.

I played Scrabble with a young Russian man who was in hiding from the people who were trying to kill him.

"This place is like a vacation," he said. "Free food and safety." He tried to guess my birthday and said he would write a philosophical treatise about me. He also understood important mathematical equations.

A young female patient asked me many times a day, "How has your sleep been?"

"Fine," I answered over and over.

"So, how was your sleep last night?" she asked me. To her credit, it was a different question.

"So-so," I said, just to give her a different answer.

There was a schedule with activities so that we could separate the homogenous hunks of time that could jam up around us and crush us. We did aromatherapy. We did dance therapy. I swayed my hips and lifted my arms so my shirt rode up to my ribcage. The counselor tugged it down and said to the men, "You have to dance or turn away." The men stared, unmoving.

We did a flower-arranging session. Everyone took great care to select and tie the slim stems and the frilly blossoms together. I cut the blossoms off the stems, tied the green, decapitated stalks together, and put them in water. They looked like asparagus. Later, they would just look like anger.

That night they placed the flower arrangements on the tables where we ate dinner. All the bouquets were displayed except mine. I flew into a rage.

"What happened to my bouquet?"

"I think it was thrown out. It didn't have any flowers on it," said a nurse.

"That's how it was supposed to be. That was me expressing myself. Why is only what you think is beautiful beautiful? How dare you," I screamed.

Then it was time for dinner and I forgot my anger as a hunk of boiled chicken was placed in front of me.

I liked being here. The rules were clear and simple, their mere existence novel and diverting. Expectations were low—we were not here to get better, just not to get worse. The people were interesting. Patients introduced themselves with their diagnoses. They spoke casually about suicide attempts, about abusive parents, about hallucinations. A vinelike intimacy crept over and between us as we exchanged stories and showed each other our scars. Squeezed inside these hallways, eight stories up, it felt like we were the last people on earth. We had been selected, by magic or nature or divinity, to feel more, see beyond, hear maybe one too many voices. We each had something wrong, wrong enough to mark our skins, glaze our eyes, circle a hospital band around our wrists. In my mind, I hovered above the city not like a person but like an atmosphere, transformed into something enormous and powerful, making people stare up at me with wonder, making them sweat or shiver. I didn't feel like I was sick; I felt like I was special.

A nurse took me to the basement in a wheelchair for the medical workup every patient was required to get. When I walked back into the hallway afterward, the nurse was no longer there so I kept walking. I didn't have any shoes on, only hospital socks, though we were allowed to wear our street clothes. I took the elevator to the lobby. I walked outside in my socks, waiting for alarms to go off, for someone to notice the psych ward hospital bracelet on my wrist, tackle me, and bring me back where I belonged. But no one noticed me. The air on my skin, the strangers crawling around me, the sheer mass of other lives being lived in my proximity seemed otherworldly. Perhaps I didn't belong here anymore. I was a patient now. I belonged up there. There I had purpose. There I was accomplished. I could be the sexiest dancer, the angriest florist, and if I tried hard enough, the sickest patient. I went back inside the lobby and took the elevator back up to the eighth floor. When I approached the main door to the psych ward, Dr. Brune, the head doctor, was standing in the hallway. I knocked on the glass door. When Dr. Brune saw me, his eyes widened. I smiled wide and waved. He took long strides to the door like he wanted to run but was stopping himself.

"Did you come back up here alone?" he asked.

"Yes," I said. "They left me downstairs."

"And you came back?"

"Yes."

Dr. Brune didn't seem to understand.

On my third day there, my mother brought me chocolate from my favorite candy shop, Li-Lac. I ate greedily. I didn't think about my mother making an effort to bring me my favorite chocolate. I didn't think of her as housing such considerations, such care. I thought only that I had gotten something I wanted. Susan, who never spoke and rubbed scuff marks off the floor, glided over and removed three pieces of chocolate from the package and walked away. Anger enveloped me. I hunched over the chocolate defensively, trying to protect what I had, not wanting to share, unable to share the moment with my mother, the woman who was trying to give me everything she knew how to give.

The next day my father flew in from Germany and came to the hospital with my mother; it was only the second time I had seen my parents together in over a decade. He asked Dr. Brune how they would know I was well enough to be let out.

"When she stops cutting," said Dr. Brune.

"How will you know if she's stopped cutting if she's in a place where she can't cut?" my father asked.

"That's an interesting philosophical question," said Dr. Brune.

I was given the Minnesota Multiphasic Personality Inventory to fill out. It was composed of over five hundred statements I had to agree or disagree with, such as: "I like to pick flowers or grow house plants," "I am afraid of fire," "I like mechanics magazines," "Sometimes I feel like my soul is leaving my body." I felt so disconnected from myself that I couldn't decide what I felt from the list of choices. I let my father fill out the MMPI for me. The only moment I thought to intervene was when he reached the statement: "My father is a good man." But I just watched as he silently and without hesitation filled in the bubble marked "yes."

The next day, my mother and father sat across from me at a table in the main room. It felt like a strange weather phenomenon, as if three different fronts had coalesced in one spot. My mother sat silently as I tried to explain to them what I was experiencing. My father leaned toward me and scribbled notes. I jiggled my leg as I drew a picture of an outline of a body, like a crime scene, then drew a spiky aura around it and then small marks emanating from the head. I told them I felt disconnected from my body and my memories and my self. My father listened, nodding his head, writing down everything I said. He massaged my feet and hands, trying to see if I could feel it. I told him to press harder until it hurt but it never did.

"You seem manic," said my mother.

"I can't feel love anymore," I told them. "I have as much access to myself as I have to other people."

My father wrote down every word.

My mother wanted to hear what the doctor had to say.

When it was time for them to leave, my father pulled out a disposable camera and started taking photographs of me, the ward, and the patients. A nurse confiscated the camera, and I felt a pinch of loss as I watched the proof that we had all been here disappear.

Back in my room, the void began to unfold inside of me. The core of who I was a tab of Alka-Seltzer dunked in water, its cohesiveness breaking up and effervescing into nothing, into oneness with what surrounded it. I wanted out of my mind and my body. At the same time I wanted to return to myself. I couldn't cut so I grabbed my notebook. I tried to write, which was how I spent my nights. My handwriting had become pudgy and loopy, like a child's. *I don't know what's wrong with me. It's become too pervasive. I think it's taken over entirely. I have no connection to myself anymore. It's as if I've memorized myself: my abilities, my proclivities, my tendencies, and I'm carrying them out by rote. Everything is too bright. It's a crystalline shifting, kaleidoscopic. If writing helps I would have to be writing all the time. I feel dizzy and hot. Weak. Shaking. Short of breath. I don't know who I am. What is this? Would I kill myself if I get crazier? Am I getting crazier? Yes.* I wrote nonstop for an hour. I begged the page to keep me safe. I wrote down a list of words: *insalubrious, surreptitious, spank, reek, lament, tacheometry.* I went into the bathroom that had no lock on the door and crawled under the sink. I drew my knees to my chest and caged them with my arms, hand gripping unrecognizable hand. I started to bang the back of my head against the wall. I said my name, my address, and my phone number over and over again.

"Alice Isabelle Carrière. One three four Charles Street between Greenwich and Washington. Two one two six seven five two four two one."

I had shattered into innumerable pieces and been scattered across immeasurable distances. Each particle had a part of me but no particle had enough of me to be me. I tried to pound the fragments back together with these words and the force of my head against the wall. The words got louder. They needed to be louder. They needed to be so loud that they flattened me back into myself. The words got fewer and fewer until I was just screaming my own name.

A nurse came in.

"You are frightening the other patients," she said.

She helped me up off the floor.

"Let's make your bed, and explain to me what's going on," she said.

"I don't know. It's so hard to describe. It's like I'm outside of myself and I don't recognize what I'm looking at. Everything feels unfamiliar, as if I'm seeing it for the first time."

"It sounds like you're dissociating," she said.

I had never heard that word, not even in therapy. The more I had tried to describe my disconnect, the more my therapist suspected I was schizophrenic, and the more alone I felt. Now, this woman I barely knew was offering me something very important. She was giving me the word.

"What does that mean?" I asked. The pumping of my heart felt like hands grabbing at a lifeline.

"You should talk to your doctor about it," she said.

"Can you get me a book or print something out for me?" I asked, gripping the bedsheet to my chest. "I need to know what this is."

The idea that what had been growing in me, the unnameable blankness, existed somewhere beyond me, in black and white on a page, gave me hope, made me feel like I could exist somewhere too. No matter how much I faded from existence and then roared back on crests of blood, I was still a person and there was a word for me.

After one week they released me. One week after that I lay in the bath, took a razor, and slid it up my left inner forearm, somehow missing all major vessels and arteries. The skin opened up and blood bloomed from the cut, the edges fading from opaque to translucent. I imagined my skin speaking, announcing the new word it had learned: *dissociation*.

2.

I was back floating around 134 Charles Street. I read all the books on dissociation I could find. I recognized myself in the flat repulsion of Sartre's *Nausea*. I understood the remote alarm, a nova raging in desolation, that seethed through Clarice Lispector's *The Passion According to G.H.* as she spent almost two hundred pages thinking about a cockroach, thinking about her thinking. I felt the same annihilating desperation in Octavia Butler's short story *The Evening and the Morning and the Night* as the characters tried to dig themselves out of their bodies. Along with dissociating, the boundaries between my moods had grown dangerously porous, happiness bleeding into despair, into euphoria, into desolation. When I felt good, it was an intense kind of good, hot steam spewing from a ruptured pipe. Then came sadness that turned vapor into liquid into stone, until my own breath drowned, then choked me. When I felt good, I spent hours reading the dictionary and writing down words. I spent days memorizing the capitals of all the countries in the world, making my mother's staff quiz me, pacing the floor muttering "Burkina Faso, Ouagadougou" under my breath. I wrote out an equation for death, pages and pages of nonsense graphs and charts and made-up mathematical symbols, with notes in the margins that said "Winnicott's aura" or "Schrödinger." The next week, I grew quiet. I stayed in bed and watched my favorite musicals, trying to locate in them what I had loved before and crying when I couldn't. I stood in the pantry reading the labels on boxes of cookies and the bottles of Diet Coke my mom was addicted to, trying to comfort myself with those concise lists of ingredients that disclosed what was inside. I'd get in the pool and see how long I could stay under water. Once I found a stray gemstone in the grout of the pool-side tiles, leftover from my mother's sessions with the gemologist, when she'd shuffle gems into lines with a credit card, like dazzling cocaine, often sending them skittering across the floor and the gemologist scrambling to corral an errant emerald. The pool room smelled of the perfumes she made with celebrity event planner Robert Isabell, rows of little black glass bottles reeking of musk and leather and bergamot lining the lip of the pool, her life up here so extravagant, so colorful, so fragrant, and in such contrast to how drained of life I felt.

I spent a lot of time in Nanny's room drinking Red Rose tea and watching TV with her. I would wedge myself next to her in her armchair, sometimes playing with the gold chain around her neck like I had when I was a baby, and we'd watch *Keeping Up Appearances*, *Antiques Roadshow*, and *Gilmore Girls*. She sometimes tried to ask questions about what was going on with me but she wouldn't know what to say, so we'd stay curled up together and wait to see how much that Victorian inkwell would go for at auction. Words were useless here, but the closeness of our bodies and the calm of her room reminded me of something solid and essential.

One night, she walked in on me cutting. It felt like she had walked in on me having sex, something so intimate.

"What are you doing?" she asked, squinting at me through the dark.

"I'm cutting myself," I said. It didn't occur to me to lie.

Pain swept over her face. She sat down on the edge of my bed and put her hand on my leg. The contact made me flinch.

"It's fine. It's fine," I said, the word turning into a moan. "You can leave."

"I'm not leaving you alone," she said.

"It's fine. I swear. I promise you can leave." The last word stretched itself out, as if trying to drag her toward the door.

She sat with me for a long time, until I fell asleep. In the morning, the razor blade and lighter I used to sterilize it were gone from my bedside.

Two weeks later, energized again, I sat at the dining room table stabbing at my computer, finishing the novel I had been writing. When I finished it, I gave it to my mother to read. She read it up in her bedroom, and when she finished it, I found a note in my room, written on a ripped-out page of a notebook with a circle of coffee stain on it. It read: "You are a success already—you have written this. Deal with it. Go to Kinko's and get it bound." I kept the note, framed it, and put it on my desk.

My mother had no idea what to do with me or what to say. The only time we spent together was Thursday nights when I'd meet her up in the pool room bedroom and we'd watch *The L Word*, a show about lesbians in LA. We'd sit on her bed eating potato chips and criticizing the fashion, the shape of their boobs, and the dramatic facial expressions they made while they fucked each other. Most days, I watched her trying to get away from me. When I tried to show her something, play her a song, or read her something, her eyes would go first: arms cocked, palms on table, gaze elsewhere. I would watch her leave.

"You're leaving?" I would say to her back.

"Yes," she would say, not looking back.

Sometimes I would try and force my way in. I walked up to her in the studio and told her I had given some guy a blow job.

"Ugh, I don't want to hear about that," she said, walking away.

I was a ghost and I tried to haunt my mother into recognition. I walked around for a week with a cut up my forearm, and she never noticed or at least didn't say anything. I would show her my cuts, shoving my arm into the path of her gaze, inviting her to walk through their openings and into me.

My mother hosted a fashion show for the designer Ronaldus Shamask. Before the party I hung out in the kitchen as cute cater waiters in starched white shirts and ties lined canapés onto silver trays. When my mother walked in to check on things, I approached her and held out my arm.

"What should I do about these?" I said, gesturing at the healing cuts on my arm. "How should I cover them up?"

I spoke louder than I needed to, making sure the servers and chef could hear me.

"Just put some makeup on them," she said, her voice low as she cast uncomfortable sidelong glances at the strangers around her pretending not to hear.

I didn't need her advice on how to cover up my cuts. I didn't want to cover them up. I wanted them witnessed. Then the party began and I gave the tour over and over, circulating like a blood cell through the halls of 134 Charles Street. After an hour, the guests moved down to the lower studio and watched as models wearing organza trapeze dresses streaked with colorful rubber paint stalked through the space and a man played a cello while reciting a poem. After the party was over, I lingered in the kitchen talking to the servers as they wrapped leftover slices of seared tuna in Saran Wrap. I didn't want them to leave. I wanted them to stay and talk to me, to offer me more food, to laugh at my jokes. I stood in the kitchen as they loosened their ties and put their coats on, and 134 Charles Street emptied out, until it was only the three of us left, my mother drunk upstairs, Nanny alone in her room with the TV on, and me in the empty kitchen, eating leftover hors d'oeuvres and drinking from the half-empty bottles of red wine.

I made my way into the library and scanned the shelves. I saw my mother's name on the spine of a book and slid it out. It was the fictionalized autobiography she had written and published the year I was born. It was called *History of the Universe*, and it was her history, which made her the universe. That felt right. It had been edited down to a modest 197 pages from nearly two thousand pages of journal entries. It was organized into five chapters—Family, Marriage, Career, Friends, and Death—and in them she described everything about everyone she knew, everything she thought, all the products she used—from Crest toothpaste to Clinique powder—and every single detail about her physical appearance. As I read her book late into the night, I was grateful for her near-compulsive meticulousness and her self-absorption. Because she believed that every thought she had was interesting, I got to know my mother; I was allowed access to her through the only way she knew how to communicate—her work. The only thing she did not describe were emotions, unless she was listing synonyms for rage. What did something so vast and powerful and mysterious as the Universe have to do with feelings? One line read: *I wish I didn't think I was the only person in the world.* I couldn't tell if it was the most arrogant thing I had ever heard, or the loneliest. The only person in the world had no one to talk to, nothing to counteract the persuasion of their own imaginings. The only person in the world got to invent reality, but was alone to suffer the consequences of its incoherence. And what about the child belonging to the only person in the world? Just another invention.

I had started snorting Dead Uncle Roy's leftover Dilaudid, the powerful opioid he had been prescribed when he was dying, that I'd

found in my mother's bathroom. When the drug hit, I felt rooted. I
felt my edges. Twelve days before my nineteenth birthday, I invited
Effie and another friend, David, over for a swim while my mother was
out of town. Effie and David watched me snort two pills and I poured
us all vodka. We went up to the pool room and took off our clothes.
David got in the water and Effie and I started dancing. I felt great. I
was a giant bunny rabbit, all wiggles and heat and softness. I bent over
and kissed David. Nausea began to insinuate itself into the warm fluff.
I staggered downstairs, still naked, and lurched into the kitchen. I
switched on the tea kettle to make some coffee. While I waited for the
water to boil I got an English muffin from the bread box. I caught my
reflection in the curved metal and it felt remote, my face just an
extension of the appliance—a knob or a handle. I slid a serrated knife
out of the knife block to separate the two sides of the muffin. Instead
of cutting the muffin, I calmly slid the knife across my right forearm
four times. It felt very natural, part of the rudimentary gestures of
meal preparation. Coffee, muffin, skin. It felt reflexive, correct. As the
blood started spilling down my arm, I slowly realized I had done
something incorrect. I picked up the phone and called Effie on the
intercom.

"Effie? Effie? Could you come down here for a moment, please?"
My voice was oddly formal.

I stared at my arm as I waited for Effie. There was no pain. It had
opened up so easily. I found a dish towel and wrapped it around my
arm. Effie and David arrived in the kitchen. Effie gasped.

"What did you do? What did you do?" she said.

"We have to go to the hospital," David said.

I went to my room to put on some clothes and attempted to put on
makeup, but David dragged me away from the mirror. We piled into
his car and he drove us to Saint Vincent's Hospital.

On the way, David said, "Just say you cut yourself by accident."

I didn't want to lie. I'd tell the nurses and doctors the truth and we'd talk about it. We'd discuss how interesting it was and they'd nod and say, "Good point." They'd understand.

When we arrived at St. Vincent's, a man with a clipboard asked me what had happened. I chattered away about the pills, the vodka, the kitchen knife. A nurse took my blood and took my clothes and hooked me up to a saline drip. Someone called my mother, who was three hours away in the Hamptons. Effie left. David came in to check on me and then left too. I was taken into another room to get stitches. I watched a doctor stitch me up, embroidering my body, turning me into a decoration. She led me back to my bed. A young psychologist arrived, looking scared. She was petite and pretty and gripped a clipboard, as if it kept her from falling to great depths. She asked me why I did this. I announced, in a clear, too-loud voice: "I am not going to pontificate to you on the proximity of mortality." I may have smiled. She paused, wrote something down on her clipboard, and left. A man at the foot of the bed next to me turned to me and said, "Wow, you have a big vocabulary."

"Thank you," I said, and smiled.

The saline made me need to pee constantly. I walked to the bathroom in my thin blue paper gown, trailing my IV. The bathroom floor was covered in urine and my hospital-issued blue socks with the nibs of rubber on them soaked it up. I felt strangely capable, welcoming the unique challenges of being a patient once again.

After the sun came up, and the drugs and alcohol were flushed from my system, I started to get antsy. I demanded my clothes and was refused.

"You almost killed yourself in three different ways," I was told.

"What would happen if I ripped out my IV?" I asked.

The doctors finally reached my therapist. I convinced her to get them to let me go. She told me she would as long as I came to see her that day and that I agreed to be put on the waiting list for an inpatient hospital. I was given my clothes and I left.

Twenty days later, I was admitted to Austen Riggs, a psychiatric hospital. In his report, Dr. Palton documented his impression of me during the admissions interview: *Attractive, very bright, and verbal young woman wearing a dress that showed a little too much of her for the weather and the occasion, and with a seductive quality.* It was a warm fall day and I'd worn a knee-length yellow dress in a stretchy cotton that showed my collarbone and my arms, but no cleavage.

My mother had driven me to Austen Riggs and was waiting in the reception area. Dr. Palton invited her into the room to discuss payment. *Things broke down*, Dr. Palton wrote in his report. *The area of finances became a sinkhole in the consultation. Although mother and her secretary and Alice had all been told in writing and/or by phone about the financial terms of admission, Ms. Bartlett arrived at the consultation without her checkbook, without having given us her or her daughter's insurance information, without having filed the fee reduction we sent her.*

Dr. Palton told us that my insurance would not cover my stay. My mother couldn't afford the treatment at that time and had assumed insurance would cover it. I watched my mother sitting on the cream sofa. I could detect no power or mystery in her. She was small and scared. I understood for a moment what I was taking from her, what my existence demanded. As Dr. Palton chastised her, I felt protective of her. We both had a naïve belief in the endlessness of everything—of resources, of good graces, of exceptions—but the demands of my illness were straining that illusion. For a brief moment I glimpsed the reality of what was happening—of what my illness meant for me and for my family, what it would take from us. My failure to keep pace with my peers, with the expectations of the people around me, would have consequences. I ran crying into the bathroom, and my mother followed me. I told her I couldn't be admitted. It was too expensive and I wasn't worth it. She told me it was all right, that we'd figure something out.

My mother made a phone call as Dr. Palton watched her from his office door. I found out later that she had called a friend to borrow the money to pay the astronomical admissions fee. The German medical insurance my father had would end up enabling my stay at Riggs. I was admitted to Austen Riggs, and those momentary realizations—that I was not just owed everything, that the world would not heel at my feet—evaporated as I moved into the white columned mansion and became a full-time sick person for the next year.

3.

The Austen Riggs Center, located on Main Street in a small town called Stockbridge, Massachusetts, was a prestigious "open-setting" psychiatric hospital for "treatment-resistant patients." We could leave whenever we wanted. Patients walked in and out freely, went to the few restaurants in the area, shopped in Great Barrington, saw movies in Pittsfield, even traveled out of the state. The nurses didn't wear uniforms, and we could lock our doors. Our meals were cooked for us. For breakfast, we could choose from omelets, scrambled eggs, pancakes, French toast. There was an enormous refrigerator in the cafeteria that held Old Chatham Sheepherding Company sheep's milk yogurt, in plain and maple flavors, and Naked smoothies. We could take as many as we liked, whenever we liked. I decided I would make up for the cost of this place by eating as much fancy yogurt as I possibly could. Sometimes, tourists would mistake Riggs for a hotel and line up at the buffet with the patients.

The residential building was a weathered white mansion with a mahogany staircase with peeling lacquer, threadbare red and yellow patterned carpets, dusty floor-to-ceiling drapes, a chandelier with dull brass finishes and missing pendeloques, and a large community room with a shabby brown out-of-tune baby grand piano with a few broken keys. My room had a bay window, fireplace, and pink sink that, I was told, Judy Garland had installed when she spent time there. The staff boasted that James Taylor had written "Fire and Rain" during his stay. The place had an impressive pedigree. My peers now were: the daughter of an NYC mega-restaurateur, the daughter of a famous Native American author, the stepdaughter of a singer whose Christmas song haunted every North American store from October until January, and the daughter of the man responsible for the fragrances in most products. Angela was an ex-junkie dwarf and a movie producer who was afraid of unattached pieces of hair. Paula was a morbidly obese lesbian who threatened to throw herself out of her shrink's window (which was only six feet above the ground). Chad was seventeen and could make himself vomit on cue, without even sticking his finger down his throat. Beth rarely spoke and made strange, startlingly loud noises deep down in her throat. Bob was a middle-aged man who had been a patient for a solid decade and hit on all the girls, asking them repeatedly, "Can I check under your hood?" He claimed it was cheaper for his father to pay for this place than to keep having to bail him out of jail or pay for totaled cars. Brad was five five, told people that he was six two, and wasn't worried because he could always fall back on modeling. Steven kept saying he was going to start a book club and stashed a gun in his room. Derek had been in a cult and before that had been a Chippendales dancer.

At Riggs, the recommended stay was "indefinite"—patients were encouraged to stay for years, or at least until their money ran out. To fill the time, people fucked each other, smoked weed on the sly, occasionally overdosed on Tylenol or Klonopin, formed cliques, bullied each other. Our main purpose was to explain ourselves, over and over, to one another. Riggs boasted a high number of self-styled intellectuals, so we proved adept at this assignment. There were activities and events to keep us patients from languishing in introspective luxury. For Halloween there was a costume party. I dressed up as Vocabulary, with words like *insalubrious* written on my arms, and felt very cute and smart. For Thanksgiving, there was a pumpkin carving competition. I carved the image of a pumpkin into a pumpkin and titled it *Narcissism*, and felt very clever. There was a woodshop; a greenhouse; ceramics, visual, and fiber arts studios; and a black-box theater whose two productions a year were helmed by a Shakespeare & Co. director and included patients and local actors. There was also an endless supply of what we, naïve and bored and entitled and sick, interpreted as "drama." An unknown man called the phones in the rooms of all the female patients, posing as boyfriends or male friends in order to have phone sex with them. I fell for it, thinking it was my friend Hicham. A fifty-year-old patient convinced an eighteen-year-old patient to take a Valium so he could have anal sex with her. Someone wrote the word *kike* on a pizza box. One girl threw a TV down the stairs because she wanted to hear that satisfying crunch. The same girl took down the giant oil painting in the living room and, with a sign saying "Free Painting," pedaled it on Main Street in the snow. If the staff found out about any of these things, the community would sit and talk about it. There were barely any rules and no consequences, and rules and consequences were the two things I needed most. My room was a mess, and I repeatedly "failed" inspection, but failure meant nothing here. I was urged to go to group therapy sessions, but nothing happened if I didn't show up. It was assumed we would be here for a very long time, and I felt no urgency, no need. The doctors and counselors expressed no urgency, implied no need. The passivity and luxury that defined this treatment would later anger me. How could we grow when we encountered no resistance, nothing that encouraged us to change? The extreme bounty—of time, of chances, of yogurt—and the extreme luxury—chronological, spatial, psychic, culinary—were like sedatives. They made the reasons for being here, and the need to overcome them, fuzzy. I wondered why anyone would ever want to leave. We were important and special and cared for accordingly. My every move so important as to be recorded by staff, my every complaint listened to and wondered about, my every random thought met with a rapt audience. If this was what it meant to be ill, I didn't know if I ever wanted to get better.

My therapist at Riggs, Dr. Lampen, was a pretty blond woman who rarely spoke, with a face that didn't move. It was as if she had a special frozen face on top of her real face. I tried to imagine her inner life, the secret hiding place behind her motionlessness, but it was so extreme that I sometimes wondered if she was real. There was no desk in her room, only two chairs and a sofa. There were no photographs, no personal touches. This was intentional. This kind of therapy relied on anonymity—I wasn't allowed to know anything about her so that I couldn't project anything onto her. It was a familiar and infuriating feeling: another remote woman. She did have a hook from which she hung her coat. That coat was the only evidence that she existed outside of this room. It hung there, heavy with meaning. Sometimes it would be wet or there would be a leaf on it, and I felt I had glimpsed something I wasn't supposed to.

I began therapy by saying what I was not. "I am not human," I said. "I don't have feelings." "I don't have a history or an identity that belongs to me." After a few weeks, I was able to name myself. "I am depersonalized," I said. "I am an only child who lived in a big house." "I pretend everything is a novelty." "I turn pain into art, like my mother."

Dr. Lampen subjected me to long stretches of silence, which made her motionlessness even more eerie and pronounced.

"I don't like quiet because I'm afraid of my own mind," I told her. She was silent.

I asked her why she was so quiet.

"I'm having a reverie about what you just told me," she said.

"I want that," I said. "I want to be able to have a reverie."

I grabbed on to that word as the one strapped-down thing in the deep space of my mind. I wanted my mind to be able to play, to wander without vanishing into the infinite, dark universe of my dissociated brain.

Every professional I spoke with insisted I describe over and over again what I meant by depersonalization—a type of dissociation I had learned about from the books and articles I'd read. It was a phenomenon most commonly brought on by trauma.

"I am incapable of knowing myself," I explained to Dr. Lampen. "I feel like I can't remember my past. I can't distinguish my thoughts about myself from my parents' thoughts about me. I feel like my arms and legs don't belong to me. I'm not real. I don't feel anything. I feel totally alien to myself."

"What does the cutting do for you?" she asked.

"When I see the blood, I feel better," I said. "It centers me and it re-establishes causality. When I cut I know I will bleed and then I know I will heal. I don't understand consequences, how one thing leads directly to another. I think that's because of my parents, how they believe we're an exception to the rules, that what applies to other people doesn't apply to us."

"What do you think the dissociation does for you? Do you think it also helps in some way?"

"I think it protects me the way hibernation protects an animal through winter," I said. I pointed to the back of my neck. "I'm located here," I said. "Silent and watching."

I felt virtuosic naming my ailments. If I didn't have an identity, I could be a rhapsody of vacancy. If the difference could not be told between me and my parents, I could be a triptych of disorientation.

There was non-mandatory group therapy, which was held in the basement, a dark, dingy-green room with overly cushy green sofas that made me feel as if I were in a stomach being digested. We were discussing the fact that Amy had taken a lighter to the phone in the hall.

"I just wonder what it means that Amy destroyed the place you speak into. Perhaps she feels she doesn't have a voice here," said one of the counselors.

"This was an act of tremendous hostility, and there is a way in which Amy isn't heard in this community," said another counselor.

"A cigar is never a cigar and I'm pissed at you," said Angela.

Amy said nothing and rolled her eyes at the floor.

"I feel as if you're burning us right now in refusing to talk about it," said one of the nurses.

I was sitting next to Kim, who had asked me three times that day how to spell *pomegranate*. For some reason, there was a tennis racket next to me on the sofa and I walked my fingers down along the strings like a ladder.

Now Amy was crying. She was telling a story about how her mother had set her bedsheets on fire one night when she was a kid. How maybe setting the phone on fire was connected to that memory. How maybe she was trying to do something like what her mother had done to her so that she could feel a sense of control over a moment when she had no control. The counselors were nodding very slowly, like their heads were applauding. Everyone said something. Everyone did the leaning-forward. Everyone looked intently at where the words and tears and feelings were coming from. I had been trying to figure out a word in the crossword puzzle that lay next to me on the sofa without anyone noticing. My eyes were hurting from looking sideways and down in the dark.

Dr. Shapiro turned to me.

"How do you feel, Alice?" Dr. Shapiro asked. He had a white close-clipped beard, white hair, and round glasses.

I looked up. "What?"

"Right now. How do you feel right now?" asked Dr. Shapiro.

I raised my eyebrows and didn't say anything. The question frightened me.

"I feel like you don't feel," said Derek, flipping his palms up in frustration.

"I've never seen you cry," said Angela. "You're so fucking cheery all the time."

They were right. I had gotten good at compensating for the emptiness by carbonating my personality until I fizzed with chipperness, then turned flat and tepid and locked myself in my room with plates of food to binge-watch my *CSI* DVDs.

How did I feel? I didn't know. I couldn't locate the mechanism responsible for generating feelings and I couldn't decipher the faint flickering of feelings that did manage to arise. But there were endless metaphors that I could mix to try to approximate awareness.

"Feelings are like nictitating tinsel caught somewhere in between where my mind has receded to and my brain kind of slumps nesciently," I said. "Feeling is me writing a sentence on a chalkboard and something following me with an eraser, erasing every letter as I write it down."

The room was quiet. I had started using huge words, often incorrectly, in every sentence I spoke, as if encrusting my speech with precious gems would blind people to its fundamental worthlessness.

"You're full of shit," said Derek, this time stretching his hands out with his palms like stop signs.

"I think it means a lot that Alice is here today. The fact that she came means that she wants to do the work," said Dr. Shapiro.

"You walk around here in those sexy outfits and you think you're so smart," said Angela.

"Who the fuck are you, really?" said Derek.

This was a good question. This was *the* question.

"I just say lots and lots of words, and then follow them with their synonyms, maybe to try and get at that one essential and preliminary thing or maybe to get as far away from it as possible," I said.

"What are you even talking about?" Angela said. "Amy is talking about how she feels and she's upset and you're just bullshitting around. Are you even listening to anything anyone else says?"

I looked over at Amy. I saw her crying. I had heard her story. It was just a story. I saw how she struggled through telling it but I didn't get it. I was so preoccupied with not feeling human that I couldn't recognize humanity anywhere else. The answer to twenty-four across was *whist*, which was an early form of the card game bridge and also an adjective meaning silent or hushed.

"How do you feel right now?" Dr. Shapiro asked again.

I knew that they were all waiting for something, but I didn't know what. I was silent for a while, and the silence sucked at the room.

"My mind is the mental colluvia at the base of the hill of my brain. It's insalubrious," I said.

No one said anything.

"I can't tell the difference between my mother and a remote control," I said.

No one said a word. Derek got up and left.

I DEVELOPED A CLOSE FRIENDSHIP with a girl named Carly. Carly was a pretty Jewish girl from the Upper East Side with eating and borderline disorders and cratered self-esteem. She had a sharp, morbid sense of humor, which contrasted arrestingly with her soft, deep kindness. She spoke in a girlish mumble, which she occasionally interrupted to spit brilliant absurdist freestyle raps. Her mother was critical and domineering, pushing her to injury on the balance beam installed in their apartment for her early gymnastics career, and the men she dated were ruthlessly narcissistic. Carly would sit on the floor of her room with Frownies (what looked like pieces of cardboard) taped to her face to prevent wrinkles on her twenty-year-old skin, and create— hand-painted phrenology skulls, embroidered journal entries, BDSM PowerPoint presentations. We spent all our time together. We drove around Massachusetts in Carly's Lexus visiting thrift shops, getting our ears pierced, singing karaoke at the local bar. She gave me my first bikini wax, the two of us sprawled on the floor of her room, laughing until we cried as we both tried to pry cooling wax off my genitals. We listened to The Modern Lovers' "Hospital" and Belle and Sebastian's "Get Me Away from Here, I'm Dying" as she dyed my hair black and we talked about how it felt when we hurt ourselves, what our mothers had done wrong, the blow job she had given fellow-patient Colin, and the sex I'd had with fellow-patient Nick while speeding down a highway at night.

I loved being a best friend. I loved being essential, being an intercessor between someone and their deepest revelations. But I was careless with feelings and information; I would get distracted or bored and turn away from these friendships with no thought for the person on the other side. I didn't know how to sustain relationships. I was still friends with Effie but now, without her right in front of me, I forgot our friendship existed. Riggs was its own world, and I forgot everything outside of it—my old friends, my sister in Europe, the needs and wants of other people. My friendship with Carly was the only friendship that mattered, until I decided it no longer did.

When a new girl arrived, I dropped Carly and spent every minute with Sophia. Sophia was a tall, gap-toothed California girl with broad shoulders and a wide, beautiful face who was less interesting and meaner than Carly but who liked me a lot. One year later, she would copy down my mother's credit card number and order three thousand dollars' worth of clothes on it. Sophia would make fun of Carly, and I would laugh along. I would pass Carly in the halls and both our gazes would drop to the floor. I felt bad but I didn't know how to fix it.

There was something repulsive but inevitable about how I treated people, something that reminded me of my parents.

I had many family therapy sessions at Riggs, sometimes with my mother and Nanny, sometimes with my mother and father, and sometimes just with my mother. When it was just my mother, she spoke about the bind she found herself in with her competing interests: her work and me.

"I'm making changes," she said. "I'm planning not to participate in any shows this year and to spend more time out in Amagansett painting."

I was hurt, but I didn't say anything. The social worker observed how we cautiously tiptoed around our needs.

We began to talk about our difficulty conveying feelings and communicating what we needed, and how we couldn't express our love and longing for each other. We noticed similarities in how we managed feelings—by withdrawing and avoiding—and we admitted that it left us feeling angry and isolated from each other.

My mother connected her inability to communicate feelings to her trauma.

"I can't cry," she said, "because it's too painful to go to that level of feeling. I was always afraid I'd damage you because of what happened to me, so I could never fully commit to parenting you."

Her brow was creased in a way that told me this was difficult for her, painful. She was trying.

"I'm jealous of your trauma," I said.

She looked confused.

What I meant was I needed something tangible to point to and blame. What I meant was I needed us to be the same, and I needed us to be different. What I meant was, I needed her.

When my father flew in from Germany for a week, we had many family sessions. "You both have such different stories," I said. "About what happened and about who I am. I can't tell what my own history is because I can't tell the difference between my memories and yours. That's why I can't make any decisions for myself. I feel like your world, your feelings, your ideas are all-consuming, and they become a bigger priority than anything I think or feel. I want you both to sit down in front of a witness and get your story straight so that I know what happened to me."

My father nodded over and over, saying "Yes, yes, yes." My mother stared into space.

"I kind of almost want you to kill each other," I said.

My father laughed and said, "Yes, yes, exactly. I can understand that."

"I need to separate from you," I continued. "Especially you, Mom. I feel confused by your history, the abuse. When I read your journals I almost believed your trauma had happened to me. I need to know what really happened to me." I turned to my father. "For instance, did you really say a daughter's first sexual experience should be with her father?"

"No, no I didn't," he said.

"Did you hear him say it?" I asked my mother.

"I don't know," she said.

My father threw up his hands. There was a limpness to my mother's gaze.

The social worker asked my parents questions about their childhoods. My parents both agreed that as the eldest children in dysfunctional, often violent households, they felt like they couldn't protect their younger siblings from death and abuse, which left them feeling helpless, anxious, and ineffectual as parents. They admitted that their drug and alcohol use played a role in blurring what we all agreed to call "reality." They were both afraid I'd kill myself, like Till. I resented the evocation of his name and that they were using him as a cautionary tale.

I had thought that watching my parents agree would shift something inside me, but their collaboration made me anxious, scared, and angry. I had only one memory of us together when I was little—I was three and they were leaving to go out, dressed in their fancy clothes, and I was dizzy from my mother's heavy-handed dose of perfume. I was weeping. I didn't want them to leave. When they left, I wept and wept, and when they came back, I thought it was because they had heard me from far, far away. It seemed I spent my life trying to manage distance, negotiate the intervals between: me and my father (his closeness a balm and a threat), my mother (her distance a challenge and a bereavement), my body and my mind (the cleaving I feared would kill me). Now that my parents were both in the same room with me, I couldn't correctly interpret their presence and their effort as the love and concern that it was. Instead, my body read their unity, however fleeting, as another threat.

I was put through psychological testing. For the first test, I had to draw a picture of myself. I finished and handed it to the doctor.

"Where is the body?" she asked.

I looked at my self-portrait. I had drawn a giant, blank oval surrounded by squiggles of curly hair. The head shape and hair squiggles took up the entire page.

"Oh," I said. I stared at my picture. "I guess I forgot."

For the Thematic Apperception Test I was shown a card with a neutral image on it and was asked to create a story about the image. In response to a card showing a boy holding a violin, I informed the doctor that the boy had dismantled the violin in order to exact revenge on his mother by fashioning an exact replica of his father's suicide. In response to another card, I explained that the "ultimate narcissist" finds another woman with her same build and hair and puts a mask on her that's identical to her own face in order to free herself of solipsism by essentially killing her version of herself in her.

"It's how suicide becomes murder when you separate yourself from yourself," I clarified.

I felt an immense pressure to come up with the most interesting stories I could possibly tell. I imagined my parents watching me, waiting for me to tell fascinating tales, to do what I was good at. I didn't know the plain language of feeling, the fundamental mechanics of observation, without the flourishes of violent imaginings. Stories were a coded language I was proficient in.

The therapist administering the tests summarized my responses in her files: *The temptation of psychotic fantasy is that it makes anything seem possible, and it distracts Alice from dizzying fears and deep sadness. She can tolerate very little stillness, softness, or passivity, instead favoring stimulating situations that provide a forum for grand ideas and imaginary scenarios.* The file summarized the testing results: *The testing diagnosis is of a narcissistic character in a psychotic state characterized by boundary disturbances, intermittently disorganized thinking, and disregard for consensually validated reality.* I was diagnosed with dissociative disorder and psychotic disorder NOS (not otherwise specified). The file concluded that:

> *Currently she cannot locate an outer psychological edge where she ends and something else—a desire for someone recognized as separate from herself, or a metrical world not subject to her fantasy—begins. Lacking a clear identity, she is nevertheless self-absorbed in the sense of being trapped in her own mind, where what little sense of relating she does have is intensely, even gruesomely sadomasochistic. Ms. Carrière lives in a world where little holds firm and everything is up for question, as if there were no limit to the power of her mind's capacity to create and destroy. She mentally turns convention on its head, and nothing is as it appears, not the structures of family or church, not the usual constraints of space and time, not even the categories of life and*

death. Her philosophizing reaches psychotic proportions and her think-
ing, though supported by a formidable intelligence and expansive cul-
tural knowledge, is so fast and so fantastic that it speeds beyond easy
contact with other minds.

Had I read that then, I would have thought that all sounded beautiful. Reading it later, it sounded very lonely.

ONE SPRING DAY, I was downstairs in the computer room, where
Angela was submitting her monthly order of boxes of lint rollers, jars
of sauerkraut, and packs of Wolford stockings, and Chad was showing
someone the NRA website. I went to use the bathroom. I finished
peeing and wiped myself. As I pulled my hand away, I felt something
dangling out of me. At first I thought it must be the string of a
tampon, but I wasn't having my period and knew I hadn't put one
in, and it didn't feel like whatever it was was in my vagina. I tugged
on it and it slid out smoothly. I held it in front of me, pinched in
toilet paper.

It was a worm. It was a worm—eight inches long with almost the
girth of a pencil—that I had just yanked out of my anus. With my
left hand I pulled up my overalls and buttoned them with difficulty.
I went to the sink and laid the worm on the edge. It was moving. The
worm was alive. It looked clean. It looked brand new. I bathed the
worm with soap and water. I wrapped it in a paper towel and put it
in my pocket.

I looked at myself in the mirror. My face looked as if it was about
to make an unanticipated acceptance speech, mouth half open and
eyebrows arched. My body was dead quiet and I was calm. Then I
felt as if a wide, heavy peal of laughter was ballooning inside me.
Something was happening that was too big to contain—things were
coming out, things I could not control. I scrubbed my hands under

hot water, so hot it steamed. I checked myself out in the mirror again. I rubbed underneath my eye to remove a smudge of makeup. I looked good.

I left the bathroom. Sophia was waiting for me outside the computer room.

"A worm just came out of my ass," I told Sophia.

I felt power. I felt pride. I smiled.

"No. No fucking way. Oh my god," said Sophia. She recoiled, screamed, waved her arms around.

I left Sophia and headed to the nurses' station on the second floor, the worm in my pocket. I walked down a long, twisting hallway covered with a light-brown carpet. My worm was the secret I didn't know I was keeping. I was my worm's secret that it was revealing to me. And the secret was that I had a body. And that body did, in fact, have something alive in it.

I walked up to the nurses' station.

"Can I help you?" asked Nurse Linda.

"I just excreted a worm," I said, voice smooth as a worm gliding through dirt.

The nurses said nothing. It seemed they were waiting for the punch line. I reached into my pocket and I took out my worm. I slowly unfolded the paper towel and laid it down on the partition between the nurses and me. There was silence. They looked at my worm. Nurse Linda's lips looked like worms. Nurse Brenda squinted as if worms were about to come out of her eyes. Nurse Debra held her breath as if her lungs were filled with worms and no air.

"I'm sorry, I've never seen anything like this," Nurse Brenda said.

"What do you want to do?" asked Nurse Debra, as if I were an expert at having a parasite ambulate out of my anus.

"I want to go to the emergency room."

I felt saner than I'd ever felt. I felt my body. I had a body. I was in that body. And inside that body there had been a worm.

"No," said Nurse Debra. "This is not an emergency."

I saw the word *emergency* in my head. *Emergency* contained the word *emerge*. A worm had emerged from my anus. Its emergence was an emergency.

"Take me to the fucking emergency room," I said.

"I'm sorry," said Nurse Debra. "This is not an emergency."

"I need to go to the emergency room."

"You are not in any immediate danger. You will have to wait until tomorrow. Then someone will be able to take you to the doctor."

I pictured an entire night alone with my worm, but also not alone because maybe there were more of them. My entire insides could be crawling with worms. I needed to know what was inside me.

"But I need to go now. I need to know what this is. Can you tell me what this is? No, you can't. You've never seen anything like this before. I need to know what this is."

"Do you feel physically ill?" asked Nurse Debra.

I felt ill with urgency.

"No," I said.

"I'm sorry, we can't take you to the emergency room," said Nurse Brenda.

I gave up.

"I want a Ziploc bag," I said.

A nurse cautiously passed the Ziploc bag to me. I tenderly put the swaddled worm into the bag. Sophia and I borrowed Derek's car and left for the hospital. I looked out the car window at Riggs at night. Riggs, lit up from inside, took on a surreal beauty. Maybe I'd be there for a decade, like Bob. Maybe I'd be happy there. But I had something in me after all, something that reminded me I had places to be, capacities I had underestimated and ignored.

We reached the hospital and smoked two cigarettes each outside. We went in and waited. The doctor called us into a room. He was perfect looking, like he was on a soap opera about emergency room doctors and he was about to take off his shirt. I told him my story, and he said, "Why don't you show me what we're dealing with?"

I unwrapped the worm and held it, my arms outstretched to the doctor, a sacred offering to a god.

I watched as he tried to conceal his alarm.

"I'm sorry. I've never seen anything like this," he said.

He left. I put on lip gloss. He returned.

"Have you been eating excrement?" he asked.

"Not that I can recall, but I wouldn't put it past me," I said.

"This is a roundworm. They are typically found in animals, not humans. I don't know how you got it and I don't know when. It could have been in there for years. I'm prescribing you anti-parasitics. Take these and give the nurses a stool sample every day for the next two weeks. This will kill any that might still be inside. You may pass a few more."

Back at Riggs, the nurses gave me a plastic seat that fit over the toilet for me to shit in, plastic containers, Ziploc bags, and brown paper bags. Every day over the next week, I defecated into the plastic contraption, carefully smeared my feces into the containers, placed them in the plastic bags, and then into the brown ones. Each time, I looked for worms. I never found another one. My worm was singular, unlike anything anyone had ever seen.

4.

I was feeling better. I felt calmer, clearer. I was on a small dose of
an antipsychotic, Abilify, and that seemed to organize my thoughts
and slow them down. I was able to have a "reverie," calmly linking
one thought to the next. I was able to cry. I had stopped cutting. I
performed, with absolute dedication and glee, in the plays put on at
Riggs, worked at the woodshop, where Eduardo, a kind man in his
seventies with vitiligo and infinite patience, talked to me about the
songs of Nellie McKay and the books of Carlos Castaneda. I borrowed
a camera from the photography studio and took black-and-white photos of everything I saw—a deserted playground, streetlight-illuminated
snow, the headless reflection in a mirror of my aunt, uncle, Nanny,
and mother, who had all come to visit. The nurses and doctors commented on my progress. We were getting somewhere.

Then I celebrated my one-year-anniversary of being at Riggs, and
Sophia and I started going into New York City every weekend. I had
earned some freedom, some latitude, I thought. We would get dressed

in my room—it was bigger and I had more clothes. I'd put on my favorite outfit—a pair of thin leggings and a tight red T-shirt that had the words I AM A VERY SICK WOMAN written in yellow letters across the chest that I'd found at a nearby vintage store. I liked when people asked me what it meant and I got to tell them I was crazy. It felt like a uniform, announcing what my job was, or a convenient name tag. We'd put on makeup, pack an overnight bag, get someone to drive us to the train station, take the four-hour train to Grand Central Station, and then grab a taxi to 134 Charles Street to drop our bags. We'd go out to bars, get drunk, climb into my bed to get a few hours of sleep, take the train back to Riggs on Sunday night, and spend the next week avoiding group therapy and planning our next weekend.

One September night in 2005, a month after I turned twenty, we went to Joe's Pub in the East Village to see a friend's show. I wore a tight striped cashmere sweater that we joked made me look like Freddy Krueger. Sophia wore a vintage Harley Davidson T-shirt with holes in it and low-rise jeans. Halfway through the show, Sophia nudged me and whispered, "Oh my God, look who it is."

She pointed to a skinny guy in two pieces of a three-piece suit with a globe of frizzy curls around his head. I didn't recognize him. I shrugged and furrowed my brow. She explained to me that he was the guitarist from her favorite band, a famous indie rock group that had risen to fame four years earlier. I recognized the band name. I had first heard of them two years ago at a party thrown by my friend Josh in LA. At the party, I met Paul, who sat in the corner with sunglasses on. I asked him what he did.

"Nothing, I'm a dilettante," he said.

Paul was five years older than me, well-dressed and funny. He talked to me all night but made me feel like it was a special favor. He told me about his best friend who was a guitarist in a famous band.

He wrote down a list of bands I should listen to: Elliott Smith, Guided by Voices, Modest Mouse, Adam Green. I thought he was very cool. When I returned to New York, I wrote him an email about buying new socks. He wrote back that it was the best thing he had ever read. Two years and a mental institution later, I still thought about Paul, and here was his best friend from the famous rock band.

"Go say hi," I told Sophia.

We approached him.

"I am obsessed with you," Sophia told Paul's best friend.

The guitarist smiled and put his arm around the petite blond standing next to him, who had a luscious Bardot pout and looked bored. I watched the blond as Sophia waited for her ardor to penetrate her icon. The blond seemed so competent at just standing there, at fitting into this cool, famous guy's armpit, that I felt I could learn from her. Sophia was trying to convey the breadth of her obsession.

"Like, literally, your band is the soundtrack to my life," said Sophia.

"Thanks," he said.

Sophia was standing too close to the guy, and her hands, which she had made into claws in front of her face to emphasize the size and force of her love, were frozen in the air between them. She wanted to say more, get deeper, but didn't seem to know how.

"Hey," I said. "Do you know Paul Elroy?"

"Yeah," he said. His tone was different from the curt "thanks" he had offered Sophia.

"I met him years ago in LA," I said.

"He's actually on a train right now coming into the city. Let me call him."

He punched some keys on his Motorola Razr and asked Paul if he knew me. Paul confirmed and said we should meet him at a bar on the Lower East Side. At the bar, as I inexpertly poked pool balls around the table, I told Paul, the rock star, and his fiancée that Sophia and I were taking the weekend off from the mental institution we were in. Everyone thought I was making a joke. I laughed and assured them I wasn't being funny, I was certifiable. I felt cool and mysterious. I invited everyone back to 134 Charles. My mother was out of town and Nanny was asleep. Paul and I paddled face-to-face from one end of the pool to the other, and back again, talking. The guitarist played us the band's unreleased new album. Sophia, drunk, begged the guitarist's fiancée to let her be a bridesmaid at their wedding. It grew light outside. The party dispersed and Sophia and I went back to Riggs later that day.

Paul and I started talking on the phone every night for hours. We talked about film and middle school and pizza toppings, about betrayal and hair. He was staying at the East Village pied-à-terre of a famous actress descended from Hollywood royalty who had transitioned rehab-inflected child stardom into a long and successful career, and the next weekend I arrived at the actress's apartment for our first date. I was late because I had been straightening my butt-length, curly hair and covering my eyelids in black eyeshadow because Paul had told me he liked straight hair and lots of eye makeup on girls. I wore a silk blouse with a brown tweed vest, tight jeans and bright yellow Manolo Blahnik heels I borrowed from my mother, two sizes too big and stuffed with insoles. Paul seemed really excited to see me and offered me a drink. He had on a vintage T-shirt with a cheeky slogan and the shape of a southern state on it, a vest, tailored black Levi's, and Converse high tops, which he dirtied up in gutters before officially wearing to go out because clean Chucks were not cool. He had huge, round eyes and a weak chin that made it look like someone was turning the volume down on his face. He disguised it with stubble. He was very funny, and we sat on the sofa laughing. As I was telling him the story of my worm, he went over to the kitchen island and started laying out lines of powder.

"It's cocaine," he said, and snorted up the lines. I watched him and continued my story.

An hour later he laid out more lines and snorted them.

"It's actually heroin," he said, as if I had challenged him. "I just do it recreationally."

We sat on pillows on the floor, and Paul played me his favorite records.

We got in the shower, and I apologized for the water washing away my heavy makeup. We got in bed and watched infomercials, laughing at the strange contraptions and the over-eager barkers. We started kissing and after foreplay that involved a blow job and nothing else, he announced that he, as a rule, didn't wear condoms. I allowed him to shove his bare penis, only half hard from all the heroin, into me, and hoped my moans were convincing. I went back to Riggs the next day, thinking of nothing but the next time I could see Paul.

I continued having family therapy sessions at Riggs, but they had a new focus: Paul.

My discharge date was approaching and my therapist was concerned about my recent behavior and my lack of awareness around it, and didn't think I was able to live safely outside of Riggs. My mother was worried too, and frightened by my relationship with Paul.

"He has too much influence over you," she said.

I scoffed and rolled my eyes, now heavily lined in black.

She tried to be sympathetic, telling me about how she had used confusion to avoid feelings, how she had a history of inviting unhealthy people into her life too.

She told me she felt disrespected when I brought Paul and his friends over to do their drugs. She told me I was acting like my father. I couldn't hear her. I couldn't see that it was her house and her life. I was oblivious to everything but doing what I needed to do to become important to Paul, but I compromised and said I'd postpone my discharge by one month.

When my father called in from Europe for family sessions, he wasn't concerned about my relationship with Paul. He thought it was normal and good for me to do "age-appropriate things." He wondered why I was postponing my discharge. He was frustrated and wanted me to leave Riggs, come to Europe, and do more "age-appropriate things."

"I'm afraid for Alice to leave here without a solid foundation and no real plan in place. She should stay at Riggs," my mother said.

"I'm afraid for her to stay any longer," my father said. "She'll end up in a hospital forever. She should leave and come to Europe."

I ended up staying the extra month I had agreed to and then left Austen Riggs "against medical advice." I had been there a year and two months. My therapist wrote in my summation of hospitalization: *She is still attracted to the position of being the child "full of potential" to be a writer, and she fears damaging this "potential" by work or by entering a process of becoming "someone" in particular. Someone, that is, who is more limited than the girl who stimulated so much excitement in the adults around her.*

"We hope to see you back here," said Dr. Shapiro, at my final meeting with the staff.

"Thank you," I said reflexively.

I was referred to a psychopharmacologist so I could continue taking the antipsychotic I had been put on at Riggs. Upon meeting with me for the first time ever and for only forty-five minutes, Dr. Gilbert sent me home with a prescription for ninety pills of Klonopin, a powerful and highly addictive benzodiazepine for anxiety that was not recommended for prolonged use and would later be linked to an increased risk of dementia, and ninety pills of Adderall, prescription speed, for ADD/ADHD. He told me that Adderall wore off every four hours, and that I should take the Klonopin whenever I felt I needed to and to get to sleep at night. After my first dose of Adderall, I went from smoking five cigarettes a day to smoking a pack and a half of the Marlboro 27s Paul smoked. I sweat through my clothes and ground my teeth. My eyeballs felt peeled open and my blood felt like it was steaming. I became reactive, hostile, and unable to read social cues. I spoke too loudly and too much and too fast, trying to hear myself over the whomping of my heart and the whooshing of my boiling blood. Each dose of Adderall made me anxious, so I'd take Klonopin like the doctor had recommended. The Adderall made me unable to sleep, so I'd take Klonopin like the doctor had recommended. I was on so much Adderall that the Klonopin didn't make me feel high or relaxed, just woozy and ravenous and sloppy. It didn't occur to me that I could question the doctor. I had learned from my mother never to question the expertise and authority of doctors. This must be what becoming well felt like.

I spent most of my time at Paul's new apartment on First Avenue and First Street (paid for by his wealthy father), where he introduced me to good music and cocaine. Paul and I had no jobs, but we followed a strict itinerary. Most evenings started at ten, when we made our way to JP Ward's, a small dive bar on Avenue A with a pool table and identical twin bartenders. I took shots of Jägermeister and drank Amstel Lights (Paul's favorite) until I puked. I'd wash my mouth out and we'd walk a block to 2A, where Stephen, the gorgeous junkie bartender who chewed razor blades, made us shots that tasted like candy—Tootsie Roll, key lime pie with a cherry on top. After 2A, we'd hit Niagara and snort cocaine to a backdrop of '60s R&B and soul, and '70s punk and new wave. If we got hungry, we'd grab pierogi at Veselka and then finish the night at Black and White, where the bartender set out ashtrays and we'd cut lines on the bar. One weekend Paul took me to Benihana with his friends who secretly told the servers that it was my birthday, even though it wasn't, and I was served a scoop of ice cream with a candle in it and everyone sang happy birthday to me. Paul and I took a pedicab through Times Square to get home, scooting jerkily through traffic and streams of people as "Clocks" by Coldplay played on an old boom box. We went to a famous comedian's game night. Paul had spinach stuck in his teeth and I panicked about whether we were in a place in our relationship where I should tell him that he had something in his teeth. I didn't tell him.

My relationship with Paul had landed me squarely at the cool kids' table. Paul's friends were very cool. They were fashion photographers (one of whom claimed to be related to William Faulkner), young rock stars who now got to be friends with older rock stars, movie stars with checkered pasts, models who were also designers (usually of T-shirts), producers, a relative of a famous Motown singer. Everyone had an apartment in Manhattan and schedules that allowed them to show up for anything, at any time. I learned that the word *party* could be used as a verb, and that was all we did. I was anxious all the time. I wanted nothing more than to impress all these people and I was terrible at it. I did crossword puzzles in bars to appear unique. When I ran into people I knew, I theatrically exclaimed, "As I live and breathe!" At the threshold of every bar, I sprayed myself heavily with an extra layer of Chanel No. 19 perfume. I had no sense of how I came off, how false and desperate. But I *was* false and desperate. I was empty and out of my mother's house, and I needed someone else to weigh me down with their desires.

Paul had never called anyone his girlfriend before. One night we were shopping at the Asian market M2M, and he called me sweetheart across a rack of wasabi peas, and I felt carbonated inside. Then he told me he would be calling me his girlfriend, because he had liked how it felt calling me "sweetheart." He was hard to win over and prided himself on not forming attachments with women. It was thrilling watching him swing from detachment to attentiveness, seeing him zoom in on me with a mischievous smile on his face. I got to be Paul's girlfriend, and that came with certain conditions. Paul demanded that I straighten my curly hair. On New Year's Eve, he got furious because I left it a little wavy.

"Why would you do this to me, especially on New Year's Eve?" he said.

He suggested I dye it dark, so I did.

Paul liked girls who wore lots of makeup, so I covered my eyelids in black eye shadow and became afraid to leave the house if I didn't have my eyes properly outlined. I had to ask, "Are we going to have sex or can I take off my makeup?"

"Keep it on. I might want to later," he'd say as he poured a box of Nerds in his mouth, eyes glued to the latest Paul Thomas Anderson movie.

Paul didn't "believe in going down on girls," so I tackled his opiate-deflated cock with intense focus and a belief that my only chance at pleasure lay in figuring out how to fold his limp penis into me and make it fun for him.

Paul told me what to wear, picking out my outfits before every night out. He told me that it would be okay if I lost another ten pounds (I was a size double zero) and then told me it had been a joke. I did what he told me. I welcomed his instructions.

I'd return to 134 Charles to host drug-fueled pool parties when my mother was out of town, or crash there when Paul and I got in a fight. Sometimes, when I came home in the morning after a night out, I'd bring the newspaper up with me and encounter my mother and Nanny in the kitchen drinking their coffee and tea. Neither would comment on the fact that I had been out all night. Neither would ask where I'd been or who I was with.

Some evenings I'd catch my mother alone in the kitchen. I'd be happy to see her and I'd want to talk. I'd sit at the butcher block table, leg jiggling from the cocaine or the Adderall, and talk to her as she got another bottle of wine from the fridge. I talked to her about the people I'd met, ideas I had for the cover of my unfinished novel I hadn't looked at in months, books I'd heard were good.

"You seem hyper," she'd say.

"I had a lot of green tea," I'd answer.

She wouldn't respond and would leave the kitchen without looking at me to go and drink by herself.

One night, after another failed attempt to initiate a coked-up conversation, when she was on her second bottle of wine, I followed her out of the kitchen and cornered her on the stairs.

"Why are you always walking away from me?" I screamed.

"Leave me alone," she said.

"No, I want to talk to you. Why don't you want to talk to me?"

"Because I don't respect you," she yelled, and disappeared up the stairs.

I stood there, alone, shocked by the volume of her voice, the passion in it. I had never heard her raise her voice like that. It seemed the only thing that could enliven her, could turn up the volume, could get her to direct words, passionate words, my way, was my failure.

It didn't occur to me that I was supposed to be leading a different life. That people my age were becoming responsible adults, building lives. Doctors had taught me that my job was to take my medication and think about how to communicate my thoughts and feelings. My mother had taught me to obey the doctors. She didn't ask me what medications I was being prescribed. If I ever spoke of feelings, she asked me if I was making it to my sessions.

I was seeing a new therapist recommended by my team at Riggs. Dr. Hart called my words "jewel-like," and we sat in her office twice a week spinning stories and sculpting metaphors. Sometimes I'd hand over gram bags of cocaine to her, saying I wanted to cut back, and she'd praise me.

Meanwhile, Paul was doing more and more heroin and had started smoking crack. I was doing more and more cocaine, paid for by the money our parents continued to give us, and on good nights we'd stay up talking and listening to music until the following afternoon. One night, a week after Stephen the bartender died of a speedball overdose, I walked into the living room to find Paul slumped over on the sofa. I shook him and his head flopped back. As I dialed 911, he sat up, laughing. Paul's temper got worse and we would walk into bars screaming at each other, dropping the argument mid-sentence as soon as the bartender handed us shots. On Valentine's Day, Paul took me out to dinner at Lavagna, the Italian restaurant he and all his friends frequented. That night I drank champagne, followed by red wine, followed by white wine. As we left the restaurant I leaned against a discarded armoire standing on the curb and vomited. Paul started yelling at me.

"You manipulated me into buying you an expensive dinner and now you're throwing it up," he screamed.

We walked to Ace Bar to play pool. After a few silent rounds, we made our way to Horseshoe Bar and ran into his friend Lilian, whom Paul believed had a crush on him. We sat in the red vinyl upholstered booth and they talked. I interjected something, and Paul told me to shut up. I went silent. Then my body lurched forward, my forehead almost hitting the table. He had hit me in the back of the head, hard. My face went hot with shock. I slid out of the booth and started to make my way to the door. Paul got up and tried to corner me, his hands extended. The bouncer came over and asked if everything was okay, and I said no and slid out the door. I leaned against the building and called my friend Leah. Leah and I had met the first day of a group therapy I was attending, and she had liked me instantly because I had asked the counselor, after a girl had a benzodiazepine-withdrawal-induced seizure, if we could have a cigarette break. Leah told me to leave the bar. But I couldn't leave. I needed to take care of Paul. I was Paul's girlfriend. I was afraid he would eject me from his world if I didn't, black-lidded and emaciated, follow his rules.

I lingered outside until I saw Paul come out, swaying. I hung up my phone and slung an arm around him and he leaned on me. I walked us home, propping him up, trying to stop him from throwing himself in front of cars. He had told Lilian to meet us at his apartment. She arrived just as we did and I saw her eyes saucer as she took in the scene. On the floor was a month's worth of the *Daily News*, pieces of paper (Post-its; pages ripped out of notebooks, ruled, graphed, blank, some with writing on them; a song lyric; a grocery item; a phone number; something reminding us of something one of us was supposed to do but never would), the celluloid skins of Now and Laters, Skittles, Sour Patch Kids, and Starbursts, which were all over the bed, under the pillows, and stuck between the wall and the bed. Heroin addicts liked candy. There were no clean dishes or utensils or pots or pans or drinking glasses. These dirty items could be found: stacked along the edge of the kitchen sink, on the bathroom floor, on the bedroom floor, on the one living room windowsill, on the two bedroom windowsills, on the one bathroom windowsill.

Paul sat on the small sofa, lit a crack pipe, and said to Lilian, "I bet you've never seen someone smoke crack before." Lilian asked if I was okay to be alone and without waiting for my answer said goodbye to Paul and left. I sat in silence as Paul smoked his crack and after a few hours I helped him into bed. He crawled to the bottom of the bed, where I was standing, put his forehead against mine, and said, "You're nothing, you don't deserve to exist. I'll put a boot in your face."

"Go to sleep," I said, then pushed him down onto the bed and tucked him in.

I felt a strange competency, as if he were my child and I was required to manage his tantrums.

When I woke up later that morning, Paul was gone. I waited in bed until he stumbled through the door the next day. He slapped on a fentanyl patch designed for terminally ill people, got into bed, and we binge-watched *Flavor of Love*.

A few days later, I woke up early in the morning, hungry. Paul was still awake from the night before.

"I'll make you some pasta with Parmesan," said Paul, from the other room. He could be nice like that.

"Olive oil and butter, too," I said from the bedroom.

I listened to his noises. The thuds and sighs and grunts and plops and bangs and clinks created an auricular comic strip of his domesticity that I followed from the other room. Then the sounds stopped.

"I cut myself," he said from the other room.

"So get a Band-Aid." I did not get out of bed.

No sound came from the other room.

"Just put a Band-Aid on it," I repeated.

No response.

"Is it bad?" I asked.

"I think so," said Paul.

I got out of bed and walked naked into the other room. Paul was standing very still and held his left hand in his right. He held it up and close to him as if I wanted to take it away from him. Blood was pouring down his arm. Paul's hand looked nothing like a hand. Everything became two-dimensional and I couldn't see what was happening, only the words to describe what was happening. I saw the sentence: "The Grand Canyon filled with blood." Then the words "the flopping open of a neatly folded ream of tough velvet" appeared over Paul's shape. The letters of "a Fabergé egg spilling its rubied yolk" stamped themselves on the scene.

Things that can be described as anything but themselves and still be true are marvelous, I thought.

I shook my head, the metaphors scattering like droplets of water. I put my hands on Paul's shoulders and moved him onto the sofa.

I forced a dishtowel around his hand, and placed his other hand around it like a tourniquet.

"Squeeze it hard. Keep pressure on it. Keep the arm elevated," I said.

I found my dress from the previous night in between the bed and the wall and put it on. I walked back out to the other room, found my purse, and packed it with: two wallets, two pink Motorola Razr cell phones, two sets of keys, and one half-empty bottle of warm ginger ale in anticipation of blood loss and plummeting blood sugar. I turned off the stove. I turned the handle of the pot in which the water was beginning to boil and angled it toward the back of the stove because it was not safe to have the handle of a pot sticking out. I saw a half-shattered drinking glass on the counter with blood on it. He had been washing a bowl, and his hand had slipped and smashed into a drinking glass, which broke and split his hand almost in half. I turned from the stove and looked at Paul silently wilting in my arrangement of him, his fingers rooted in the squishy red dishtowel. I found a roll of paper towels, unreeled it, and crammed the pristine paper blossom into Paul's fist, red roots sprouting instantly.

"Let's get you to the hospital," I said.

I picked up my purse from the floor and Paul from the sofa and I exited us into the hallway. I locked the door with one hand, holding Paul upright with the other. I led us down the hallway, opened the door one-handed, and we fell into the morning. I ran ahead, my arm raised, trying to catch a cab. I looked behind me at Paul, and I watched as he began a slow-motion free-fall toward the ground, then swung his body at the last minute in a circus-act arc that kept him in his looping stride. I ran back and let him fall against me. I walked us down the block, keeping my right arm up, trying to hail a cab. No taxis stopped for us. I kept us upright until we reached the curb, where I let him slide down me and sit. I called 911.

"Yes, hello. I need an ambulance at the corner of First Street and First Avenue. Northwest corner. My boyfriend has a severe laceration of the left hand. It is almost completely severed and he is bleeding profusely. Please hurry."

A man approached.

"I called an ambulance. I saw you guys. He looks pretty bad," he said.

"Yes, thank you. Everything is under control. I called an ambulance. It's on its way," I said.

I turned away from the man and hoped my ambulance came first. I wanted it to be mine.

Paul was leaning heavily against my leg, bleeding. He stared at the pavement.

"Can you light me a cigarette?" he asked.

I looked down at the top of his head. His hair was greasy and stringy.

"I don't know if that's a good idea," I said.

He was asking my permission. I got to decide for him and that felt good.

"It'll make me feel better. I swear," he said.

"Okay. Fine. Just one," I said. I wanted a cigarette too. I lit two and gave one to him.

The ambulance slung itself onto the curb. Three EMTs hopped out and arranged themselves around us. One unfurled Paul's split fist. One EMT, into a walkie-talkie, said: "Yeah, it's pretty bad. He almost cut his hand off."

One of the EMTs pulled me aside. He came too close and spoke at me in weak bursts of aerosol spit.

"Has he been taking any drugs? Is he on something right now?" he asked.

Now I got to tell his story. I felt powerful.

"He has a long history of frequent and heavy drug use. He has a serious heroin addiction in addition to frequent crack and cocaine abuse. He claims he's clean at the moment, but he's an addict, so I can't confirm that with any certainty. I know he has been self-administering methadone to come down. He may be on it right now. I don't know the exact dosage, but I presume it's high, given the severity of his heroin use. I hope that's helpful," I said.

"I thought so. His pupils are pinpoints. And he looks dirty. You look clean," said the EMT.

"Thanks," I said, feeling like I had won an award, best actress in a crisis.

"Can I have a drag of that?" asked the EMT, pointing to my cigarette, as if we were close friends. I felt flattered and disgusted.

"You can have it," I said. I gave him the cigarette.

I left the EMT and walked around to the back of the ambulance. Paul had already been packed inside, quivering on the padded vinyl bench. I pushed past the two EMTs and sat down next to Paul. I intercepted the clipboarded forms as they were passed to him. I would fill out the forms because I knew all the answers and I had neat handwriting. I would be thorough.

The ambulance began its carnival of urgent lights and motion. Paul reached for my hand with his good hand. I let him hold my hand, even though I didn't want to. His hand was little and exhausted and wet. I could catch him before he nearly fell. I could elevate his arm and hold the phone to my ear and walk him upright down the street. I could remember to turn off the stove. I was indispensable. I was a basic need. My handwriting would be legible despite the reckless driving. The information I gave would reveal him. In this crisis, I felt alive. I did not want to sit and hold his little okay hand.

We arrived at St. Vincent's. I knew this place. I'd been here before. I knew the system. I was in the system. But we were not here for me. This time, someone else had cut themselves open.

We were taken to Trauma Room 3. Paul sat on the bed. He was limp and hunched over like a half-deflated pool toy. A doctor entered.

She numbed his hand with a large syringe and began to suture the wound. Left with nothing needing my white-knuckling, I exited the building and sat on the steps. In my purse was a pillowcase that said Saint Vincent's Hospital on it, which I stole from Trauma Room 3. Tiredness began to erode the spiky peaks of adrenaline. It started to rain. I lit a cigarette. Paul was okay. I had conquered this crisis. But this morning of over-full moments would pass, and I would be nothing again.

5.

When Paul's hand was healed, he flew back to LA, telling me every week he would return in a week. His aunt called to tell me she had found syringes in the trash. He came back to New York City on Valentine's Day and there were bruises on his forearms. We went to a fondue restaurant and he nodded out over the steaming pot of cheese. "Jet lag," he said. I believed him. Then he returned to LA and never came back.

That summer, my father came to New York for my twenty-first birthday. We sat at the dining room table at 134 Charles Street. He had written a screenplay and wanted the two of us to do a table read. The screenplay was about Dracula biting a "junkie prostitute" and getting addicted to heroin through her blood, and the prostitute getting addicted to drinking blood. Dracula and the prostitute fell in love. My father was going to play Dracula and he wanted me to play the junkie prostitute. When we reached the part when Dracula bites the prostitute and they fall in love, the words—writhing on a bed, kissing and sucking with urgency and desire became too much for me. I stopped reading.

"I'm hungry," I said.

I went into the kitchen and put a pot of water on to boil for pasta and my father followed me. He talked to me as I unboxed the spaghetti, found some pesto, and put it in a bowl.

"Every father secretly wants to sleep with his daughter," he said.

I was struck with numbness, as if I'd been bitten by something poisonous. My skin went hot. I couldn't speak. I forced myself to evaluate what he had said like I would a painting created by a long-dead artist with intentions muddied by time and context. Something that had nothing to do with me. *Just say something smart,* I thought. I heard the top of the pot rattle as the water boiled.

"I think the water's boiling," I said and turned away from him.

That same year, my father was crucified. A photograph of my half-sister, Elena, had appeared in a newspaper without her mother's consent, so Bettina sued. Instead of paying the 5,000-euro fine, my father decided to go to jail and used his imprisonment, in collaboration with the popular tabloid *Bild Zeitung*, to bring awareness to the rights of unmarried fathers and their children. In Germany, at the time, unmarried fathers often lost their custodial rights in separations. My father organized a coalition of three hundred people, mostly fathers who had lost children through separations and custody disputes, to gather in front of the Federal Ministry of Justice in Berlin to crucify him. My father, thin to the point of emaciation, was tied to a large cross, naked except for a piece of cloth around his hips and a "crown of thorns" on his head. Around him stood fathers dressed in old-fashioned prison uniforms, chanting and holding signs that read: END THE WAR AGAINST FATHERS, EQUAL CUSTODY FROM BIRTH ON, and FATHERS ARE ALSO PARENTS. My father struck poses—head thrown back, mouth open; head slumped lifelessly forward. He and his army of bereft fathers eventually managed to get the law changed.

The story was near perfect. It had villains and disenfranchised masses and a charismatic leader upon whom misfortune was repeatedly visited and a triumph over power. My father's mythologizing was complete. To the public he was father, martyr, Christ. To me he was slippery and far less noble. I never considered that he had his own reasons for doing this, for fighting. That he had another daughter he loved. That he had priorities beyond me. I saw the grandiose, public gestures he made to protect his relationship with my sister, and I felt angry and jealous and abandoned.

I DECIDED TO APPLY to Columbia University to finish my undergraduate degree. Paul's absence meant I had time to be something other than a girlfriend, and it also meant the end of our grueling schedule of bar hopping and narcotics. I was excited to be in school and threw myself into my classes. I felt hyped up—I was, after all, still on Adderall. My brain whirred with ideas and I'd shoot my hand into the air and quiver it until I was called on. I loved having to show my student ID, saying over and over to myself, "I am a student." I made the dean's list my first semester. Then I started seeing a new psycho-pharmacologist who diagnosed me with bipolar and generalized anxiety disorders, justifying the former with the observation that I dressed differently at each session—sometimes in a colorful sundress, sometimes in tight black jeans and a vintage band T-shirt. Along with my new diagnoses came more meds: the antipsychotic Risperdal for potential hypomania, the mood stabilizer Lamictal for mood swings, Trazodone for depression, more Klonopin, more Adderall, and the sedating antipsychotic Seroquel, because the Adderall made me unable to sleep. The Seroquel combined with the Klonopin made me insatiable. I stood in front of the fridge at 2 a.m. gouging out pieces of cold chicken from a carcass with my hands and shoveling them into my mouth. I woke up in the middle of the night and put a spoonful of chocolate pudding, which I'd left next to the bed, into my mouth and fell back asleep before I could swallow it, waking to my cheek glued to the stained pillowcase. Twice I fell asleep on a half-eaten Milky Way bar, and once on a wedge of brie. I started to gain weight. I was prescribed medications to counteract the side effects of the medications—Topamax and Liothyronine for the weight gain from the Seroquel and Klonopin, Lyrica and Gabapentin to file down the amphetamine teeth that lined my brain.

As I was prescribed more pills, I was diagnosed with more disorders, whose symptoms often resembled the side effects of the pills. I wasn't ruminating obsessively because I was on prescription speed, but because I had obsessive-compulsive personality disorder. My emotional lability was because of borderline personality disorder, not because my brain blazed into a chemical conflagration every morning only to be doused dead by downers at night. I started to think of myself as a machine that ran on pharmaceuticals, an appliance designed to obliterate feelings. I had learned from my mother that feelings were not welcome, and now I was learning they were pathological. There was no such thing as sadness, only clinical depression. Joy and motivation were only harbingers of hypomania. Feelings, good or bad, meant that something was wrong. If I felt sad, I called Dr. Sarini and requested a higher dose of my mood stabilizer. If I felt suspiciously okay, I suspected I was becoming hypomanic and called to get my antipsychotic increased. When I decided, after reading Kay Redfield Jamison's memoir of her struggle with bipolar disorder, that I should be on Lithium, I left a message for Dr. Sarini, and the next day a prescription was called in to my pharmacy. My hands turned purple and I felt swirly and deadened. I left another message saying I had decided to stop taking it. I was curious about the full potential of stimulants and requested every form—Ritalin and Concerta along with the Adderall. Prescriptions for all of them appeared and I would alal.

experiment with taking one, and the next day, the other. Dr. Sarini told me repeatedly that psychopharmacology was "trial and error" and that this haphazard prescribing was the way it was supposed to go. This was me taking care of myself. He told me I would need to be on medication for the rest of my life. My mother's belief in these doctors never wavered, and she still never asked about my medications or how I was tolerating them.

When I visited my father and grandparents in Lübeck, they asked me what medications I was taking. As I ate my liverwurst toast, I listed all the pills.

"So you have pills to wake you up and pills to make you sleep," said my father.

I resisted. It wasn't like that. There were good reasons. There had to be. Opa, a psychiatrist, shook his head and hauled out his giant reference books to look up the compounds.

"They bring you up and they bring you down. This is not the way," he muttered.

I got defensive. I thought they were trying to stop me from getting help.

My diagnoses explained and explained away every part of me. I held them aloft and visible like a sign at an airport, using them to identify myself even to strangers. My alleged bipolarity was often the first trait I announced about myself, opening myself up like my heavily high-lighted *Diagnostic and Statistical Manual of Mental Disorders* (DSM). The medications were the necessary accessories to this identity. When I traveled and had to put all my pill bottles in a Ziploc bag to go through security, I felt a bolt of pride as TSA agents pried it from my bag and examined it. What must they have thought of me? Were they intrigued? Impressed? Intimidated? That they might think I was sick never occurred to me. I could not abide the simplicity of sickness. I was not just sick, I was special.

My sessions with my therapist reinforced this belief. We discussed nothing concrete. She was in constant contact with my psychopharmacologist but expressed no concern or thoughtfulness about all the medications. Twice a week, every week, we discussed the idea of me, the idea of my parents, the idea of being a human among humans. She praised my eloquence, asked me about my dreams, matched me metaphor for metaphor, helped me abstract myself further. I was always honest with her because I was talented at being a patient. I feared averageness, I told her. I feared limits, I feared the quiet in which I would be forced to confront that I might be average and be averagely limited. But the average person was not on nine medications with seven diagnoses. I was still exceptional.

Another doctor was added to my entourage. My mother and I started going to a family therapist. Dr. Kaufman's face was soft and bulbous, as if his features had taken shape from the mushy wax of a slowly melting candle. He would welcome us into his office, remove his shoes, put his feet up on a foot stool, and take a sip from his plastic cup of Orangina, which sat next to a fresh liter of the stuff. During the session, my mother and I sat on the floor in the hallway outside his office with the door propped open, so we could smoke cigarettes. Dr. Kaufman commented on my weight, congratulating me when I was skinny, then asking me why I had put on extra pounds. Hopped up on Adderall, I made long speeches about feeling neglected or having no identity of my own. My mother listened, struggled to find feeling words, and deferred to Dr. Kaufman, who decreed that every time she got drunk and criticized me, she had to buy me a dress. Nanny attended some of the sessions, and Dr. Kaufman used her as a witness, to confirm or deny the validity of our statements. The sessions were endless and useless, and I begged my mother to stop seeing him, but he was renowned and expensive, and she was convinced he could fix us.

. . .

MY MOTHER WAS HAVING a hard time. She was broke. Her extravagances had caught up with her.

"Should I sell this house?" she asked me one afternoon.

I was on my way upstairs.

"Sure, why not. It's full of ghosts," I said, and walked away.

The house was sold. We stayed at 134 Charles Street for six months, packing it up. The week of the move, my mother flew to the Caribbean with Nanny, leaving me alone to finish packing up the first twenty-three years of my life. I took my Adderall and drank Red Bull all day as I sorted through stacks of photographs, middle school French exams, my Silver Cross baby carriage, the desiccated jack-o'-lantern I had carved fifteen years ago and kept in a Ziploc bag. My very last night in 134 Charles Street, I sat in the empty living room at four in the morning, after having stayed up all night haphazardly throwing things into boxes, weeping, listening to "Hey Jude," and putting cigarettes out on the floor that was no longer mine. I stared at the living room, empty of my mother's uncomfortable furniture, the walls bare of her massive paintings. The house felt weak and afraid, and so did I. I lay on the floor on my side as if I were cuddling 134 Charles. I was scared to leave the fortress that had defined me for so long.

In a trunk I found all the cards that my mother had written to me when I was a child. When I finished going through everything in the trunk, I sat down and read them, saving a letter she'd written on the occasion of my fifth birthday for last. It read:

Dear Alice,

You will be five tomorrow. Today you jumped, ran, all over the house being happy about being five. "I'll be five, I'm going to be five, when I'm five I'll . . ." You told me that when you became five you wouldn't wet your bed anymore and you'd be able to lift heavy things. You wanted a chocolate cake with chocolate icing; and strawberry icing, separate from the chocolate icing. You wanted your father (Papa, Mathieu, Daddy) to be here, and you will have both. You want many other things: rainbow ice cream, a locket, your dinner now, a story, 2 stories, a pretend game, 3 movies, all the way through. What you have is your father—Mathieu. Your mother—Jennifer. Your Nanny—Denys. All of us wish you the very best, with all our love for the beginning of your big girl life. You are pretty, intelligent, lively, sensitive, kind, gentle, fierce, wild, and strong. You are the great joy of my life. Congratulations at five.

Mom, Mommy, Maman, Jennifer

That night, alone in the house, I wrote my mother a letter:

Dear Mom,

Your letter, and my finding it, is really the culmination of a slow, necessary process—of me realizing you are a real person separate from me, and of finding my way to you. I remember when I first realized that I love your work. I remember when I first admired your style. I realize I have something not many people have. I have a role model, and I hate that word. I think I fight you so hard because you remind me of everything I am afraid I will never be. Maybe I accuse you of neglect because I neglect myself. I am so terrified by my admiration and love for you that I lash out at you. I find your love for me devastating and inexplicable. The more I realize how much you do for me and how much you love me, the more scared I am that I have depleted you. That I have misused and abused you. I am scared that I will never be able to be that person you wanted and believed I could be. I want to live up to your dreams for me. You need to know that you have lived up to my dreams for a mother. You wrote as if you were writing something(one) into existence. Even then, you spoke to me as a person. Now, we are negotiating what we mean to each other and how we express that. What we want from and for each other. Maybe I treated you so poorly because I didn't understand that you needed me too. I know I still fight you at certain steps, but I am starting to understand the value of the direction in which you are trying to point me. I am sick of wanting to be victimized, I am sick of being sick. I am trying to push away the guilt and regret and self-loathing. It's easier to feel damaged than it is to realize I've been lucky and loved. In you and Nanny I have had everything. I am sick of symbols. I don't want a life of metaphor and turns of phrase. I feel as if I have been talking my whole life. Talking around things, talking over people, talking myself in and out of things, talking myself up, talking myself down. I am ready to listen. I want a relationship with you. Maybe then I won't feel so scared all the time.

> *I love you,*
> *Your daughter (and fellow alien),*
> *Alice*
> *December 2008*

I closed the door of 134 Charles Street behind me for the last time and caught a plane to meet my mother on the island of Nevis. I arrived that night and handed her my letter. She took it to her room. I was at the bathroom sink when I heard her come back in. My breath caught and my heart quickened. My mother came into the bathroom.

"This is very nice," she said.

"Well, it's all true," I said, instinctively raising my arms for an embrace.

"Why don't you keep it for me?" she said. My arms found their place at my side again.

She handed the letter back to me and went back into her room.

After the sale of 134 Charles Street, my mother bought a house in Brooklyn. Nanny moved in with my aunt and uncle in Tribeca while it was being renovated, and my mother moved into her tiny cottage in Amagansett. I moved into my first apartment, on West Seventeenth Street. My mother and I, no longer held together by 134 Charles Street, drifted further apart. When I moved, she gave me a box of all the utensils she didn't need, so I arrived at my new apartment with a pizza slicer, an ice cream scoop, skewers for roasting marshmallows, and a set of grapefruit spoons, both of us hoping I was prepared for real life.

ONE EVENING, I got a call from Gregory. I had met him through the famous guitarist at Dangerous Studios in New York City. He was a music producer and songwriter who had been in a band that was signed to RCA in the '90s and was producing the guitarist's first solo record. Gregory was fifteen years older than me, handsome, charming, talented, funny, well-dressed, and had a shih tzu named Spike who wouldn't stop growling. When he lit my cigarette he told me to look away so I wouldn't look cross-eyed. I stared at his dimple. I went to pet Spike, but he growled at me. I tried to remember Paul was there with me. I'd see Gregory whenever Paul and I went out, which was almost every night. We liked each other immediately and had long, passionate conversations in the dark corners of bars. One night, we found ourselves alone together at 4 a.m. on the Lower East Side under a streetlight.

"All I want to do is kiss you," one of us said.

"Me too," said the other.

We stared into each other, the moment dilating with our desire and deliberation. It was thrilling to want that hard.

"We can't do this," I said.

I had to get back to Paul, and Gregory had to get back to his girl-friend of sixteen years.

Now, two years later, both of us single, I asked Gregory over the phone, "Do you want to come over and tuck me in?"

"Have you ever been properly tucked?" he asked, and I laughed.

That night, he walked up the stairs to my apartment and I greeted him at the door.

"I have to warn you, I'm a drunk," he said.

I heard: "I have to warn you, I'm drunk," so I said, "Don't worry, I'll catch up."

He was wearing a three-piece, taupe corduroy suit with a T-shirt that he had painted a tie onto. He had big, expressive eyes and shaggy brown hair and a huge, dimpled smile. In my apartment, I poured us drinks and dropped the needle of my vintage record player onto Elvis Costello and the Attractions' *Armed Forces.*

I settled on the sofa next to Gregory.

"So what have you been writing?" he asked.

"Well, I wrote a novel about the necessity of perverse relationships, how masochism is a kind of art," I said.

"What is the necessity of perverse relationships?"

I fumbled for an explanation. I hadn't expected him to ask follow-up questions.

"I'd like to read it," he said.

"How's the producing going?" I asked.

"It's good. I like to see how much I can do with as little as possible. Some of my best stuff was made in my kitchen with a cheap micro-phone. No one listening is going to know or care what mic I used or what compressor; they just know if they like it. I just want little

Johnny down the street to put on his headphones and go, 'I'm not alone.'"

"Were you little Johnny in his room alone?" I asked.

He laughed. "I still am."

He grabbed my neck and pulled me into a kiss.

That night we had sex. Afterwards, I lay on my back, laughing. "What the fuck was that? So that's what it's supposed to feel like?"

"You have a sex smile," he said, grinning. "You can't stop smiling."

I hadn't before known what it felt like to not be able to get enough of someone. I hadn't known what it felt like for someone to make my pleasure not only a priority but a party. After that first night Gregory just didn't leave. We collected his stuff from his friend's apartment, where he'd been staying since he'd broken up with his long-term girlfriend. We fucked four times a day, breaking my sofa, keeping us indoors for days. The rest of the time we talked, listened to music, wrote together, and drank.

We sat on my floor drinking whiskey and writing a song we titled "High Class Problems." I had always been afraid to sing, but he encouraged me.

"Just recite it, like Lou Reed," he said.

He strummed his guitar and I leaned toward the laptop speaker we were recording into.

"I got high," I sang. Gregory held up his hand for me to pause. I paused. Then he motioned for me to continue. "Class. Problems."

A car alarm started blaring in the street, and he harmonized with it. We did a few takes of the first verse and then got distracted by a red rubber ball, which we rolled back and forth across the floor at each other while he told me about his life.

He described how he was alone a lot as a kid and would spend days in his room listening to records, typing out the lyrics of his favorite songs. He'd spend hours playing a note on his little plastic organ, humming in unison, then altering his pitch so he could feel the dissonance in his body. He played in what he called the Me and Me band, where he'd record himself singing and playing on one boom box, then press play on that boom box while recording on another while singing a harmony with the first boom box. I told him how I had spent hours alone in my room listening to my audiobooks, how I'd recite my actions to myself like I was my own narrator.

He told me about his twenties: the band he had formed, getting signed to RCA, touring with the Verve Pipe and Lenny Kravitz, modeling for *L'Uomo Vogue* and doing runway for Issey Miyake. He told me how he had started ordering pain pills online from Málaga, Spain, and had moved on to snorting heroin, a habit he would keep hidden for years—a high-functioning and productive junkie—and would only break by becoming an alcoholic instead. I told him about my cutting, about my mother who didn't seem to like me, about my father who didn't seem to know the right way to like me. He wasn't awestruck and he wasn't shocked. He asked me many questions—about what I loved and what I feared, about what I actually was trying to say when I obscured my meaning with metaphors and big words. He listened hard, and it made me feel weightless, no longer heaving up the effigy of myself made out of pills and catchphrases and scars.

Infatuation developed rapidly, a superbug that put me down hard and fast. We created an intense, insular little world, in which each tiny gesture—a kiss, a laugh—felt huge, the magnification in a dew drop. I couldn't bear to leave him for any amount of time. I tried to go to class but turned around and ran back to my apartment just as the uptown C train pulled into the station. We flung ourselves at each other until the paste of us could mix, participating in the invention of a novel compound. We said "I love you" to each other right away, over and over, many times a day, as if our bodies, metabolizing the other's fervor too fast, required more and more and more sustenance.

Of equal vigor was Gregory's alcoholism. He was honest with me from the beginning about how far gone he was.

"It's like I'm trying to kill myself by jumping out of a first-floor window over and over," he told me.

I witnessed up close the grueling routine demanded by his illness. He drank a liter of vodka a day, and at night I'd wake to see him in front of the refrigerator, the freezer door open, drinking straight from the bottle to quell the shakes. My sheets became saturated in acrid alcoholic sweat. He dry heaved over the toilet in the mornings. As Gregory's illness blazed, the medications I was taking flinted the tinder of my pathologies.

"I'm going to scare you off," he said.

"I'm going to scare you off," I said.

"I'm on a grand adventure," he said, spreading his arms wide. "I know it's foolish and I know it's irresponsible and I don't care. And if ever you don't want me here, I'll leave."

"I want you here," I said.

Three months later, I had to fly to the Caribbean to meet my mother. In the middle of a blizzard, I dressed Gregory in his three-piece suit, put a MetroCard and forty dollars in his pocket, wrapped him up in his coat and a warm hat, and sent him into the snowy night. He had nowhere to go, but I, an oblivious rich kid, didn't understand what that really meant.

Gregory had continued to scrape together enough money to sustain his drinking and stay in youth hostels by producing the records of Manhattan brats impressed by his résumé, but the money had run out. He called an old friend who got him a ticket to Fort Myers, Florida, where he waited out the winter in his former tour manager's apartment, overlooking a trailer park. I visited him for Valentine's Day. We rode bikes around Fort Myers, wrote songs on a friend's pontoon, laughed when a parrot landed on my shoulder. We had such loud sex that neighbors would holler "oh god yes" at us from their trailers. When I arrived home, I opened my email to find an MP3 attachment titled "Carrière." From my computer speakers, in a voice about to collapse under the weight of its sentiment, Gregory sang: "Carrière, Carrière, I want to carry her away." By the end, as he repeated the lines "Without you I'm only half me. Without you I only have me," I could hear the sorrow in his voice.

Gregory was subsisting on baked potatoes and rice. His royalty checks and former tour manager paid for his alcohol. Once spring arrived, he flew back to New York, relying first on family, then on his charm to keep a roof over his head. He eventually ran out of favors. After detox in a hospital, rehab in Pennsylvania, a relapse, a bus trip back to New York, and a realization he really had nowhere to go, he ended up at Men's Educational Alliance PRIDE Site One—a sober-living center on the Lower East Side. Most of the residents were reluctantly sober convicts, mandated by the courts to be there. Gregory's counselor was a former champion whistler and his designated "big brother" was an ex–Barnum & Bailey Circus clown with a snaggletooth and an anxiety disorder, whom Gregory dubbed "Johnny Panic" after the Sylvia Plath book. At night, Gregory would lie on the top bunk in the twelve-by-sixteen-foot room listening to his three roommates snore. One guy gasped in his sleep and then made a high-pitched noise that sounded like a little girl calling Gregory's name from far away: "Greeeeeeg." The guy in the bottom bunk had a baritone snore that would vibrate the bed. Johnny Panic would exhale and then fall into a long silence that was exploded by a violent, gasping inhalation. These sounds formed a relentless sonic locomotive that tore through Gregory's sleepless nights. He didn't have any ear plugs or headphones, so he'd wad up toilet paper, soak it in spit, cram it in his ears, and wrap a pair of pants around his head. After 6:15 a.m. wake-up and breakfast, Gregory swept, mopped floors, and cleaned toilets. For the first seven days he had to be escorted at all times—even to the toilet for his withdrawal-induced diarrhea and dry heaves—by other residents. The residents were allowed to take a "med walk" four times a day, where they walked to Tompkins Square Park, rolled loose-leaf tobacco, which was the only kind they could afford on the ten-dollars-a-week stipend, and smoked. He tried to comfort himself with the fact that he was in his old neighborhood. To calm down, he would chant to himself, "I am in the East Village on East Tenth Street by Tompkins Square Park. I'm home."

One morning, after four months of sober confinement, Gregory walked out of Men's Educational Alliance PRIDE Site One, across Tompkins Square Park, and through the band-sticker-covered door of Doc Holliday's, where he asked the Bettie Paige look-alike bartender for two double whiskeys, paid for with the royalty checks that had continued to arrive and that he'd secretly cashed and kept waded in a sock in his drawer. To sleep, he found a flophouse, which was one giant room, the floor of a warehouse, separated by partitions topped with chicken wire to prevent people from crawling into other people's space. A man with white tufts of hair puffing like smoke from his open shirt handed him a can of bug spray and told him to spray himself and the room down because of the bed bugs. In eight months, Gregory would be curled up under a blanket in a small room in Brooklyn, unable to eat anything except flakes of salt, his hair falling out from malnourishment, his feet numb from neuropathy, drinking. In another eight months, he would be curled up on a bench in Tompkins Square Park, unrecognizable and waiting to die.

I tried to keep track of him. He wasn't allowed a cell phone at PRIDE Site One, so I resorted to calling his ex-girlfriend, who didn't know where he was. I called another girl he had been staying with, who refused to give me any information about him. When he regained access to his phone, he was too preoccupied with his slow suicide to pick up when anyone called. I called every hostel I could remember him ever having mentioned, including one called, unforgettably, "Lollipop," but they refused to release information about their guests. I thought about him all the time, but I would soon become distracted by a threat even greater than my heartbreak. As Gregory was folding in on himself like a napkin twisted into the shape of a person, my symptomatology—derived from illness or the medications allegedly treating that illness—was stretching, finding its legs, about to bound off to the very limit of where I thought my mind could go.

6.

That summer I visited my father in Berlin, where he was shooting a telenovela called *Anna und die Liebe*. I was twenty-three and I looked after my sister, who was twelve. We'd take the train to the suburbs where my father was shooting and spend the day in his dressing room. We'd run lines, eat snacks, and take selfies. We wandered the Berlin suburbs talking and singing songs—Regina Spektor's "Fidelity," an Italian lullaby, and a song by a Moldovan pop trio I'd heard on German MTV.

"You're going to be very beautiful," I said to Elena.

"I don't want to be beautiful," she said. "That doesn't interest me."

I laughed. I respected that.

I loved my sister and I was impressed by her. She was confident and decisive and very diplomatic. When my father and I fought she'd silently place a note on the table that informed us of our bad behavior and instructed us to get along and then walk away. I wondered sometimes who I was to her. I wanted her to love me. I wanted to be important to her. But I was also jealous of her, even though she was only twelve. My father was protective of her and never yelled or threw tantrums like he had around me. When she'd misbehave or refuse to do something, he was patient.

"Why aren't you screaming at her?" I'd scream at him. "You weren't like this with me."

I was still being prescribed Adderall, which left me with a relentless, irrepressible boiling inside my brain and my chest that I needed to match with constant stimulation and movement on the outside. I dragged Elena all around Berlin, compulsively shopping with my mother's credit card and visiting tattoo shops to see if they could tattoo the first lines of my novel onto my forearm. My friend Leah was also in Berlin, and we went out one night with her friend Friedrich. We walked from bar to bar, trying to decide where to go. We'd walk in and I'd immediately say, "No, not here" and insist we leave. Nowhere we went felt right. I needed to keep moving, keep searching for that perfect, elusive place. I thought I was being discerning, that my indecision and insatiable need were relatable and they too were in search of something they could never find, but later that night, Friedrich said to Leah, "I hope your friend gets the help she needs."

To bring myself down, I drank alone at night, whiskey and vodka straight out of bottles I found in the apartment where we were staying. My sister, perhaps in an act of helpless defiance, took my phone and secretly documented my binges. Photos of me asleep with my mouth wide open clutching a near-empty bottle, photos of overflowing ashtrays and empty liquor bottles lining the windowsill would mysteriously appear in my photo library. One night, after my sister had gone back to Venice, I found a baggie of cocaine in a purse I had packed. My father used to tell me that when I turned eighteen, we could do heroin on a beach together, and I thought this would be the perfect opportunity to fulfill one of our fantasies. I also knew he used to love cocaine (which he had stopped using when Elena was born) and I wanted him to do it with me.

He declined so I laid out a line on the coffee table and snorted it.

"Isn't it so crazy I just randomly found this?" I said. "I had no idea it was in here and it crossed an entire ocean to surprise us, like a gift from the gods. Fucking wild, no?"

He was eerily quiet. I was used to him twiddling his fingers and sucking on a cigarette and following the little cards on the screen as he played Skat. But now he was completely still, lying on the couch. He stared into the distance. I bowed my head to do another line. He erupted from the couch, towered over me, and stabbed a finger into the air between us.

"Don't you ever fucking do that in front of me again." His words held a cracking force but were low and level.

I was speechless. All the images of our shared transgressions swirled around me. I thought this was what he wanted. Just the two of us getting into trouble, doing things normal assholes didn't do, because they couldn't understand, because they were too boring or stupid or prudish or American. I thought this was who he wanted me to be. But I had fucked up and he was rejecting me.

After years of sexualized words and gazes—my father's and other men's—I was concerned that my father was no longer sexually attracted to me. I had been tracking what I thought was his waning interest for a while. When the pills first made me gain weight I asked him if I was the same size as my mother when they got married.

"No," he said. "She was slim."

Something inside my chest collapsed. I had failed. I was watching a light in his eyes dim. The more my body changed, the bigger or smaller it got, pumped up or whittled down by meds, the more I worried about my fluctuating worth. I had at first thought it might intrigue him, as other facets of my sickness seemed to. When I was seventeen and we were visiting his friend Karl, my father walked into the living room and removed any remotely injurious object (pencil, stapler, lighter, sharp-edged picture frame) in a flamboyant performance of parental protectiveness. When I came to visit one year and showed him my Ziploc bag full of nine medication bottles, he made me pose with it and took a picture of me holding the bag aloft, smiling. But he seemed frustrated by the physical changes and I became attuned and sensitive to his irritation. Before flying to Berlin, I had lost twenty pounds and would overhear him on the phone telling people how great I looked and how much weight I'd lost. Every time I went to visit him I mapped the hills and valleys of my body, desperately trying to decipher if there was beauty still in its shapes.

It was a strange circuitry of worry and responsibility, pride and shame, pathways lighting up and crossing that should never have intersected. I had started to see the world differently, but I couldn't figure out why. Every movie I watched that contained a scene when a father was affectionate with a child, I anticipated a dark turn. Every time I saw a father be affectionate with a daughter in public, my bones ached with suspicion and a queasy trepidation. I interpreted every physical gesture, any moment when skin met skin, when a gaze lingered, as hazardous, inappropriate. I didn't know how to identify a father-daughter relationship that was safe. There was always, in every touch, the potential for treachery, for transgression, for taboo. It confused me why people around me couldn't see it too.

I had recurring nightmares about my father. They took place in hotel rooms, like the ones we stayed in in Europe while he was shooting movies. We were in a bed together and he started touching me. I pretended to be asleep and I didn't stop him. Sometimes in the dream I murmured "Daddy." I used a term I had never used to remind him of who he was while he was doing what he was doing. In the nightmare I began to get turned on, often orgasming into wakefulness to then be slammed with a soaking shame. It took me days to recover from those nightmares.

I couldn't figure out why this was happening, why I was feeling and doing all these things. I wondered if it had something to do with my mother's abuse. Had I inherited it somehow? Had those words in her journals infected me? It was hard to know what had happened to me. My father had given me words and ideas, ones that did not belong in a father's mouth or the mind of a daughter. He had treated parenthood as a reckless experiment. But compared to my mother's nightmarish memories, my own experiences paled in comparison. I was also beginning to feel at home in this place I occupied with my father, and, sitting on the floor of a Berlin apartment, tempting him with this powdered Eucharist, I tried to keep us there.

I returned to New York at the end of August and had to move apartments because I had been kicked out of mine for smoking too much. I was alone again. 134 Charles Street was gone. Gregory was gone. My mother was at her cottage in the Hamptons, while the building she had bought in Brooklyn was being renovated. I would call her and try to keep her on the phone.

I called her once when I knew she was in Brooklyn, visiting the construction site.

"Do you want to spend some time with me?" I asked.

"Is there something wrong?" she asked.

"No, I just want to hang out with you. Don't you want to hang out with me?"

"I'm going back to Amagansett," she said, as if she had an important appointment, which she did not.

"But you don't have to," I said. "If you wanted to, you could hang out with me."

There was a long silence.

"I have to go out to Amagansett," she said. We hung up and I cried.

Dr. Sarini had recently put me on Zoloft. The other medications were all doing something: adding sweat, flesh, bottomless hunger, trembling alertness. The Zoloft combined with the Adderall made my mind and body vibrate. I could not be still. During the day, I cleaned my apartment for hours, organizing and reorganizing its

contents, arranging and rearranging the furniture. At night, I got
dressed up in clothes that were too tight for me, now plush from meds
and mood swings, and went out alone to my favorite bars. At Marie's
Crisis—a show-tunes bar in the West Village—I met George. George
was gay, effusive with his compliments, and eager to party. I took him
to the Beatrice Inn, the exclusive lounge frequented by celebrities,
downtown socialites, and the offspring of Middle Eastern royalty.
"Private party tonight," they'd say if they didn't want you in there.
After talking excitedly at each other until three in the morning,
George and I went back to my apartment and passed out in my bed.
Over the next two weeks, he would come over (from where, I didn't
know), tell me to try on outfits and jewelry for him, and we'd topple
out into the night. Then pieces of jewelry went missing and he stopped
coming around. I came across a photo on George's Facebook page of
him wearing a necklace of mine. Alone again, my mind gnawing on
this betrayal by a man I didn't realize I didn't know, I called my father
in Germany. I talked to him about George stealing from me, large
gulps of air punctuating my sentences as I kept forgetting to breathe.
My father must have noticed something in my voice, because he
begged for time off from his desperately needed acting job and booked
a flight to New York, arriving three days later. I was excited to see
him and we had a nice few days. We read each other our writing and
he cooked me dinner. He built me a bookshelf. The third evening,
while I was in bed watching a TV show on my laptop, he lay next to
me and put his arm around me. All the breath went out of my body
and I froze. I stared at the screen and felt my mouth go dry. He commented on the show and I managed to make a gurgling sound of
agreement. When he finally released me from this septic cuddle, I felt
dizzy and weak.

The next evening, I started texting George. Did he know the
punishment for grand larceny? I asked. I drank beer after beer and
sent text after text. I declared to my father, also many beers in, that

we needed to go to the police and report George. At the police station, I held out a printout of the Facebook photo of George and my jewelry and explained to a police officer that this guy had stolen from me, jabbing my finger at George's two-dimensional neck, making the paper buckle and thwack. My father tried to interrupt. I could smell the alcohol on his breath, but not the boozy steam that puffed from my own mouth. I felt my father's tall frame vibrating at a high frequency as I stood there, oblivious to my own shivers of derangement.

Back at my apartment my father told me I should just drop it. "Drop it, drop it," he repeated. But I could not. This was all that mattered. I was enraged he couldn't see that. I felt hollowed out, my thoughts, sharp and stinging, spraying themselves across my mind like fire-hosed acid. I screamed at him to get out of my apartment. He grabbed my only set of keys and stormed out. When I tried to call his cell phone, it rang uselessly from my kitchen counter. I felt trapped. My heart smacked against my rib cage, my thoughts thrashed at my brain. I grabbed one of my orange pill bottles and swallowed five Klonopin. I grabbed another brown glass beer bottle and drained it. The door opened and shut and my father was in my living room again. I ran into the bathroom and locked the door behind me. I dismantled a razor blade, wedged myself between the closet and the washing machine, and began slicing up my left forearm. My father banged on the door, begging me to open it.

"You love the drama," I screamed. "You love this," I said as I did snow angels on the bathroom floor, bleeding.

He begged me to open the door.

"You'll just make me go to the hospital," I said.

"No. I won't. I promise. Just open the door," he said.

My father called my mother in Amagansett. My mother called my friend Leah, who came over. When she arrived, I unlocked the bathroom door and came out. She helped me wash and dress the wounds and gave me a croissant to eat, to fill my stomach and absorb the pills. I went to sleep in my bedroom, Leah watching me breathe, and my father went to sleep on the couch. He returned to Germany two days later and called when he landed to check on me. My mother never mentioned what had happened that night.

It was spring, and the weather was turning. The days got warmer and then hotter, mirroring the escalating temperature of my mind. Alone in my apartment, I turned my attention to my body. I discovered a rash on my thigh. I interpreted that ruddy patch as a hazard symbol, warning me of something—but of what? I had long feared I was susceptible to HIV. Memories of my mother's friends who'd died of AIDS flooded me. I scanned my body for any abnormal sensations. But being in a body always felt strange to me. I examined my tongue. Did it look whiter than usual? Were these signs of thrush? I peered into the toilet to examine my stool. Was this normal stool? I turned to WebMD. The more symptoms I put in, or the less related they were, the more likely it seemed that I had HIV or multiple sclerosis. I hadn't been tested since all the unprotected sex I'd had with Gregory, and I became convinced I had HIV. I made an emergency appointment with my gynecologist.

"What brings you here today?" she asked.

"I don't want to show it to you," I said, sitting on the exam room table, sweating and trembling.

"Why not?"

"I'm scared it's HIV and I'm scared for you to tell me it is."

"Just show me."

I lifted up my skirt.

"That is a sweat rash," she said. "Because it's hot outside. It'll go away in a few days. If you want you can put some Cortisone on it."

I demanded an HIV test, but when the results came back negative, I was convinced that the infection was not detectable yet, an invisible threat known only to me. And if I didn't have HIV, I knew there must be something else wrong with me. I went to my GP and told him I felt like there were electric currents pulsing in my head, did he know what that meant? No, he didn't. I went to a proctologist, a dermatologist. They found nothing. Monitoring my body consumed me. Any illness I contracted, I knew, would be insidious, tricky, stealthy. It could be anything. It could be anywhere. My body seemed porous and susceptible and liable to turn against me at any moment.

Two weeks later, the imaginary illness spread from my body to other machines. I became convinced I had been hacked and that my computer communications were being monitored. I stared for hours at the computer logs, watching in real time as the computer told itself in its own language what it was doing. The numbers and abbreviations meant nothing to me but I knew they were detailing every breach, every malign intrusion, which would become clear if only I knew the language. I printed out the system logs, convinced that somehow as the logs moved between their digital form and the printed page, the truth had been intercepted and destroyed. Somewhere, invisibly, wirelessly, in the air around me, fatal distortions were occurring. I sent myself emails written to "them" because I knew they were monitoring my email. They were changing the order and content of my text messages, too. I held my breath and choked back tears of terror as I updated my Facebook status to: "I HAVE BEEN HACKED. DON'T BELIEVE ANYTHING THAT IS WRITTEN ON HERE" or googled how to change my social security number. This preoccupation with infection, with the permeability of borders, with the mutiny of mundane machines—my body, the devices I used to live— took over my life.

I tried to get help. I called AppleCare and explained the invasions I was enduring.

"You should buy chicken wire and surround your house with it," said the AppleCare specialist.

"But I live in an apartment," I said.

"It's just as effective if you put the chicken wire all around the inside of your apartment," he said.

I scribbled these suggestions down in my notebook.

"There's also a special paint you can put on the walls that will make the signal bounce off of them," he told me.

I thanked him and hung up. As I googled "paint to protect against hacking" I realized the AppleCare specialist had been mocking me, and then realized the call must have been intercepted by the culprits.

I went to Tekserve, the computer-repair store. It was a hot summer day, and I arrived with giant sweat stains under my arms and a glistening face.

"My family has been hacked," I told the man at the desk. "The FBI is helping my mom but I just want to make sure my stuff is okay too." I calculated that these embellishments to my story would legitimize me.

"Look for a virus," I said.

"There's nothing here," the guy said, after quickly scanning my external hard drives.

I went back a week later.

"It's FBI girl," said one of the employees, smiling.

"Yep, that's me," I said, smiling back, flattered he remembered me.

I did in fact call the FBI. I spoke to someone who told me to slow down because I was sounding crazy.

"Why would anyone want to do this to you?" he asked.

"I don't know but don't you think that proves that I'm not crazy? If I were crazy, I'd be making up reasons why. So admitting I don't know shows I'm not crazy."

With every passing week, the incursions got worse, and I was called upon to invent new ways of protecting myself. One morning in July I woke up to find that the doorknob on my front door was sagging. I called the police, and soon two officers arrived. It was the afternoon and I was in a vintage pink slip with crescents of yesterday's makeup under my eyes.

"Can you still lock it?" asked one of the police officers.

I closed the door and twisted the lock and it locked. I opened the door.

"Okay, well, was anything taken?" he asked.

"Um, not really. I don't think," I said.

"Well then we can only report this as damage to property since the door can still lock and nothing was taken."

"Well, stuff has been messed around with recently," I said. "Pages were ripped out of my notebook."

The police officers looked at each other. One of them shrugged and said, "I'm sorry, miss, but we can only report this as damage to property."

There was something about a doorknob's being taken apart just enough while still being functional that unnerved me. This was a statement, loud and insolent and mysterious. Were they mocking me? Telling me they could get in if they wanted to? To thwart the invasions, I stacked my dining table chairs in front of the door and snaked ribbons of vintage lace through the legs. If the lace was broken, I'd know that someone had tried to get in. It didn't occur to me that the lace was irrelevant, that the chairs would clatter if someone tried to enter. But these were no ordinary intruders. They were cunning, I knew, and I needed to be smarter and sneakier and more creative than they were in order to defeat them. I didn't realize then that I was the intruder—mastermind of both barricade and breach.

By late summer I was convinced I was being chloroformed and gang-raped in my sleep. Going to sleep was like willfully drowning myself, holding myself under with booze and Klonopin until I could pass out, until my ceaseless vigilance could be momentarily submerged. When

I woke up I inspected my underwear for signs of sexual assault. Any discharge on my underwear and they went into a Ziploc bag and were stored in what would later be labeled my "manic box."

In my "manic box" was:

Ziploc bags full of physical evidence I had collected and labeled. The evidence included: flakes of plaster, strands of hair, lint, sediment from my fire escape and balcony, loose screws, a used Band-Aid, cigarette butts, a torn six of clubs playing card, a dismantled bicycle bell.

hundreds of pages of printouts of computer systems logs

two laptops, dismantled and put back together with tape

an external hard drive containing hundreds of photographs and screenshots of: "possible associates"; rooftops of buildings; all the graffiti on any surface within a three-block radius of my apartment, which I had collected and studied in an attempt to detect a pattern; suspicious cars and vans parked near my apartment; text messages that I did not recall sending or receiving, which I believed to have been altered remotely so as to skew events.

a notebook with: the license plate numbers of cars parked around my apartment, dates and times of phone calls received and made, the letters of people's names and Facebook posts arranged into anagrams that would reveal their secret communiqués.

envelopes labeled "dubious info" containing receipts (taxi, deli, bar), business cards, paper phone-number tabs ripped from a suspicious-looking guitar-lesson advertisement, all found within a one-block radius of my apartment

A soggy receipt in the gutter held secrets. A flyer for a production of *The Phantom of the Opera* was a message, a coded threat. I'd walk around and around my block, scouring the concrete for new evidence, updating my catalog of license plate numbers. But every time I meticulously archived the rotten flower petal, the broken hair tie, the new combination of letters and numbers, I became more disoriented.

Everything I encountered glowed with a radioactive menace. Everyone I encountered took on tremendous significance. They were all connected. Anyone could be one of them. The taxis I got into had been waiting for me. The men who asked for my number on the street were monitoring me. Something had been set into motion, a vast machine that knew where I was, knew what I was doing, could match my mounting fear with more menace. The more embattled I felt, the bigger and stronger and faster the enemy machine became.

By late August I knew I was being constantly monitored. Eyes and ears were on every part of me every second, in a drenching scrutiny. I was listening to one of my favorite childhood audiobooks. In between the narrator's sentences I heard, "Yo, D, what up?" come through the speakers. I realized they had bugged my apartment and I had tapped into the frequency they were using to communicate. I unscrewed all the light fixtures and peered into the wiring in the ceiling. I unscrewed all the outlets and pried around inside them with a screwdriver. I continued to look and examine, searching for proof. I tried to dismantle an old iPod, but the sleek design would not yield its insides. While I was trying to shove the edge of a knife in between the flush seams I heard people outside my door. I ran outside and followed two young men out of the building.

"Were you just inside that apartment building?"

"Um, yeah."

"What were you doing in there?"

"What?"

"Do you know how to open these things?" I asked as I tried to force a fingernail under the track pad of the iPod.

"I want whatever you're on," said one of the guys and they laughed and walked away. I retreated back into my apartment and took my afternoon dose of Adderall.

I bought a camera disguised as a desk fan and spent hours watching the footage. I convinced my mother to pay for people to sweep my apartment for bugs. Two men arrived with machines in black boxes.

"But what if they know that you're here and they've turned off whatever they're using to surveil me so your machines can't pick it up?" I asked.

"That's not how it works," I was told.

My mother sat on the sofa, silent. Her silence and her rare presence confirmed to me that I was right to be so diligent about my safety. Maybe it was because she was familiar with unbelievable stories. She had, after all, been used in a murderous sex cult.

"There's nothing here," said the de-buggers.

I convinced her to hire a forensic computer analyst to look at my computer.

"I can't see anything wrong with this except for these weird things you did to it. What is 'in a sieve they went to sea'?" he asked.

To throw people off my scent I had renamed my computer in settings after a poem my Scottish middle school librarian had read to us.

"There's nothing here," said the forensic computer analyst.

No one could identify the threat so I was forced to live a daily life constantly under siege by something only detectable by me. I had to eat and communicate and sleep and shop and sit on the subway and answer the phone all while the surge of adrenaline threatened to shred my veins. There was a hot, granular quality to my thoughts. The blood thrumming in my ears was hot white noise. Sweat continually covered my brow and darkened my underarms. My speech was breathless and speedy. When I was not at home I could barely breathe or concentrate. When I was outside, my mind spun with images of them prowling inside my apartment, going through my

things, embellishing their elaborate methods of surveillance and torment. After a while I couldn't take it and I'd stop whatever I was
doing, make an excuse, and run home. One day I fell up the stairs as
I sprinted toward my apartment. I entered on my hands and knees.
There was no one there. I hadn't caught them. So I just decided not
to leave.

I managed to send my Columbia advisor an email saying I would
not be able to return to school in the fast-approaching fall, and she
sent me the paperwork for a leave of absence, freeing me up to build
my entire life around this threat.

I ordered American Spirit cigarettes from the corner deli and
Duraflame logs to keep the fire burning even through the sweltering
days because it made me feel less alone. I ordered food from FreshDirect.
I bought two industrial-sized garbage cans so I wouldn't have to take
out the trash often. The garbage sat inside the giant bins in the middle
of my living room and festered. I stopped washing dishes. I ate cereal
out of Tupperware with a ladle. I ate spaghetti from a vase with tongs.
I used an old bowl of split pea soup as an ashtray. My appetite faded
completely and I ate only sliced turkey and carrots, and only when my
body absolutely demanded it. I barely slept. I was cutting every day
and then switched to burning, giving myself two deep partial-thickness
burns, causing nerve damage that would last for years.

One day Effie came over. She saw the cuts and burns on my arms
and the dark circles under my eyes, smelled the rotting trash, and
asked me what was going on. I told her all about the break-ins and
the rapes and the surveillance. She spent the night and left before I
woke up, leaving the door unlocked behind her because she didn't
have a key, which convinced me she was in on it. I texted her: "I'm
onto you. I know what you're doing. You're working with them."

"What are you talking about???" she texted back.

No one in my life could be trusted. When friends called, I'd make
them confirm their identity through a series of questions, and when

satisfied, would launch into the latest update of my persecution. Eventually they stopped picking up my calls. As people fell from my life, I agonized over who was doing this to me. Who had had access to me? Who had been in my most intimate spaces? Was Gregory the culprit? I hadn't heard from him in months. Was he the mastermind of my torment? Maybe everything I'd ever believed or felt had been a lie. Maybe this—this invasion, this war—was the only true thing in my life.

At night, I crouched at the windows, scanning the other buildings and examining each dark silhouette. Overwhelmed by all the eyes that could be watching, I taped spare bedsheets and towels across the windows. The only connection I had to the world was the swathes of sky let in by the skylights in the ceiling. The sky was a living force as the apartment bulged with heat from the sun.

In September, my mother got me a kitten. I named him Bracket. One morning, while in my bedroom examining my mattress with a flashlight—picking up strands of hair and placing them into a Ziploc bag—I heard noises out in the living room. I held my breath, terrified. Bracket was in the bedroom with me, and I reasoned that they wouldn't hurt an animal so I cracked the door open and pushed him out into the other room. I thought the presence of the cat might chase them away. I also felt if I sent him out into the room he would transmit the information to me. Part of me wanted to see them and confront them. Part of me was scared for my life. Perhaps some deep part of me knew there was nothing there and that would be more terrifying than anything else.

I waited in the bedroom as I heard them leave. I could hear very distinctly the sound of multiple footfalls going down stairs. I opened the door. The apartment was empty except for Bracket standing on the dining table. I ran to a drawer and grabbed the largest knife I could find. It was early still, and my eyes were dry and stinging from lack of sleep. I sat on the sofa and gripped the knife with both hands, trying to remember to breathe. As I sat there, I saw myself. For a brief moment of clarity I saw how far things had gone, sitting on the sofa with a knife surrounded by my refuse, and I saw that I could not find a way back or a way out. I cried.

I had an appointment scheduled with my psychopharmacologist and two hours before, the buzzer rang. It was my mother's assistant, sent by her to bring me to the doctor. I sat in Dr. Sarini's office jiggling my leg, talking rapidly of break-ins and rapes and surveillance. After listening for a while, Dr. Sarini said, "You have to choose. Either you take these new medications I'm going to prescribe or I'm calling an ambulance right now. I've sent people far less symptomatic than you to the psych ward."

"I'll take the pills," I said.

I started taking Depakote, Trileptal, and Zyprexa—two mood stabilizers and a heavy-hitting antipsychotic—in addition to all my other pills, including the Adderall. My mother came to visit me one week after I went on the new medications. She slept in my bedroom and I slept on the sofa. I had been instructed by Dr. Sarini to double the dose of Trileptal that morning. I took the two pills and went back to sleep for forty-five minutes. My mother was preparing to leave when I awoke. I sat up and walked into my bedroom, where she was packing. I stood in the doorway. She turned and looked at me and asked, "What are you doing?" My arms and legs were jerking like marionette limbs on strings.

"I don't know," I said. "I'm not doing this on purpose."

I made my way back to the sofa and lay down. My eyes were rolling back in my head and my tongue began to move uncontrollably in my mouth.

"Call the doctor," I managed to say, gesturing to my cell phone.

"It sounds like an overdose," Dr. Sarini said. "There's not much you can do. She just has to ride it out."

My mother brought me a garbage can and I threw up in it. She filled a glass with water and put it to my lips but my mouth and tongue were contorting too much for me to drink from the glass. She crouched next to me as I writhed on the sofa.

Hours later, when I had regained control of my body, my mother left.

Dr. Sarini maintained that I should stay on the new medications—and the old ones, including the Adderall. The new pills didn't take away the paranoia, they merely blurred it. I felt heavy and deadened, the bonfire in my brain now cold, heavy ashes. My hair started to fall out, clogging the drain, snaking around my fingers. I collected the hair every day and stored it in a large envelope, more evidence of wrongs committed. I developed cystic acne, painful and hot. I spent long stretches in front of the mirror squeezing pimples until my chin was smeared with blood. I gained forty pounds. My hands felt weak, dead at the tips of my arms. Glasses of water fell from my grasp and crashed to the floor. It didn't occur to me that it was the medication doing all this to me. I thought it was just my stupid body.

Nanny took care of me in my medicated haze. She was the only person I saw. Nanny, now eighty-three, would travel to Chelsea from Tribeca, climb the steep staircase, balancing on her cane, and stay with me. At night, she rubbed my eyelids to help me get to sleep, as she had done when I was little. We shared the only laugh I can remember in those twelve months. We were trying to put together a laundry hamper, but the components had been mislabeled. We spent a fruitless hour trying to make the parts fit, dissolving in laughter each time we failed. From time to time I would point out evidence of the torment being inflicted on me, and she would nod and agree that, yes, that vase had been moved. Yes, maybe that van had been parked there too long. Even in my delusion, she would never leave me alone.

I had been seeing my therapist throughout what I was told was a manic episode, and I had grown frustrated with her. She seemed not to believe me. I wanted solutions, and she just wanted to talk. I needed to figure out how to protect myself, and she wanted me to reflect. I would have barely any memory of our sessions over the year I was manic. But I would have the beautifully worded case study she would write about me. When she eventually revealed the case study to me a year after my manic episode, I felt betrayed. The woman I had been confiding in had been studying me, turning me into a beautiful, terrifying object lesson. She gave me the dramatic pseudonym of "Juliet," a *theatrical name*, which, she explained, *expresses an aspect of the complex narcissistic and perverse elements in her parent's obsessions with her, obsessions, to be sure, also accompanied by neglect.* I was reduced to a story, and not even my story was my own.

In the case study, she wondered: *How much did the delusions mask Juliet's rage and wish to deplete the mother? . . . How much was she the designated enactment of the father's wishes and envies in this regard? . . . How much did {these invasions} replicate the psychic and sexual invasions of the father? . . . Who did what to whom?*

Who did what to whom? It was a question that had haunted my family. What had happened to my mother? What exactly had my father done to me? How many of my symptoms were the result of the American psychiatric complex invading my body and my mind?

7.

Dr. Sarini recommended a treatment center in Florida where he sent many of his patients, and I agreed to go. I was twenty-five. While most of my peers were getting their master's degrees, getting married, and progressing in their careers, I was being admitted to my latest treatment center.

This time, I wanted to get better. The last year had scared me. And I was tired.

The night before I left for the treatment center, I called my father.

"If you get better—" he started to say.

"If?" I screamed. "If? Why would you say that?"

"I don't know if you'll survive," he said. "I hope that you will but I can't predict the future."

I was ravenously angry.

"What am I supposed to say?" he said.

"You're supposed to lie to me," I screamed.

When I arrived, the center's psychopharmacologist took me off the Depakote, Trileptal, Zyprexa, Klonopin, and Adderall, but put

me on another stimulant called Vyvanse, which functioned like
Adderall. Forty minutes after I took my morning dose I was chain-
smoking on the porch, telling stories about my childhood and sweating through my shirt. Then I would be told by counselors that I
talked too much and could we figure out what to do about my
sweating problem? Beyond the huge words and complicated metaphors I continued to use, I also gesticulated wildly to a point beyond
mere animation, possessed by a crazed and indecipherable sign language. My therapist, Diane, told me to sit on my hands, but then I
just swiveled my neck back and forth, as if a current were flowing
through me. I wanted to take advantage of this place. I knew that
I was lucky to have another chance, and I wanted to get well. I
wanted to be calm and receptive and thoughtful, but the medication
wouldn't let me.

There were strict rules at the treatment center. We had to keep our
bungalows meticulously clean—no water spots on the mirror, no dirty
laundry in the hamper. We had to be on time—if we were late to
group therapy, we were barred from the room. We had jobs—writing
down the messages left on the one communal telephone, walking the
treatment center dog, Sophie (who was on antidepressants herself).
There were strict regulations surrounding our interactions—sexes
were kept separate, and if we developed a close relationship with a
roommate, they'd reassign us. If we failed to follow the rules or fulfill
our responsibilities, there were consequences—they'd confiscate our TV,
revoke our day passes to leave the property. Patients were encouraged
to tell on each other, and the daily Community Meeting was a forum
where we voiced inexpert opinions on the behavioral, personality—
even physical—traits of our peers, and were celebrated for it. One such
Community Meeting focused on telling Albert, a near nonverbal
schizophrenic who made no eye contact, that he smelled. Albert sat
silently in his folding chair staring at the floor as patient and counselor

alike told him how gross he was, asking him questions—How often did he shower? Did he know personal hygiene was an important part of getting and staying healthy? Did he own deodorant?—he did not have the words or neurochemistry to answer. After the meeting, Albert continued to smell bad but the community had done its job. A special meeting was called to address the "issue" of me and my friend Dean—a young trans guy with soft features that twitched occasionally from the tardive dyskinesia he had developed from his antipsychotics. We were close, considering getting even closer, and when we weren't smoking cigarettes on my porch, we were watching TV in my bungalow, my head in his lap. Two patients, who would watch us through the window, told the counselors something was going on between us. At the meeting, patients and counselors demanded to know the nature of our feelings for each other and if anything physical had happened. Some were confused about whether Dean was "a lesbian or a straight guy," demanding he explain "what" he was. After forty-five minutes, Dean was begging, out loud, for it to end. That night, he came into my bathroom and lifted his shirt, revealing the seven gaping slashes he had wrought on his chest. I hugged him, trying to keep our chests from touching.

I was placed in trauma group. I didn't request it but my New York therapist, Dr. Hart, had informed my therapist at the center, Diane, about my father, and it was determined that I should be in trauma group. I had to fill out a Trauma Form—a chart where I had to list all the moments when I had felt violated, that had given me "trauma," how I had felt about it then, and how I felt about it now. There was only enough space for cursory answers. My tiny letters snaked around the page until I ran out of room, so details had to be forfeited. Once a week, four of us sat in a circle in Diane's dim office with the door locked. The type of therapy we did was called Chair Work. When it was my turn, I sat in a chair in the middle of the room. Diane got up, grabbed another chair, and placed it so close to me that it touched my knees. This would be where I put my father. I pushed back in my chair. I felt uncomfortable; I told Diane I was afraid. She told me to decide how far back the chair needed to be for me to feel comfortable. I motioned to her to push it away, again and again, until it reached the opposite wall. Diane told me to decide how my father would be sitting in the chair. Did he need handcuffs or did I need bodyguards? I chose two bodyguards and I told her that he needed to be tied to the chair. There needed to be a plank that his head could be tied to so that he couldn't thrust his entire body forward. Diane told me to pick a "me" at a specific age and place her next to my chair. I picked seven-year-old "me." Seven-year-old me was wearing a striped shirt and had a bad haircut. I liked her. Diane told me to look at her and say: "I wasn't there to protect you then but I am here to protect you now. I won't let anything bad happen to you ever again."

I repeated the lines to seven-year-old me.

Diane told me to pick an incident and tell my father about how it had made me feel and what it had done to me. She went to her desk to look for my trauma form, but she couldn't find it.

"It's okay," she said. "We can do this without it. It just said something about touching your dad's penis, right?"

I twisted around in my chair.

"No," I said, the word long and stringy with surprise.

"So pick another one and let's start," said Diane.

She told me to close my eyes and tell my father about the incident I had selected. I recited the story of my father making me lick the tears from his eyes.

"You used me to fill yourself up," I screamed at the chair with my eyes closed.

I listed every incident I had written on my trauma form—from the tale of a toe in a cunt to a Lolita on a horse to a pimp in sunglasses.

I felt the other patients watching me. I felt cuddled by their rapt-
ness. My skin grew hot and tears slipped from my scrunched-up eyes.
Diane whispered to me to give my father back his shame. This was
the script we were given in trauma group. Every session of Chair
Work ended with our giving the perpetrator back their shame. The
idea was that they were shameless and we, the victims, held their
shame for them.

"I give you back your shame," I yelled.

"Again," said Diane.

"I give you back your shame."

Diane asked me if she could put her hand on my back. I allowed it.
The confident tenderness of her touch ruptured something inside me,
my snot and tears the fluids of this strange paroxysm. I looked around
the room and saw the other patients staring at me with love in their
eyes. They called me brave and amazing. One patient declared that
my father was a monster. I felt giddy and incandescent, covered in the
glitter of their admiration. Diane asked if she could give me a hug. I
sank into her enormous fake breasts, which were draped in angora and
saturated in perfume. Falling into her fragrant bosom while my peers
chanted their support, I felt caught in the frenzy of religious fervor—a
preacher laying hands on me as I spoke in tongues, ejecting Satan from
me, filling me with a faith that would save me as long as I never
questioned it.

Diane had an assuredness that unnerved and sedated me. Her memory was bad and she often confused the details of her patients, but she
was unwavering. She took a shred of story and stitched and padded
until it became something plush and inviting I could hug to myself,
ambiguity plumping up into shapely certainty. I told her of the night
in Hamburg when I was eight years old and my father had been reading to me in bed. I went to the bathroom and saw spots of blood on
my days of the week underwear. When I showed it to him he said,

"You must have broken your hymen." I didn't remember anything else except that I had learned how to ride a bike that day. Under Diane's care, I started to believe my mind was resisting me, that something more had probably happened that I was blocking out. Any dark pockets of non-memory were significant and sinister. Not remembering couldn't mean that nothing had happened but rather too much had happened. Diane later told me that she moved very slowly, intentionally taking her time getting me to say, "I was molested." When I named my father a molester, I was told I was strong, brave, and special. I was a survivor. That felt good.

The language in trauma group was fairytale-like—"icky," "monster," "survive," "persevere," "overcome." I was ready to commit fully to my character, to the story of the molested girl who had overcome her monster. Diane told me never to speak to or see my father again, so I put him on the list of people who weren't allowed to have their calls put through to me or have any information released to them. She told me no good could ever come from someone so evil. The simplicity felt thirst-quenching. I was ready to consume great quantities of this new solution until I felt completely myself. In my previous therapy, words had been soft and pliable. Now they were hard and inflexible. Once you called someone something, that's what they were, that's what they had always been, and that's what they would be forever. I loved stories and now I had one almost like my mother's, both with monsters whose shadows had been enlarged by therapists. I would later tell that story, embellished by Diane, to anyone who would listen. In doctor's offices or dark bars, I would announce my father as the monster I was taught to believe he was. It was my new identity.

I pictured my mother in another dim room confiding in Dr. Bernard all her hang-ups—her pain during sex, her promiscuity, her difficulty talking about feelings, her drinking, that time she had walked in on her father fucking a family friend. She laid them out like colors on an artist's palette as Dr. Bernard dipped the tip of her expertise in, creating images of such enormity and vividness that they crowded everything and everyone else out. I pictured her and Dr. Bernard shaping the amorphous clay of her fears into the forms of Bertie and Russell and "Monkey Boy." My mother was a brilliant artist, and she must have applied that same ambition and rigor to her psychotherapy. It reminded me of how she described surviving Yale: "I was terrified my first semester, but then I just started building huge stretchers that interfered with the people working near me." To deal with her fear, she created enormous, intrusive structures—a canvas or a memory—so large and so overwhelming they interfered with the people living near her.

Dr. Bernard was either a perpetrator or a victim herself. Either she had believed just as strongly in the myths she and my mother were telling together, or she was the ruthless mastermind of a nonconsensual scientific experiment. I would encounter Dr. Bernard's name again, years later, when I watched the documentary *Three Identical Strangers.* It told the story of identical triplets separated at birth who reunited and discovered that they had been victims of a disturbing scientific experiment that involved dividing triplets and twins into different socioeconomic households, withholding any information that the children had siblings, and documenting what happened. The doctors behind the study were Dr. Viola Bernard and Dr. Peter Neubauer— my mother and father's therapists, respectively. Finally here was proof that the people tasked with my parents' care, the people responsible for shaping their lives and, ultimately, mine, were real-life villains.

Now here I was, sitting in a therapist's office, sweating and squirming from prescribed medication as a therapist misinterpreted my trauma form, made up stories, and told me what words to call myself.

Parts of what Diane said were true. My father had transgressed. He had said things that shouldn't have been said. He had been derelict in his parenting in a way that had lasting effects. But did that mean the only way forward was to disavow him, to cut him out of my life as my mother had? Burn it all down and never think about it again, as she'd done with her journals? He had been the parent who asked how I was, the one who had tried to intervene in the treatment that was making me worse. Was silence the only way forward, the only path of healing? I had been told to do many things by doctors. I had been told to take the pills that roiled my brain, and I had done it. And now I'd slug down this story like the obedient patient I was, not questioning if I could be something, or someone, more.

Toward the end of my five-month stay, my mother came for family weekend. The patients and their parents sat in chairs in a circle as Blake, the family therapist, facilitated the session. Each family, when it was their turn, sat in chairs in the center. When it was our turn, I stood up and removed one of the designated "parent" chairs. My mother sat in the remaining one, and I sat in the one across from her.

"You're the only one here who only needs one seat for your parent," Blake said. "How did that make you feel, to take one away?"

"Normal," I said. "Fine."

I talked about my father and the "sexual abuse."

"She's an accomplice, right?" I asked Blake.

Blake nodded.

I was angry at my mother.

"You're an accomplice," I said to her.

Her reactions were barely discernible, her face waxy and stiff with bewilderment. I started to cry.

"My heart is breaking, I just want to hug her," said one of the patients.

"Me too," said my mother.

"So do it!" yelled one of the parents.

The audience was rooting for me. They were protecting me. My mother got up, walked over to me, and placed her arms limply around my shoulders. She stood there for a few seconds and returned to her chair. The hug had not given me what she'd intended, it had given me something else. It had given me its shortcoming, which was far more useful to me.

"Honestly that just felt so awkward," I announced. "I'm so not used to physical affection from you that it just reminds me of how uncomfortable it is." I was glad the hug had been hollow. After all, what was I without my mother's disinterest?

8.

After leaving the treatment center in July 2010, I moved into a studio apartment with no air conditioning in Delray Beach, Florida. I got a job at the Boys & Girls Club and continued seeing Diane. I loved working with the kids and I loved having somewhere to be every day, but I tingled with restlessness. I didn't know how to drive, my friends from the treatment center moved away and moved on, and I'd get uncomfortably drunk on my own. The one person I wanted to talk to was Gregory. I had no idea if he was still alive. I decided to call him, and, with each ring, I pictured a different dire scenario—frozen on a park bench, living under a bridge, long dead and buried. When I heard his voice, I felt a scratching in my chest, something trying to get out and fly to him, and an involuntary smile spread across my face. I pretended I had called by accident, embarrassed about something, although I wasn't clear what. When I'd last spoken to him, he'd barely made sense, ending his sentences with the remark: "Don't you know I don't make any sense? Don't you know I don't know what I'm saying?" Now, his voice sounded clear, his words distinct, not bending and sliding in his mouth like they did when he was drunk. He sounded calm and measured. He told me he was three months sober. He described the final days of his alcoholism and how MusiCares, the not-for-profit organization of the National Academy of Recording Arts and Sciences that helped working musicians get sober, had agreed to pay for one last rehab in Nashville, which is where he was now living. I told him about my treatment center, about Diane, about how everything made sense now that I knew my father was a monster and that I would never speak to him again. We talked late into the night.

"I'm still in love with you," I said.

"I'm still in love with you too," he said.

I scooped ice cream into a bowl in the kitchen, illuminated by the light from the refrigerator, and smiled into the phone. That electric feeling between us had not been dampened, not by my year of near-lethal madness, not by his unsuccessful suicide-by-substance. We said good night and talked every day after that.

After four months in Florida, I decided to go back to school, re-enrolled at Columbia University, quit my job, flew back to New York, and moved in with my mother in her new house in Brooklyn.

The address was 315 Vanderbilt Avenue. It had been a building for the Candy and Confectioners Union, and then a preschool. Like 134 Charles Street, it was not initially designed to be a residence. My mother's bedroom looked out onto a garden through an entire wall of glass. Her bathtub was in the middle of the room, right behind her bed, and the toilet was similarly exposed in the corner. There were two floors of studios and no guest room—only a room for Nanny. I moved into the storage room, which had no door and no furniture. I tipped boxes on their sides to create shelves for my clothes. I was back in a house with no locks, and now, no doors. The bathroom closest to my room didn't have a shower, and Nanny's was outfitted with an uncomfortable geriatric walk-in tub, so I bathed in my mother's bathtub in the center of her bedroom. I rubbed soap under my armpits as I gazed out the wall of windows onto the eight-foot boulder my mother had imported from the Hamptons, listening to her smoker's cough erupt from her as she lay on her bed next to me. I was back living with my mother, bathing next to her in a glass room, boundaries porous as ever.

Some days, I would sit in her studio with her as she worked. She was working on a massive piece that was more than 158 feet long, even bigger than *Rhapsody*. She couldn't come up with a title so she asked me to help her. She explained what the piece was about and its relationship to *Rhapsody* and another piece called *Song*. I stared at the rows of square metal plates with colorful dots in varying sizes, black and white squiggles, monochromatic house silhouettes, that wrapped around the walls.

"Recitative," I said. "The part of an opera closer to ordinary speech that advances the plot."

She loved it. She named it *Recitative*.

And in that moment we were joined. She had needed a word and I had had the right one.

NANNY WAS EIGHTY-SIX AND RETIRED. She had decided to tie her life to my mother's instead of moving back to England to be near her sister, Thelma. When my mother and Nanny moved into the Brooklyn house, Nanny's life shrank. When we lived on Charles Street she knew everyone in the neighborhood. Nanny's best friend, Helen, lived just three blocks away on Bleecker Street and they had tea every week. She would walk the dog and chat with the couple who owned the laundromat next door and loved to gossip. In Brooklyn, she knew no one and had no responsibilities, but she tried to keep a strict routine. She fed the cat at 5:30 a.m. and then prepared breakfast and brought it to my mother, balancing on a cane and pushing a metal cart. She then lay on her bed watching the news or just staring out the window, waiting for my mother to need something. I would sit in her room, drinking wine, and listen to her talk about her past, telling the same stories over and over and over again, while my mother's anxious dog barked all day.

I was under Dr. Sarini's care again too, and he reintroduced the Adderall and Klonopin and steadily increased the number and doses of medications I was on. I had re-enrolled at Columbia to finish my degree but I was having trouble getting to class. I'd watch TV all day, skip class, and drink with my mother at night. When it was time to complete an assignment, I'd panic and sit frozen in front of my laptop, eyes fixed on a TV show. My sizzling anxiety was the only thing that got me out of the house, but not anywhere I needed to go. It sent me walking the Manhattan and Brooklyn bridges at night, even in the middle of a snowstorm. I walked for hours, waiting for the sear of panic to dissipate. At night, I'd lie in bed and talk to Gregory on the phone. He talked to me about his recovery, about how losing everything had changed his life for the better, and how his desperation had been a gift. He was working the twelve steps of Alcoholics Anonymous, and it was having a profound effect on him. His pursuit of specialness, he explained, had destroyed him, and now, through the humble execution of small, repeated gestures, and a commitment to something other than himself, he was rebuilding his life, repairing relationships, and he was happy. He used words like *acceptance, service, humility*, and *surrender*, and I thought of how different they sounded from the words I had been given to heal. He told me about the singles he was producing out of a motorcycle repair shop, the artists he was collaborating with, the first song he had written sober. Then, some nights, sitting on the porch of the halfway house he was living in, he'd lower his voice to a whisper and we'd have phone sex.

My therapist, Dr. Hart, whom I had also started seeing again, told me she'd rather see me back in a mental institution than living with my mother in New York. I left her office and called Gregory.

"Can I come live with you?" I asked.

He said he had to talk to his sponsor. He was apprehensive about making any big decisions only one year into his recovery.

"You're two sick people," his father said, when Gregory asked his advice. "How can two sick people take care of each other?"

I took another leave of absence from school and in April 2011, Gregory found us a house to rent in Nashville and arrived in a U-Haul truck he had driven straight from Nashville to pick me and my stuff up.

I loved the little yellow house Gregory had chosen for us, and we spent weeks scouring vintage shops for weird furniture to furnish it with. We planted vegetables in the backyard. In a nearby graveyard, Gregory taught me how to drive in his boat-sized 1986 Mercedes with no power steering. He took me to a Beatles laser light show at the planetarium, an amateur circus by the Cumberland River, and a honky-tonk lesson at the local American legion. For my twenty-sixth birthday, he stuffed a piñata with twenty six pieces of paper, each with something he loved about me written on them: "I love your 'why' questions. I love the way you sleep talk. I love your gift. I love your upspeak. I love the way you read me like you wrote me." We adopted a cat. We built puzzles and listened to audiobooks.

Underneath all these moments still bounced my medications, the amphetamine altitudes and depressant depressions leaving me unable to find secure footing, and the hulk of my new identity—molested survivor repressing memories—heaved beneath the delicate skin of my new life. During the day, Gregory would record artists in the motorcycle repair shop and I'd chain-smoke cigarettes and binge watch *Law & Order: SVU*. Then he'd head to an AA meeting and I'd drink two bottles of wine in my attic office. He'd come home and find me curled in a closet, drunk and weeping about what my father may or may not have done to me.

"What am I not remembering?" I wailed. "What else did he do?"

I knew from my mother and from Diane that there could always be more, something below the surface that could come up and swallow a whole life whole. Since I had been warned not to have any contact with my father, I punished myself for missing him.

The walls of my office were covered with sticky notes, like I was a crazed detective, of questions and theories about my family. I gathered all my hospital bracelets that I had kept over the years and put them, as if they were an award, in a frame on my desk, where I sat every day trying to write. I was working on a collection of short stories about every time I'd ever brought myself or someone else to a hospital, these interventions the only important things I had ever done, crisis after crisis the heartbeat of my life. I wrote a story about seducing my father into sleeping with me. At the moment of penetration, I asked him what he was doing, and described his face as it collapsed with shame. I wrote and wrote, reliving those moments of chaos and inventing new ones, from the safety of my desk, just as my mother had relived her memories, in all their ferocity and falsity, in oil on canvas. I was— with my cigarettes and my wine and my search for answers—closer to my mother than I had ever been.

There was a difference, though. I had a partner who was kind and patient and devoted to me. And I wanted to be a good partner. But it was hard to focus on someone else when I was so preoccupied with myself. The amphetamines and the alcohol didn't help. I'd start drinking and then I'd start fights, cornering Gregory in the living room moaning, "You hate me, don't you" as he quietly tried to slip by me and hide in the bedroom. Sometimes he'd beg me not to drink, sometimes he'd yell, but he'd inevitably hold my hair back when I puked and make sure the water glass on my bedside table was full. It didn't occur to me that being around me was not only dangerous for his sobriety, but utterly unpleasant. One night I went out with a friend and called Gregory very drunk, just to say hi. He told me he had had enough, that he couldn't be around me when I was drunk, and that he was going to sleep at the motorcycle repair shop. I got my friend to drive us to a gas station, where I purchased a three-foot-tall greeting card, writing out shakily with a Sharpie: *Sorry I'm a wreck. I love you.* I surprised him with it at the motorcycle shop, where he was asleep on the front office floor. I thought for sure this toddler-sized trinket with a dramatic inscription would fix everything, but it only made him more upset.

Still, Gregory was patient and saw something in me he didn't want to give up on. As he made us dinner the next night, I sat at the dining table complaining about my anxiety, my emptiness, how I didn't know who I was or what had happened.

"That's everyday, normal existence," Gregory said as he chopped garlic. "Anxiety and not knowing who I am is the baseline, I just improvise on top of that."

"So what do you do about it?" I asked.

"I try to take care of other people so I don't have to think about myself, about whether or not I know who I am. How much ginger do I chop?"

"A tablespoon," I said. "But you at least have a center. You know who you are. Your identity is solid."

"Are you kidding?" he said. "I feel like a child's drawing version of myself most of the time. I'm just pretending to be the kind of person I want to be."

As I chopped the onions, I thought about how Gregory was the strongest person I knew. I thought about how he metabolized shame and regret and turned them into fuel for his unrelenting considerateness. He was kind and gentle in a way I had never experienced before, and he thought of the people he loved constantly, in the same compulsive way I thought about my own mind. I watched Gregory as he carried out his love for me, as he paid attention to my words and asked me questions, as he anticipated my needs, my desires showing up in his actions and the objects they manipulated—a glass of water, a sweater when it was cold, a favorite song to wake up to—like inadvertent mind control. He could predict what would send me spinning, what my mind would fixate on, and would help me try to stay in the present. He had an irrepressible optimism that was directly proportional to how nihilistic he knew he could be, and I watched him take care of himself, nurture his recovery and nurture me, put one foot in front of the other despite the "swirling depths of despair," as he called them, that spun beneath our feet. As I wiped onion-induced tears from my eyes, I tried to imagine the churning slowing, the vortex decelerating, the void slowly filling. I couldn't yet picture what that life would look like, but for the first time I didn't have to live it alone.

I got a call from Nancy, one of my mother's studio assistants. My mother, now seventy, was living on Coca-Cola and potato chips and wouldn't get out of bed.

"I really think you should come here. She's not well," said Nancy.

I arrived at my mother's house at around seven at night. Gregory had stayed in Nashville to work. Her bedroom was dark. I stood in the doorway and said softly, "Mom, Mom, I'm here." She sat up, crossing her legs under her. She blinked.

"Am I upstairs or downstairs?" she asked.

"You're downstairs," I said.

"But am I in Charles Street?"

"No, you're in Brooklyn," I said. Anxiety gripped my guts and squeezed.

"I don't think I know where I am," she said.

"Well, you're right here in your bedroom on the first floor in Brooklyn on Vanderbilt Avenue. That's your garden out those windows, and your studio is in the next room. Upstairs is the kitchen, and Nanny lives here too."

"Is it daytime or nighttime?"

"It's nighttime. I get confused too when I wake up in the middle of the night. Try and go back to sleep," I said.

Over the next few days, I observed my mother's behavior. Something was very wrong. She accused me of taking a raincoat that was hanging in the closet right in front of her. She'd ask me questions over and over again, and, when I told her she'd already asked me, didn't she remember? she'd pretend she hadn't been paying attention the first time or just wanted clarification. But there was something in her sentences, a tell that belied her claims: the pause right before her justification told me that she was as confused and unnerved as I was. I went over to my aunt and uncle's apartment.

"Something's wrong with her," I said. "She can't remember things."

I told them what I had noticed. They told me nothing was wrong.

"That's just Jennifer being Jennifer," my aunt said.

What appeared as symptoms happened to resemble my mother's defining traits. Her whole life, she would forget things she didn't want to remember. The act of forgetfulness liberated her from responsibility, from discomfort, from having to interact with other people on anything but her own terms. That's how it had always been. But now it was different.

I ignored my mother's excuses, I ignored my aunt and uncle, and for the first time I listened to my own intuition. I took my mother to her GP, who referred her to a neurologist.

"Does it look like I have something just terribly wrong with me?" she asked the neurologist.

"I've only just met you," he said.

"Well then would you want me to have something terrible?" she joked. I laughed. It was something I would say to a doctor.

"Now why would I want that?" said the doctor. He didn't get it.

"Oh, I don't know," said my mother. I felt protective of her. I could see her weakness, her fear, and I could see her using repartee to fight against it.

"Spell *world* backwards," said the doctor.

"Dr. Roseman was doing this the other day," she said.

"How about you spell *world* backwards. I don't want a story," said the doctor. I was getting angry. Why wouldn't he want a story? Wasn't the fact that she remembered and could tell this precise story an indication of the thing he was trying to figure out? That the world, backward or forward, still lived inside of her?

"Well, it's *world* and backwards. Same way as frontwards except backwards," she said. I was impressed with this answer, proud, as if she were my precocious child. I felt like I too were meeting her for the first time. As if this bizarre setup had allowed me access to her as a real person, a person who made weird jokes at the worst possible times. I was starting to realize how terrified she must be.

She had to draw a clock and draw shapes. She had to write the sentence: "Today is a rainy Tuesday in December." She had to list all the animals she could think of: "dog, cat, beetle—or is that an insect?—elephant, tiger, water buffalo, snake, silverfish." She had to name a piece of furniture, a fruit. He gave her three words to remember later: *apple, table, penny.* She had to touch her left ear with her right thumb.

"Stick it to my left thumb?" she asked, pausing with her hand in the air, her thumb sticking out.

The doctor repeated the instructions, and she raised her other hand, thumb out.

She had to count backward from a hundred by sevens, which I would never have been able to do even on my best day. She made it to eight-six.

Who was president? Bush. (It was Obama.) What month? The beginning of winter.

Her deficits flew at me like arrows.

The doctor asked her how many nickels were in a dollar thirty-five. She paused. We all waited in silence, watching as the numbers wouldn't come, the answers stayed obscured.

"That's . . . so depressing," she said, to herself, to the numbers and dates and presidents and clock hands that refused to materialize for her.

The doctor was silent.

"How many did you ask for?" she said.

"How many nickels in a dollar thirty-five," he repeated.

I watched my mother.

"How about how many nickels in thirty-five cents?" the doctor said.

"Six?" said my mother. "Seven? Six?" The doctor just stood there.

"This is truly horrible and scary," she said.

I was frantically going through multiplication tables in my head.

"How about in a dollar?" said the doctor.

"Twenty," said my mother.

"In a dollar thirty-five?"

"Twenty plus . . . I don't know." She gave up. I wanted to hug her, but I didn't. Hugging her as she sat there alone and scared would have felt like touching a sacred statue, something I was not allowed to interfere with without cosmic consequences.

"What were the three words I asked you to remember?" said the doctor.

She looked around the room as if the words were hiding there, scrawled on the frame of the Gustav Klimt poster, embossed on the white paper that lined the exam table. They were not there. She looked at me. *Apple, table, penny*, I thought so hard I felt for sure she could see them crammed up behind the glass of my gaze. But I couldn't help her.

She was diagnosed with dementia. Over the next week, I found notes she had written to herself: *What's wrong with me? Suicide thoughts. Run tests for neurology. Went to doctor because I felt drugged. Memory loss. Anxiety. Cold symptoms. Helen McEachrane called. I haven't called her in a long time. Have I been sick a long time? Call all people I still want in my life. Devise systems for everything I have trouble with.*

I found a list:

1) How did I get this way?

2) When did I get this way?

3) What did doctor say?

4) How could it happen so fast?

For the first time, I saw her cry. It was a quiet, tidy cry—just a sheen of wetness in her eyes, the sides of her mouth turned down. She made jerky movements as if trying to throw the emotion and the reality off of her. She began to threaten suicide. While looking for socks in her drawer I found pill bottles, full, stuffed inside a pair of socks.

"Mom, why do you have pills stuffed in a sock?" I asked her.

She was dozing on her bed and her back was turned to me. She did not roll over to look at me.

"I just want to have them in case I decide to off myself," she said as I watched the back of her head.

I knew she wouldn't have the follow-through. She was terrified of death. Even the way she phrased it, "off myself," seemed like something she had heard in a movie and liked the way it sounded.

I returned to Nashville and sat down with Gregory to discuss what we should do.

"We should be near her," I said. "We need to go back."

Gregory was apprehensive. New York had violently ejected him, and the thought of returning scared him. But he would go back for me. We rented an apartment seven blocks away from my mother's house in Brooklyn. I re-enrolled at Columbia.

I decided to major in psychology even though all I cared about was books and writing. After so many years spent analyzing my own deficits, I was convinced all I was qualified to do was think about what could go wrong with a mind. I got a job babysitting two children. On the days I didn't have class or work, I'd visit my mother and Nanny. I'd show up at the house four nights a week with a bottle of wine for me, and a back-up bottle, also for me. My mother would already be a few glasses in and we'd drink and smoke and I'd spend hours regaling her with stories from my past, desperately trying to entertain her, generate the conversation she no longer could. I'd ask her questions and when she couldn't answer them I'd answer them myself.

"What's the craziest sex thing you've ever done?" I asked.

"I don't know," she said. "What's the craziest sex thing you've ever done?"

"I had sex with someone while driving down a highway at night," I said.

"What?" she screamed and laughed.

I told her about the time I'd slept with a family friend she knew.

"How was it?" she asked. I described it in graphic detail and she choked on her wine, laughing.

Sometimes she'd share with me what was going on inside of her, and I'd listen, rapt, the ashtray between us filling with butts, the bottles of wine emptying.

"Do you ever get an image stuck in your head and you don't know why it got there but you can't get it out?" she said one day.

"Yes," I said.

"Well, I keep seeing these big whirling blades. Ugh."

"Ugh," I said.

"Well, it's okay because I invented a use for them," she said.

"Like what?"

"Well, they slice through sausages."

Each visit she offered another peculiar dispatch from her interior: "I just lie here like an ingot," she said one day. "Like a piece of lead. I'm in twilight all the time."

I looked for clues in her musings, as if, taken together, they would form a portrait of her illness, which maybe we could stash in a closet and it would deteriorate instead of her.

Sometimes she'd be more direct, and those words, without the padding of metaphor, struck me deeply.

"I don't trust anything I believe right now," she said. "I feel like there's a piece missing. I think that piece may be me."

I felt a pressing obligation to collect all the bits of her I had coveted for so long—her humor and her charm and her brilliance. I needed to get to know her before it was too late. I gave her the "Proust Questionnaire." We sat on her bed cross-legged, with our ankles tucked under us, ashing our cigarettes in the seashell she used as an ashtray.

"What is the trait you most deplore in yourself?" I read from the list of questions.

"Self-involvement," she said. I was surprised that she had such casual self-awareness.

"What is the trait you most deplore in others?" I asked.

"Boringness."

"What do you consider the most overrated virtue?"

"Honesty," she said.

"Why?"

"Because people feel compelled to tell everyone everything and there's quite a lot I don't want to know." I was that person she was talking about, an indiscriminate oversharer.

"What is the quality you most like in a woman?" I asked.

"Not talking too much. I don't like anybody to talk too much," she said.

"What or who is the greatest love of your life?" I asked.

"I don't have one," she said. None of us had stuck. Not her first husband whom she had married at twenty-one. Not my father. And not me.

204 EVERYTHING/NOTHING/SOMEONE

"If you could change one thing about yourself, what would it be?"

"Everything," she said. I looked up from the screen of my laptop where I was typing her answers. This struck me as unusual, an uncharacteristic humility, maybe regret. "Just because it would be something to do," she clarified.

"What do you consider your greatest achievement?" I asked.

"Continuing to do work."

"What is your most treasured possession?"

"Books."

"What is your most marked characteristic?"

"Bluntness."

"What is it that you most dislike?"

"Not getting my way," she said.

"What is your motto?" I asked.

"Just do the work," she said. That was the only advice she had ever given me. Just do the work. I didn't know how much longer she would be able to live by her own motto, or if it was something I could ever live up to. A few months after her diagnosis, she had gotten to work, and made an enormous plate piece simply titled *Dementia*. On each plate she wrote out the word—in cursive, in dots, in all uppercase, in all lowercase. "Dementia" over and over, as if she were trying to use that brutal word to soothe herself, as if, through the force of her work, she could transform calamity into comfort.

"What is your greatest regret?" I asked.

"I don't have any," she said. I wanted to believe this was because she couldn't remember any, and not because she didn't care about the consequences of her actions and inaction. I felt torn between anger, envy, and sadness. She had lived a life of silence and work and gratification, and she regretted none of it. I wanted to force regret on her like a straitjacket, bundling up everything she had lost and everything she was about to lose in an embrace she could not avoid.

I didn't know how long she would still know who I was, or know who she was. I found my copy of the book she had written, *History of the Universe*, and I asked her to write an inscription to me. I told her she couldn't just sign her name, that I wanted her to write something special, just for me. I left the room. I was afraid—afraid she would have no words for me, that the thought of me would leave her as blank as her illness did. After ten minutes, I came back into her room and picked up the book. She had written:

For Alice, you are my universal history.

In the threat of illness was also an opportunity. Through simple acts of caring I would find what had gotten lost between us for so long. She developed an infection in her abdomen—the old site of her hysterectomy surgery had opened up—and the doctor taught me how to unpack and repack the wound. At home, I would help her take off her leggings and roll down the band of her underwear. I stood her in the bathtub, telling her stories, and gently let the water run over the wound, soaping it as carefully as I could. She didn't argue and she didn't complain.

"I don't like this," she said matter-of-factly.

"I think that's good," I said. "I'd be worried if you did."

"I guess that's true." She laughed.

I dried her off and she lay back down on the bed while I gently bandaged the wound.

Her neurologist ordered an EEG, and I had to keep her awake all night long, without caffeine. We sat shoulder-to-shoulder on her bed as we watched the reality show *My Strange Addiction* on my laptop.

"But why?" she screamed as we watched a woman eat drywall.

She covered the screen with her hands, laughing, as another woman stung herself with bees.

"How do you think she does it?" she asked as a woman talked about her love affair with a carnival ride.

We discussed various ways love could be made to a machine as the sun rose.

A few months later I noticed her ankles were swollen so I brought her to the ER, where they told me she was almost in heart failure. Gregory came to meet me there. We sat next to my mother's bed and Gregory distracted her. He was wonderful with her. They had first met years ago at the height of his alcoholism. He had come over to the house and met my mother in the kitchen. We had always kept the butter in our toaster oven to keep the cat from licking it, and when Gregory saw it he said, "Nice to meet you. I love your butter dish. It looks just like a toaster oven."

My mother laughed so loud that I jumped.

He was good at distracting her from uncomfortable situations.

"Look at that shadow," he said pointing at the wall. "Doesn't it look like a dragon?"

"No, it looks more like the dragon's grandfather," my mother said.

"That's so true," he said.

I sat and listened as they talked. Gregory could encourage the best parts of people, their inventiveness and playfulness. I wished I could be like that with my mother. I wished I could meet her where she was instead of always wishing she would finally chase after me. I watched Gregory as he calmed and entertained her, trying to memorize the vocabulary of care he was so fluent in.

I went home and Gregory stayed with her until they found her a permanent bed. She was moved to the ICU because it was the only place they could administer nitroglycerin.

The next morning she called me.

"They tried to make me sleep on the floor," she said.

"I really don't think anyone tried to make you sleep on the floor," I said.

The nurse told me my mother had panicked and ripped out her IV. She'd run around the ICU, screaming, insisting they were trying to attack her.

"It's called ER psychosis," she told me. "It's not uncommon."

I felt connected to her in that moment. I recognized that impulse, remembered that need to flee the confounding forces conspiring against me.

When they moved her to a private room, I slept on a cot next to her bed. A few days into what would be a six-week stay, I was told she had developed an impacted colon. The nurse responsible for manually disimpacting my mother's colon said they were understaffed and asked if I could help her. I agreed without hesitation. I held my mother's hand as the nurse began the process. My mother yelped, screamed, "Stop," and pushed the nurse away.

"Mom, we have to do this or you won't be able to go to the bathroom," I said.

"I don't care," she said.

"You can even die from it," I said.

"Fine, then I'll die," she said.

"Well, first you'll have to stay in this hospital even longer. Is that what you want?" I asked.

"No," she said, the threat of discomfort more terrifying than death.

"Can we try again?" I asked.

"Okay," she said.

The nurse asked me to hold her down. I pushed down on her shoulder and let her grip my wrist. The nurse reinserted her fingers, and I felt my mother's hand hit the side of my head. Then she pulled my hair. Then she sank her teeth into my arm. I didn't know what to do so I laughed.

"Mom, you just bit me!" I said.

"Sorry, sorry, sorry," she said.

"It's okay," I said. "I wouldn't expect any less from you." She gave a weak laugh.

The next day, a nurse requested my help in holding her down as they reinserted her catheter. We had never figured out how to be intimate with one another, but now, as I pinned her down to make her well—my body so close to hers, accepting the hug of her jaws, her panicked yanks—I realized I had, in a circuitous way, finally found myself in my mother's arms.

Meanwhile, Nanny was getting weaker and weaker. She fell and broke her hip while I was visiting her, and I held her hand and stroked her hair as she was hoisted onto the stretcher. In the hospital she suffered the first of two strokes, leaving her with aphasia that made her words roll around in her mouth and her mouth unable to properly eject them. A month later, she suffered sepsis from a bite from Bracket the cat, who was now Nanny's cat, leaving her temporarily paralyzed from the waist down. A month after that, she was diagnosed with heart disease and had to have surgery. She became so thin, her body so slight and stooped, that she was like a punctuation mark moving through space, an ambulatory parenthesis shuffling across the room. I took her to doctors' appointments and Gregory took Bracket to the vet. I filled her pillboxes and washed her feet. Next to my notebooks and flash cards for school were piles of Nanny's bills and insurance forms and bank statements, for which I was now responsible. Next to my class schedule was a list of my mother's and Nanny's doctors' appointments and lists of their constantly multiplying medications.

When I was little, Nanny always seemed to be preparing for something, and the way she prepared was to worry. She kept crumpled-up tissues in the sleeve of her cardigan. She told me to bring an umbrella but then cautioned me to not get it stuck in the subway doors. She warned me against wearing a necklace while I slept in case it strangled me. I thought of the quirks of her care as I tried to manage the logistics of her aging. I thought of her bearing witness as I tried to make her shrinking life bigger. When Gregory and I came over, Nanny talked and talked. Once she had our attention, she didn't want to let it go. She loved Gregory and would come alive when he walked into the room, telling stories and making jokes. He was much better than I was at sitting and listening as she told the same endless stories over and over. She'd continue to talk to us even after we'd left the room, and I had to decide whether to linger at the threshold so she could finish a story with no end, or choose to walk away. She talked to herself more and more frequently. Not just the usual eruptions of frustration or the accidental out-louding of an observation, but whole conversations.

These were the days when Nanny started to cry. I had never seen her cry before and it frightened me.

"I just don't know. Sometimes I get sad," she would say.

As she cried she said, "Damn! Damn!" I tried to imagine how her life felt to her. Was it occurring to her now that nothing was hers? That the things she had accomplished were not measurable by any known standards? She existed in traces, in people. She was the uncredited voice in the back of the heads of all the people she had cared for. She lived in someone else's home, and she was being cared for by someone else's child.

We were both afraid. We were afraid of what my mother's illness meant for both of us. I felt like I had nothing to give Nanny. I couldn't protect her. I couldn't even figure out how to comfort her. I sat there, watching her cry. Sometimes I'd try to tell her how much she meant to me, try to list all the things she had given me, try to lend bulk to her withering life.

"You saved me," I said. "You protected me so well."

She wouldn't look at me. She stared out the window.

"If it weren't for you I'd probably be dead," I said.

She'd respond with a scoff, or the subtlest shake of her head, refusing my words.

That Mother's Day, I bought my mother a box of Jacques Torres chocolates, and I bought Nanny one too, but Nanny's box was smaller. When I presented them with their gifts, Nanny made a joke about being a half-mother, or a less-mother. I felt a pain in my chest. I hadn't wanted to hurt my mother's feelings by suggesting they were both my mothers, even though that's what it felt like. And I hadn't realized that something as simple as the dimensions of two boxes could render so vividly the pain and ambiguity of our unique situation. I felt angry at myself and sad for Nanny. I hadn't wanted to make her feel small, to make her feel less than, but I was scared that if I gave her a gift whose measurements reflected how I really felt, I would end up shrinking my mother down to nothing.

I wanted to connect with Nanny, but, still prescribed uppers and downers, I'd end up sitting in her room, scrolling on my phone, counting the minutes before I could leave. I'd come home exhausted and sad and angry, and Gregory would cook us dinner and quiz me for my Spanish test. Many nights, I'd drink until I puked and start fights with Gregory when he returned from his AA meeting. I felt scrambled, so many feelings happening at the same time, and under the constant whisking of the Adderall, the sloshing of the benzos. I was so anxious and on so much amphetamine that I'd moan myself to sleep, while Gregory rubbed my back to try to help me calm down. It still didn't occur to me that I could get off the medications. They seemed not like a separate part of me that could be safely excised, but part of the essential network of who and how I was—just as critical and inextricable as my veins or nerves. Dr. Sarini had told me I'd need to be on medication for the rest of my life, and I believed him. I'd take my morning pills and want to start fights with my aunt or my mother's assistant, writing long, rambling emails or texts, which I read to Gregory before hitting send. He'd tell me to wait. He'd beg me to give it twenty-four hours and see how I felt. Be patient. I'd send the emails or texts anyway, oblivious to the damage I was causing. I didn't

realize how much energy it took for him to try to haul me back from
the powerful amphetamine pull toward discord, time and time again.
I tried to fight the current of my volatility by showing up for my
mother and Nanny. I tried to take cues from Gregory—his attentiveness, his patience—straining to resist those spinning eddies of lability.
When he noticed I was particularly far away—dissociating or trying
to keep up with the torrent of anxious thoughts—he would extend his
hand for me to shake and say, "Hello, nice to meet you in this moment."
There'd be a pause as I returned to myself and then I'd smile and clasp
his hand, pumping it up and down, his hand the only tether that
could keep me here.

That winter, we got married in my mother's garden, in the beautiful aftermath of a blizzard. I found an eighty-six-year-old humanist
minister online who claimed to be "weatherproof." I carried a bouquet
of plastic flowers I had played dress-up with when I was five years old.
My mother and Nanny were the only witnesses, and we signed the
marriage license on top of color charts in the downstairs studio.

I was suddenly living a life where things were happening that
weren't just in, or about, my own mind. For the first time I had to
stop constantly thinking about what was wrong with me and pay
attention to what was wrong with everyone else. I was unused to being
needed, and I craved and resented it. As I crouched on the floor
washing Nanny's feet, I felt pulled in two directions. I wanted to give
her more than just a foot bath, and I also didn't even want to give her
this foot bath. I ran my soapy hands over her gnarled feet, trying to
press into her the care and love I knew existed in me, to bathe her like
she had bathed me. But I felt so many other things besides care and
love. Anger pinched at me. Guilt shouldered in and I was pummeled
slowly by its great, muscled form. A dazzling sorrow, cold and clear,
drenched me. I was fighting, constantly, the invisible bodies of anger,
fear, and sadness as they blocked my way, pounced onto my back,
skittered around in my stomach, splashed me stunned. I couldn't

connect to Nanny the way I wanted to because I couldn't reach her through the horde.

The details of my mother's decline vexed me too. A lifelong smoker, she had a gruesome smoker's cough, which would overtake her especially when she laughed. Making her laugh was one of the things I liked doing the most, but she would start coughing uncontrollably and then vomit. When it didn't bring her to regurgitation, her laugh gave her illness away. She laughed at stories I told her or TV shows, but there would be too much of the laugh, too loud and too often, as if she were doing it just in case it was a moment when a normal person was supposed to laugh. Clichés started to take over her language. She would say "keep your fingers crossed" or "just relax and take it easy" or "well, that's something to think about"—phrases nonspecific enough to sound like an appropriate response to almost anything. In each infuriating banality, I heard the grinding of her forgetting, the slow work of the disease. She developed an infuriating naiveté. She pretended to not know or be able to figure things out. When I told her exercise was good for her, she said, "Really?" When I told her smoking was bad for her, she said, "Really?" When I told her humans needed to drink water or eat vegetables or take showers or brush their teeth or not eat bacon every single day she said, "Really? Why?" I could never tell if she really didn't know or understand, or if this was some childish game she liked to play to try and get out of an activity or keep pace with a conversation. So much of what she did made me angry. Inside this anger I missed the mother I no longer had. I missed the mother I never had. I missed the mother I couldn't have. I hated that woman who couldn't remember anything, the woman who was turning back into a child. I hated the woman who still felt like a child, who couldn't tell that all of this anger was an endless ocean of sadness.

And yet, as her illness progressed, I noticed an unexpected change in her. She became tender, curious. She liked to lie in bed smoking

cigarettes and drinking coffee, but wanted to be involved with everything that was happening outside her door. The kitchen of her cottage
in Amagansett was directly outside her bedroom, and at the slightest
noise, she'd say: "Hello? What are you doing?" I would explain to her
that I was pouring a glass of water or going to pee. She would laugh
and say a long and loopy "Oh . . ." Any comment I made to someone
else and "What are you talking about?" would come bounding from
the other room. Then I'd explain about the dry cleaning, or the dog's
visit to the vet, or about how maybe this bread was stale. Gregory
made a game out of her endless questions. When he was in the other
room and she asked, "What are you doing?" he said, "I'm putting
roller skates on the dog," as he poured a glass of water. She laughed
until she coughed.

"Well, how does he like it?" she asked.

"Well, he's not as good at it as the cat, but he's working on it."

Every time I came over, she'd ask me how I was and was not shy to
tell me she missed me. Whenever I had to leave she'd throw her arms
around my neck, clutch at my hair like an infant, and tell me she
didn't want me to go. "Stay, please." When I struggled with something, she said, "How can I help?" and even though she no longer
could, her inquisitiveness felt nuclear, decimating—a simple question
able to raze thirty years of distance. My sordid, tumultuous history
wasn't relevant any longer. It only mattered that I showed up. After
years of begging for her attention, she was finally interested in me. I
was the only person she wanted to spend time with. She could also
finally name feelings. It no longer occurred to her to avoid emotions.
She would say something made her sad instead of just getting another
glass of white wine. There was a heartbreaking joy in seeing her able
to make that tiny admission. She also seemed content without the
excesses that had marbled her life. She was no longer a person amplified by fame, swollen from money, or made tiny and shrunken from
avoiding feelings. When everything that had defined her for so long

disappeared—her constant need to work, the memories of ritualized sexual abuse, even her desire for alcohol—I was able to see what had stuck. And what had stuck was me.

For my birthday that year, Gregory and I went over to my mother's house. Gregory put a box in front of me, and I unwrapped it at the dining room table. In the box was a stack of index cards with descriptions, in my mother's handwriting, of me. I sat at the table and flipped through them. "Alice likes cats," I read aloud. "Alice has brown hair. Alice can swim. Alice is romantic. Alice is smart. Alice has courage. Alice is a wife. Alice is fun. Alice cares. Alice is thoughtful. Alice is a Democrat. Alice is pretty. Alice takes a ride. Alice lives in New York. Alice is concerned. Alice is real funny. Alice creates. Alice is groovy. Alice demands. Alice is a Greek Goddess. Alice brushes her teeth. Alice can be daunting. Alice is a daughter. Alice is human." It had been Gregory's idea. He had gone over to her house a week before my birthday and asked her to describe me. I was silent. I was stunned. I held in my hands a miracle—my mother, Gregory, and myself. I held my past and I held my future. Gregory knew me. He knew my fears—of being forgotten, of having never been known. It seemed my mother knew me too. Gregory had given me what I had always wanted: words to describe who I was, from the woman who didn't like to talk, the woman who thought she was the only person in the world. I framed those notes and put them on my wall: proof we had all been here, three humbled humans, telling each other we existed.

9.

I was practicing the ballet of small, repeated gestures that made up my life with Gregory. I was early for every class, my performance earning superlatives from my professors. I made the dean's list. Gregory was recording bands. He encouraged me to write, and we wrote songs together.

My mother sold her Brooklyn house and moved out to Amagansett, which was too small to accommodate both her and Nanny. My aunt and uncle took over the management of my mother's care. She now had caretakers looking after her and was happy living by the beach. Gregory and I decided that we would move back to Nashville after I graduated that year and agreed that we couldn't leave Nanny, now eighty-nine, behind.

"I can't let Nanny's biggest fear come true," I said. But mostly I didn't want my fears to come true. I didn't want to picture me without Nanny.

"We'll take her with us," said Gregory.

The next day, we told Nanny we wanted to move to Nashville and that we wanted her to come with us. She started to smile and her eyes filled with tears.

"I'll have to learn a Southern accent," she said, smiling wide. "Yeehaw."

Nanny needed a place to stay until I graduated and we could make the move, so Gregory and I moved her and Bracket to a nursing home four blocks away from our new apartment on the Upper West Side. We helped her settle into her room, unpacking boxes and coaxing the cat out from under the unfamiliar bed. We brought Nanny down to the dining room, where residents were required to eat dinner. I helped her into a chair at a table with three male residents. I kissed the top of her head and said goodbye. We paused in the doorway and watched her. I was nervous the others wouldn't welcome her, that she would get her feelings hurt. But as I watched, Nanny started laughing. She leaned forward and said something to the gentleman next to her, who leaned forward to receive her words. She laughed again.

Every day she had new stories to tell—about her occupational therapy, about walkers being stolen, about her speech therapist. She told me, laughing, the story of a fellow resident who had called her into his room to ask for her help in taking his pants off. Because of her aphasia, we sometimes couldn't understand her words, but her joy was loud and clear. She made me a bracelet in occupational therapy and presented it to me proudly. She was excited to move to Nashville with us, and started talking about the future more than she did the past.

On November 12, 2015, seven months before we were scheduled to move to Nashville, six months before I would finally graduate, I was at a friend's house on the Upper East Side having dinner. Halfway through the dinner, my phone rang. It was Gregory telling me the nursing home had called him. Nanny had fallen and was on her way to the hospital.

I pushed my plate away, grabbed my coat, took the elevator down-stairs, and flagged a cab. As I slid through the dark I felt like an explorer, a cartographer of the moment. Was this the moment when Nanny's end appeared, the bottomless drop-off I hadn't been expect-ing, but maybe should have been? I had imagined it so many times, what it would look like, what it would feel like, but I had never imagined it would be so still and silent. The sound had dropped out of everything and an anesthetic inertia filled me as I wove through Central Park in the dark. As we pulled up to the hospital and I paid and thanked the driver, as I announced my arrival to a woman behind a desk, my words felt independent of me.

"Hi, sorry, I think my grandmother is here," I said.

"What's her name?"

"Oh, sorry," I said, and spelled out her name.

I apologized again to the woman when she told me Nanny hadn't arrived yet. And then suddenly Gregory and I were hugging in the empty waiting room with the *Law & Order: SVU* theme song playing in the background. We were directed to a room in the ER and as we approached it I saw Nanny through the doorway. She was lying on a gurney with a blanket up to her neck. She was pale and a vicious pur-ple bump the size of a baseball protruded from her forehead. A plastic tube extruded from her mouth, the stalk of an exotic plant, as if the injury had made her something more than herself, something rare and strange. Through my shock, I could not see a badly injured woman, I could only see indestructible Nanny and her powers of survival.

Two doctors approached us and told us she had hit her head and was being taken for scans. It would be helpful, they said, if we had the power of attorney forms. Gregory went back to our apartment to get the papers. I sat and waited.

Two doctors appeared and led me into another room. One began to speak but I interrupted.

"Should I sit down first?" I asked.

"Yes."

"So it's not good," said one of the doctors. "Her brain moved three centimeters from the impact, and she has a brain bleed that looks like it's been there for a while. The neurologist will be calling you very soon to decide what you want to do."

They walked away. I sat staring at my hands. A few minutes later, a nurse told me that the neurologist was on the phone.

"I'm so sorry you're going through this," the neurologist said.

"Thank you. What's the prognosis?"

"Well, that partially depends on what you can tell me about your grandmother. She's your grandmother, correct?"

"Sure. What do you mean?"

"What I need to know is what kind of life would be worth living for her? What would she consider a good quality of life?"

"If she couldn't speak or feed herself she wouldn't want to live," I said. I was surprised at how quickly I had answered. This was the biggest decision I had ever had to make, deciding what life meant for someone else. But in this moment, I realized I knew Nanny.

"Well, that answers a lot for me. In this case, the best we can hope for, with surgery going perfectly, is that she would need to be on the tube for the rest of her life."

The cry leaped out of me before I even notice it had formed.

"Okay. Thank you," I said, shaking as I put the phone back in the receiver.

When I returned to the waiting room Gregory was there with the forms. I told him what the doctor had said and he began to cry. We gripped each other tightly.

They wheeled Nanny back from the scans and into a small room and I squeezed into the space beside the bed. Her left eye was shocked open, the pupil unfocused and unmoving. One of the doctors appeared in the threshold of the room.

"I'm so sorry that it wasn't good news," he said. "You have some decisions to make."

"If she'll never have the tube out I think there's really only one option," I said.

"Right," he said.

My eyes landed on his name tag, which announced him as Dr. Doctor.

"Your last name is Doctor?"

"Yes, yes it is," he said. He smiled a tiny smile, which he then quickly wiped from his face. Tonight I didn't care about the story this would make, the unbelievable detail of a doctor named Dr. Doctor.

I went outside to call Nanny's sister, Thelma, in England. I knew the news would be conveyed just by the ring at such an hour, by it being my voice on the phone. There could be no other reason I was calling. I told Thelma what had happened and that there was no hope for recovery. My voice wobbled. Thelma's voice, usually high-pitched and girlish, now was clotted and rough as she repeated, "Oh, oh, Alice." We said goodbye.

I called my aunt Julie.

"If you want to say goodbye we are at Mount Sinai on 113th Street. You should come now if you want."

Julie brought us satsuma oranges, which we ate as we watched the beeping machines.

"Could she really not pull through?" Julie asked. "It seemed like she squeezed my hand just now. She can't see through that eye? Squeeze my hand if you can hear me," she said to Nanny.

I felt angry at her hope. Of course she couldn't pull through because that was not how this story went. We had entered into the one where she didn't make it. There wasn't any plot twist here.

The doctor asked, "Are you ready?"

"Yes," I said.

The doctor removed the tube. Buttons were pressed and the hiss that had been in the background went away. Nanny stopped breathing. Minutes passed and my blood rushed to my ears and my heart clanked. Then, with the sound of something heavy being dragged along the ground, she took air into her lungs again. We watched Nanny breathe. And then we watched her not breathe. It went on and on. Violent stillness and silence and then violent movement and sound as she ripped air into her. I held her hands in mine and I spoke to her.

"Thank you for everything you did. You saved me. You protected me. I promise I will be okay. Gregory will keep me safe. I will look after Bracket. You were so strong and so brave. You kept everything together. You kept me together. I love you so much. Everything will be okay. It's okay."

I repeated myself over and over. "Thank you." "It will be okay." "You saved me." I talked and talked. Everything I had ever wanted to say to her surged through me. I kissed her forehead. I said goodbye. We left.

She lived for seven days. Then one evening, during dinner, my phone rang. Nanny was dead.

She was Nanny. But her name was Eileen Denys Maynard, and she died.

Gregory went over to the nursing home to clear out her things so I didn't have to. He wept the whole time he folded her wool sweaters and long pleated skirts into cardboard boxes, placing the little lavender sachets she used to keep them smelling fresh on top of the clothes. In storage, she had boxes of photographs, stacks of Playbills, bins full of blank postcards and old calendars. Later, when we went through my mother's storage for our move to Nashville, we found many more boxes of Nanny's. She had also kept everything of mine. She had packed up all my childhood clothes, all my passports, all my toys, all my books, all my drawings and French tests and book reports, the creatures I had made out of old osso buco bones, the bear she had stitched for me, the mat she had sewed for my preschool nap time. She had protected my past. And I kept everything of hers. I kept all her clothes—the long wool skirts, the sweaters from Scotland, the white linen aprons from governess school. I kept all her photographs, all the souvenirs she had saved from the Concorde—a crystal ashtray, a Walker fountain pen with the airline's logo on it. Among her things, I found a photograph of the two of us in a hammock. I was a baby asleep on her chest, as she rested her chin on my head. I recognized the feeling of packing myself into her, tucking myself between her arms, under her chin. I recognized the feeling of tracing the cuticles of her fingernails. I also found all the notebooks she had kept detailing her experiences with my family, all her frustrations with my parents and her fervid desire to protect me, to help me be understood, laid out in her tiny script, her dyslexic words. As I read her notebooks, read her story, our story, I was learning all the ways language and love lived inside of me—as infection, as weapon, as heartbeat, as cure.

III / Someone

1.

In May 2016, three months before I turned thirty-one, I finally graduated. My mother, my aunt, and Gregory attended. It was exhilarating to get attention for something that didn't involve me hurting myself. We ate coconut cake and laughed. My mother's studio manager gave me a stack of books by Joan Didion. I wanted to do more things that made people happy for me, that made them feel good to be around me.

A month later, Gregory and I moved back to Nashville. I got a job at the Boys & Girls Club and started work on a memoir. Gregory recorded artists and wrote songs. Every month, we hosted charades nights with all our friends. We planted a garden and fought squirrels. I found two kittens in a hollow tree, so we had four rescue cats. Gregory's parents moved to Nashville from Pennsylvania to be near us. We had never been thought of as the reliable ones, the ones worth tying a life to, and suddenly his parents were trusting us to pick out a house for them, sight unseen. I found a new psychiatrist and decided to wean off my medications, Adderall first. It scared me how effortless it was to go off it, and how much better I felt. My heart stopped crashing around in my chest, my leg didn't slip off my other leg on a sweat slick, my jaw loosened. I could hear and notice what was going on around me, and inside of me. I wasn't on edge all the time. I had fewer arguments, I asked more questions, I was more patient. People started treating me differently. I had always been the friend that people shared their darkest secrets with, but now I was the friend who could be relied on. With the guidance of my psychiatrist, I started tapering off the other medications. I wanted to see who I was underneath all the pills, what parts of me—feelings and thoughts and sensations—suspended in the chemical permafrost, would emerge and proliferate. The last medication to go was the Klonopin, the highly addictive anti-anxiety medication I had been prescribed for almost fifteen years. Research had just come out that prolonged use of Klonopin was associated with a greater risk for dementia, and I was still on a high dose. The withdrawal from Klonopin was notoriously difficult and could be lethal. I called it the Murphy's Law of withdrawal: anything that could go wrong went wrong. There was diarrhea and flatulence, there were hand tremors, there was skin crawling, there were temperature fluctuations, there were appetite changes, there were cold sweats, there were chills, there was insomnia, there was nausea, there were headaches, there were heart palpitations, there was forgetting, there was a lack of focus. I developed a tic where I twirled my hair constantly—while I was talking to people, while I was driving, even lying down in bed. I wore a shower cap around the house all day so I couldn't get at my hair. I felt an invisible hand choking me—strong fingers wrapped around my throat as I went about my day. But I wanted to know who was on the other side of this drug, and I used my dissociation, also made worse by the withdrawal, as a tool, treating each new symptom as a curiosity, a discovery to be examined and cataloged.

After spending months tapering off Klonopin, I was medication-free for the first time since I was sixteen. I felt better than I ever had. I felt streaked with joy, beams of sunlight painting over the gray of my brain. I sat on my front steps and stared at a tree and felt completely overwhelmed by the idea that I was able to sit on the steps of my house and look at it. Gratitude replaced the discontent I had been scratching at all these years. Along with joy, I felt rinsed with sadness, clear and fluent. Gregory and I invented the "Safety Cry," where every Sunday we picked an uplifting but cry-inducing film so we could cry together. It had been hard to cry on Klonopin, and I now discovered that I loved crying. It had a lingering narcotic effect that left me drained and sated at the same time. I had always been afraid of being alone, being quiet with my own mind, and now I welcomed it. I took long drives by myself, delighting in my autonomy, only possible because I felt I was becoming a person, separate from everyone else, brimming with myself. The medications had blunted my orgasms but now they were so intense I would often burst out laughing in the middle or scream, "What the fuck is this?" or leak tears from my eyes. One lasted five minutes. No longer needing to mediate the effects of prescription speed, I was able to stop drinking, which made everything even better. The constant feeling of wrongness, of being in the wrong place—whether that place was a house, a country, or my own body—was replaced by a sense of arrival, of landing.

After four months without Klonopin or alcohol, I was in a state of bliss, a bliss that I could safely pry away from pathology. I wasn't manic, I was well, and well felt so foreign and so fantastic that it registered as euphoria. I looked at things with a swelling, oozing love that I would have previously only attributed to drug trips depicted in movies where a character licks a tree or cries at their own arm hair. My self-loathing had dissolved. I stood in a yoga class, staring at myself in the mirrored wall, and was overcome by the realization that I loved myself. I loved Gregory even more than before, which I hadn't thought possible. I was getting the first natural sleep I had gotten in twenty years. I liked my job. I was volunteering at Planned Parenthood and the Nashville Adult Literacy Council. I had deep friendships and was rekindling important ones from my past. By our second year in Nashville, I had finished the memoir I had been working on. By the third year, I had signed with a top literary agency in New York City. My life had heaved and sloughed off an obsolete version of itself, revealing something fresh and new, tender with possibility.

In early June 2019, I was having menstrual cramps. I was curious about holistic treatments, and my GP had recommended CBD oil for everything and anything. I did research all day and read only glowing reviews about the safety and benefits of CBD. I drove to my local organic market and bought a bottle of the most potent formulation. I had researched dosage but the consensus was that it didn't really matter because nothing bad could ever happen with CBD oil. The worst that could happen, I'd read in the *New York Times*, was that you'd sit on your couch with a bag of chips and zone out.

I took the first dose of 60 mg when Gregory and I went to his parents' house for dinner and a movie. Halfway into the movie I felt twitchy, my eyes felt gritty, sandpapery, but it was subtle. After the movie we went home and got in bed. I had read that the correct dose for sleep was 160 mg, so I took two more droppers full and went to sleep.

I woke up around 1 a.m. As I slipped into consciousness, I realized I was gone. I realized, too, that there was nothing doing the realizing. I couldn't locate myself anywhere. My "I" had vanished. There was a feeling of a heavy, slick rope slipping through my fingers, fast, and then I became the rope, I was the thing sliding away, fast.

I groaned and squirmed on the bed, trying to lock something into place, trying to hold any part of myself down. I was cartwheeling through a roaring emptiness. I was on the verge of blacking out, but panic withheld that merciful unconsciousness from me. My heart was slinging around in my chest, a bowl of gelatin on a high-speed train. A booming heat overcame me. I ripped off my nightgown and flailed my legs trying to fan myself into coolness. I crawled off the bed and opened the linen closet on my hands and knees. I reached my arms inside and dragged out all my old pill bottles—pills I kept in case of emergency. There had to be something in there that would make this stop. I was shaking and couldn't hold the bottles in my hands so I knelt on the floor with them spread around me and tried to see the labels and read the words, but the numbers and letters disintegrated and lost all meaning.

"What's wrong, what's going on?" Gregory, now awake, was standing over me. I gurgled a few times before I could speak over the frantic galloping of my heart. I didn't know where the words came from or how they took on sound. "Something's wrong," was all I could manage. I started tearing at the pill bottles. I screamed and screamed as I tried to bring a palmful of pills to my mouth. Gregory knocked the pills out of my hand, wrapped me in his arms, and managed to pin me to the bed. Still screaming, I tried to wrestle away from him, twisting beneath him. I needed to get away. I needed to get away from what was happening inside my mind. I was witnessing something I wasn't supposed to. The experience was too big for me, it didn't fit inside me, and I blew apart. I screamed and screamed, at a life I knew was ending, a life that had just begun in so many ways, the life I had always wanted. I knew I was dying.

"I love you," I said to Gregory, my face pressed into the bed. "I'm sorry."

I went completely limp. I could feel him drag me up from the bed. Floating above my body, I saw a mass of heavy nothing spiked with limbs that dangled, flopping in Gregory's arms, a coil of something that was unwinding itself, losing its shape, slipping away.

"You're okay, you're okay," he said over and over as he struggled to lift me up and hold me against his body.

Somewhere inside the emptiness, I saw the glowing marble of the life I had finally achieved. A voice—my voice—told Gregory to get me under the shower. He dragged me to the bathroom, turned on the shower, and put me under the spray of water. I told him to make it as cold as possible. I sat under the freezing torrent until my body was wracked with shivers. My breath came faster and deeper and for a moment I started to feel like I was finding my footing. The cold hooked itself into my mind, dragging its bucking, sliding form back to me, back to my contracting muscles, my wildly beating heart. For a brief moment, I felt nudged toward wholeness again. I told Gregory to make me slowly warm, and he turned the water temperature gradually hotter. The moment my body stopped shivering, though, the connection was lost, and I returned to the terror of spinning through blankness. I motioned for him to crank it back to freezing until I could shiver again. We continued like this for three hours. Gregory had given me three Klonopin and we were both waiting for me to pass out. I begged for more medication, but he refused. After an hour of shivering and warming, I couldn't get cold enough and started to panic. Gregory packed my body with Ziploc bags full of ice and I finally began to shiver again. I became afraid of what would happen when the hot water ran out and we would have to turn the shower off. I knew I would disintegrate completely and be gone. Gregory found a recording of shower sounds on YouTube and cranked the volume up as he slowly turned the tap off. He collected all the blankets and towels we had in the house and piled them on top of me. I lay in the bathtub, Gregory sitting on the toilet watching over me, until the meds knocked me out.

Over the next four days, I could barely eat or drink. The sensation of food, even water, inside my body felt like something terrible was being done to me. My body would get cold and then hot. Nausea sloshed over me. My limbs tingled and my hands shook. In my chest was a nest of fat, writhing worms, my heartbeat frantic beyond rhythmicity, terrorized out of cadence.

On day five, I went to an emergency appointment with my psychiatrist who diagnosed me with panic disorder and PTSD. She put me on propranolol, a blood pressure medication to help with the physical symptoms of panic; Klonopin; and Seroquel, the sedating antipsychotic I had been on before, to knock me out at night. The panic and dissociation were debilitating, exhausting, and took up every inch of my body, all my attention, and every second of my life. According to the *DSM*, dissociation is *a disruption, interruption, and/or discontinuity of the normal, subjective integration of behavior, memory, identity, consciousness, emotion, perception, body representation, and motor control*. There is nothing it does not touch.

I was preoccupied with where my thoughts came from and how they were still being generated without me here. Everything familiar—Gregory's face, my purring cats, the angles of my home, the gestures of my body—became terrifying and strange. When I lay in my bed, extending my arm to take a sip of water from the glass on my bedside table or throwing an arm over my head, I flashed back to all the gestures I had made as I tried to twist myself back into my body. When Gregory wrapped me in his arms at night, I remembered the weight of him on top of me as I had screamed and squirmed beneath him. Gregory's face terrified me. We were so close and spent so much time together that he normally felt like an extension of me. And since I had become unrecognizable to myself, the sensation of looking at his face was horrifying and surreal. It was the same with my own face. I couldn't unlock or lock into place that it was me, my face. Every time I accidentally caught sight of it, brushing my teeth or if I forgot to keep my gaze down at my hands—equally unrecognizable as mine—I felt that nauseating drop that preceded a plunge into blank panic. I was not real, yet I was conscious. Nothing was actually happening, besides the mundane movements of living, yet every moment was stranger and more terrifying than it had ever been. I woke every morning with dread sticking to me like sand. I constantly scanned my body and the world for potential hazards. At any moment I could tip and fall into the endless emptiness. My body told me I was under assault, and the assailant was my own mind. I didn't know how to avoid the trigger if the trigger was consciousness. My days were spent scheming ways to survive the moment, assessing each second for its surreality and unlivableness. I knew that with dissociation, the more I questioned it—wondered at the origin of my words or inspected the joists of reality—the worse it would get. I worried, too, that even if I returned to some kind of normal connection to reality, to myself, I would not be able to recognize it. I was afraid I had seen too much, glimpsed the secret mechanisms behind everything I was and everything there was, and I would never again be able to accept the simple, solid, absolute state of existing I had recently enjoyed. All I wanted was to return to myself. Just at the moment when I had become a person, someone I recognized, I became the most nothing I had ever been.

Words were the only thing that tethered me to some splinter of myself. I sat under a tree in my backyard and wrote about every single detail of every moment. It calmed me, but I knew I couldn't write forever and I didn't know what would happen when I stopped. An enormous wave was about to crash over me, tug me under, and send me spinning, and writing froze it at its cresting. I wrote gratitude lists. I wrote lists of likes and dislikes, trying to remind myself of who I had been. I wrote down what had happened to me, trying to prove that I was a person something had happened to. Technically, barely anything had happened. I had been asleep and had woken up and somewhere in between I had been stolen. Dissociation and PTSD were psychological responses to traumatic events, but I was traumatized not by an external event that my mind was trying to escape, but by the experience of my mind escaping itself. The event was the response, the response was the event. And words, their powers of differentiation, were all I had to name the before and the after, to announce the thing that had destroyed me, and, I hoped, to declare the thing that would save me.

I listened to the audiobooks that had filled my mind as a child. I started thinking in the third person again, as I had done when I was little. The only way I could bear to look at my reflection in the mirror, as I washed my unfamiliar face or my alien hands, was to narrate what I was doing in my head: "She is brushing her teeth," "The water is warm." But this desperate reliance on words stretched their functioning dangerously. There were terrifying moments when words started to become disarranged and then dismembered. I would be listening to an audiobook and suddenly wouldn't be sure I understood the words. I would be reading a book and the words would become the black, inert lines that they in fact were, my mind no longer able to elevate them into meaning.

Two months later I was still nowhere to be found. In this splintered state I needed older touchstones. I needed to go back to the beginning. Back to what had built me. Maybe then I could figure out how to be the architect of my renovation, build a bulwark against a mind that kept tearing itself down. I went to visit my mother, searching for something she could not give me. I sat across from her in the Amagansett living room, watching her eyes floating in the white static of her mind, as I floated in my blankness behind my eyes. Nanny was dead. There was only one person left: my father.

After three decades, after all the courtroom allegations, after Diane's confident assessment, after reading the statistics that 99 percent of all cutters, 99 percent of all bed wetters, and 99 percent of all dissociaters had been sexually abused, after years of being an ocean away from him, my father was as unreal to me as I was to myself, as towering a villain as my dissociation. I decided I would confront my father. I would tell him my story, ask him his, and write it all down.

Gregory and I took long walks around the neighborhood and talked about my rescue plan.

"I need to go there and find out what really happened," I said.

"What if things go wrong and it's not safe? This could make you much, much worse," he said.

"How could I be worse? I'm already nothing. I'm not here. I'm gone."

Gregory was silent.

"I can't keep going like this. I don't want to have to kill myself. I need to do something drastic," I said.

"Okay, then let's do it. But I think you should have strict rules. Don't just go into this unprepared," he said.

I called Diane, my therapist and trauma counselor from Florida, and told her I was going to see my father and confront him about our past.

"You're fucking crazy," she said. "You'll never get what you're looking for. You're trying to play a game he's been playing much longer than you, and he's way better at it."

I realized it might be a terrible idea. But there were no pills that could fix me. There was no more money for another fancy mental institution, no time for ten more years of introspection. I needed to find my own way out.

I emailed my father and asked him if we could Skype. I wrote about my dissociative break. I still felt I could tell him anything—that had not changed. He wrote back and we set a time and date to talk. I had not seen him since my manic episode eight years earlier. As his image filled my screen, I was filled with a mix of hope and fear. He was framed in a tight close-up, his face behind a scrim of cigarette smoke.

"Hello? Can you see me?" he said.

My body struggled between a melting relief and a rigid apprehension. I stared at his face, which had aged in a way that surprised me. For a moment, I forgot I was in this moment too, as if I were watching him on TV.

"I can see you," I said.

We exchanged no pleasantries, and I launched into the story of what had brought me back to him.

"Usually with dissociation," he said after I had finished, "there's some sort of core trauma, and I can't figure out what yours is."

I paused. I felt my body go hot.

"I have an answer for that if you want it," I said.

"What is it?" he asked.

"Well, I've actually been thinking about this for a while. I think it would be interesting to have a conversation, a dialogue between a person who has lived the consequences of trauma however you define it and the person who contributed to that experience of trauma." My opacity sheathed me. I knew I needed to slide the truth out of its ornate casing and let the blade fall however it may, but I didn't know how to ask my father why he had invited me into sexuality. Why he had said all the things he had said. I didn't know how to tell him he was part of the reason I split off from myself.

"I think with trauma there is sometimes a temptation to try and find one singular event that caused a massive upheaval. But it can be more than that. It can be an accumulation of small-seeming violations that can last a lifetime," I said.

"You're absolutely right. You're absolutely right," he said. "Trauma does not need to be one event. It can be a context, a situation, which is lasting. That's very insightful, what you say, and that is true."

I had forgotten how good it felt to be affirmed by him, even if he didn't understand fully what he was affirming. He always overdid his concurrence and it had always made me feel special.

"You did a lot of things that really damaged me. There are things you did and said that had lasting effects," I said.

"Well I should go into therapy with you," he said. "You should be my therapist."

"Well . . . I could come to Paris and we could sit down and talk about the last thirty years," I said.

He agreed, clearly not realizing what he was agreeing to. I was scared but I was also far enough away from myself that I felt like nothing could get me. My dissociation, for how much it tormented me, presented an opportunity. And I would take it.

2.

Gregory and I departed Nashville for Paris in October 2019. I had always loved airports. There were rules, and I knew them. It felt good to obey, to move swiftly, to be efficient and ready for anything. When I was little, flying across the Atlantic Ocean twice a year, I learned the names of the flight attendants on each flight and took Polaroid pictures with them. I craved the over-salted, semi-frozen airplane food. Now, twelve years since I had last been in Paris with my father, I held my passport open, and recited my name to the TSA agent. I had both passports with me, the blue and the burgundy, the American and the German, and I studied each one, the same name, the same face, different versions of me that had lived in such different worlds. Gregory was beside me. I was making this trip with someone who, despite how insubstantial I felt, was full of me—full of my love and of love for me. We didn't know what awaited us, but I was propelled by the desperation my dissociation had ignited, and I had beside me the person even it could not drive away.

As we approached the Paris apartment in a taxi, I saw my father waiting outside. I was afraid of how I would feel when we embraced. When he hugged me I laughed out loud, something old and automatic. I didn't know if feeling happy to see him was bad. We were greeted inside the lobby by the concierge, who had lived in the building for forty years. She recognized me and gave me a big hug. The elevator smelled exactly the same as I remembered. It was made of lacquered oak and rectangular panes of glass and was extremely tiny: I used to race it, sprinting up the winding, carpeted stairs as the elevator glided alongside and then above me, its dark, shining bulk ascending like a sea monster, window-eyes glinting and cables trailing like tentacles. The apartment was so full of light, so familiar. My father had left on my bed the hippopotamus stuffed animal I had had as a child. I jammed my face into its fraying flank, trying to dive back into the oldest parts of myself, the parts I hoped still existed. I stood on the terrace with Gregory and scanned the zinc roofs and blue sky for the thing that would bring me back. As I walked through the thresholds of my childhood—the lobby, the elevator, the huge metal front door—I waited for the walls of myself to stack back up, the doors to settle back under their lintels, the triangle of roof to drop back over my head. I announced all the things I remembered to Gregory, pointing out the tin ornaments my mother had painted, the sharp edge of the fireplace where I had split my lip open as a toddler, my voice getting louder and louder as it tried to carry over the abyss and reach me. I had wanted the force of this place, the powerful fist of nostalgia, to punch me back into existence. But as I exhausted the memorabilia and memories, I realized it would take more than this to return home.

My father's partner of fifteen years, Colombe, prepared a delicious meal of lamb chops and caramelized endives. I had first met Colombe when she had come with my father to visit me for my twenty-first birthday. She was a beautiful, intense, fiercely intelligent woman with a mane of coarse curls who had been the editor in chief of French *Vogue*. I had liked her instantly, and had been confused about how such formidable women could be so duped by my father. Over dinner, Gregory told them his story of recovery from drugs and alcohol. He told the whole story, not leaving out any details. They were impressed and moved. While Colombe and my father chain-smoked and we spread cheese on little boiled potatoes, I read aloud from question cards I had brought with me.

"What annoying behavior of yours do you blame your mother for?" I read.

"Falling in love with critical women," said my father.

"What lie do you keep telling yourself?" I read.

"Probably the one I'm not aware of," said Gregory, and we all laughed.

"That's intelligent, that's subtle," said my father.

"What's the funniest thing your inner child wants?" I read.

"A hug," said my father.

"I want gigantic shoes that I can bounce really high up and down with," said Gregory.

We laughed.

I hadn't realized how much I wanted Gregory to know my father, to be known by him. I was surprised at the lively ease of the evening, but I was wary of it too.

After dinner, my head was spinning from exhaustion. I lay down and closed my eyes and immediately felt unsafe, all the parts of my mind becoming loose, too loose, threatening to wobble apart as I moved from consciousness into sleep. I felt a bolt of nausea in my gut and my skin got hot. Oh fuck, it was happening again. My heart started to throb and the avalanche of dissociative panic threatened to bury me. I took a Klonopin and a Seroquel, grabbed my pillow, and made my way to the bathroom, in case I needed to put myself in the shower again. I spread a towel on the tile floor and lay down next to the bathtub. My stomach churned as I waited, hoping for my medication to sneak past the panic and ambush me into unconsciousness. Suddenly, the door burst open and Gregory raced to the toilet. Instantly, my stomach cramped. When Gregory was done, I sank onto the toilet, ecstatic with relief. This was food poisoning, not my mind breaking down again. I was here and I was safe.

THE NEXT DAY, I took Gregory to the Jardin du Luxembourg, where Nanny and I had spent so much time together. We ate waffles with powdered sugar, which I'd loved as a child. We watched the carousel turn. We listened to the tock of boules hitting as white puffs of smoke rose from the cigars of the old Frenchmen who came every day to play. We smelled the shit from the ponies who lifted their tails and made their deposits as they swayed along the paths, children on their backs. Two bright-green parakeets wound in and out of the horse chestnut trees. As I surveyed the idyllic scene, I felt in danger; my chest twitched with anxious heartbeats, rivulets of sweat trickled from pits to wrists. As a group of elderly Parisians practiced tai chi nearby, Gregory and I went over the rules of the impending confrontation with my father, discussing contingency plans for if he got drunk, if he got angry, if things got out of control.

My father and I had decided to begin our "therapy sessions" the following day. I unpacked all the journals, spanning twenty years, I had brought with me and stacked them on the dining table next to his pile of notebooks, spanning fifty years. At the appointed time, we sat down, facing each other across the table.

Gregory stood next to the table and addressed us.

"You both need to follow the rules," he said. "First of all, there is no alcohol consumption allowed during these sessions." I looked at my father. We had come up with that rule for him. The last time I had seen him, he had been drinking seven beers a night. He noticed us both looking at him and said, "Yes, yes okay."

"One person gets to talk for up to half an hour without interruption, with the exception of questions for clarification," continued Gregory. "Then the other person gets to respond without interruption. If it gets too heated or too difficult, either person can walk away at any time. Just say, 'I need a break,' and take a pause. If you can't follow the format and can't resist interrupting, I'll be in the other room and if I hear yelling I'll come in and encourage a break."

I thought about the temper and impatience I had inherited from my father, the litigious style of arguing I had learned from him. I hoped we'd be able to follow these rules. It helped to know Gregory was in the next room, listening to the rise and fall of our voices, monitoring for signs of distress.

"Sometimes Alice and I will have what I call 'friend talks,'" said Gregory. "We take anything personal out of it and she'll tell me something about me that she doesn't like and I'll listen as if I'm just a good friend of hers. And sometimes I've done that and I've said, 'He sounds like a real asshole.' It validates her reality and it helps take the potency out of how upset she is with me so I can listen to it without being reactively defensive."

"Yes, yes. That's very wise," my father said. He had the demeanor of an eager, impatient student, his pen poised for note-taking, his shoulders thrust back.

"Any amendments can be made to these rules as you go," said Gregory. "Are you ready?"

"Yes, I'm ready," said my father. "I don't know what I'm ready for, but I'm ready."

"Good luck," Gregory said and left the room.

I pressed record on my phone and placed it on the table between us. My father lit a cigarette. I watched his cheeks cave in as he inhaled.

We each had a notebook open before us, and we uncapped our pens. I pulled ten yellowed pages from a folder and laid them on the table between us. It was the final divorce judgment.

"I wanted to give you a chance to tell your side of the story," I said.

He read the papers, the cylinder of ash on his cigarette lengthening. He sighed.

"I remember how it started," he said. "Jennifer came up to me one day and said that since New York is not a no-fault state she had to have a reason to divorce me. There are three reasons which constitute fault in a marriage. One is adultery, one is abandonment, and the third is physical violence. Since I had not abandoned Jennifer but she had abandoned me, that didn't work. I had committed adultery with the Spanish actress, and I had always admitted that, but since Jennifer and I had sex after, it counted as forgiven. So that didn't work. And the third one, physical cruelty—I never raised a finger to her. She was desperate. I didn't want a divorce. I spoke to a friend who was a lawyer and I said, 'There are no grounds for divorce,' and he looked at me and said, 'That's what lawyers are for. We invent them.'"

I wrote those last three words down in my notebook and underlined "invent."

"They came up with this idea of inappropriateness. They accused me of having an 'unduly stimulating' relationship with you," he said, quoting from the files. "I was an extremely interactive father. That was our defense. It was probably very stimulating for you, but not only sexually. I taught you languages, we talked philosophy, we invented stories, we played Scrabble. In the course of the trial they said that I was a very interactive mother—ah you see!" He laughed at his Freudian slip. "A very interactive father. And that Jennifer was an aloof mother. Some perceived me as being too close to you for a parent. And I was devastated by the way that was used against me instead of in my favor. My whole behavior during that time in the first, let's say, four years of your life, was determined by two things. One was that for the first six months of your life, Jennifer and you had very little physical contact because she had contracted an infection in the hospital and was in excruciating pain and couldn't hold you or breastfeed you. The second was that you were allergic to formula and cow's milk. The only thing you could keep inside you was goat's milk. And I went to get it every morning at a little shop on the corner. In the first years of your life I was mothering you very much."

I pictured him filling up empty spaces—filling me with the milk I couldn't get from anywhere else, filling the space between me and my convalescing mother, and now, filling the gaps my mother's silence and her forgetting had left behind. Circumstances had made him the final authority on our history. I stared at the waveform on my phone as it recorded the peaks and valleys of his rendition. I was wary of him and the pages that were his to fill. My chest got hot, thudding as he stapled these facts onto the blank spots of my story. I didn't know what I wanted from him, what I needed him to say.

"I also felt I needed to protect you from Jennifer," he continued.

"From what?" I asked.

"From her damage and from her aloofness. That's what I wanted to do all along since you were born," he said.

"Protect me?" I said. "It says in these files that you were against therapy for me. Did you think I shouldn't be in therapy?"

"I was afraid for you and for me. During the trial, I was specifically against the court-ordered forensic psychiatrists. I remember a scene that terrified me. When I met with one of the forensic psychiatrists she asked, 'Do you take showers with your daughter?' I said, 'No.' 'But you did? Until what age?' she asked. I said, 'Four.' And she said, 'Did you ever have an erection when you were taking a shower with her?' and I said, 'No.' She looked at me and said, 'How do you know that Alice wasn't aroused?' And then I remember in my mind saying, 'I didn't check whether her clitoris was hard.'" He scoffed. "I thought it was disgusting. These were the moments when I said, 'What world am I living in?' That's when this term of inappropriateness really started to be discussed. Would I be able to hold a child back who was about to cross the street at a red light—or was it inappropriate? I was against forensic psychiatrists because I had the feeling that therapy was not there to help you, it was there to prove their case. Over years of this trial every single problem you had was monocausally attributed to me. I really thought that they would brainwash you. And you were getting worse. And then you told me Dr. Shore had hit you."

He read through the pages. "Wait," he said. "It says here: 'When the question of therapy for Alice was raised, Dr. Neubauer recommended that they see Dr. Shore.' Yes, this is interesting. I must have raised the question of therapy for you, in my sessions with Dr. Neubauer. It was I who brought you to therapy in the first place." He threw the papers down on the table. "You stayed in treatment with Dr. Shore for a year and you were in an even worse state by the end. And not only because of how I behaved. It was the whole atmosphere. Which was lies and wars and exaggerations and defensive behavior on my part. Poor child.

"And no one ever proposed a session with you, me, and Jennifer," he continued. "No one ever had the idea during this whole fucking trial when you were gliding into mental illness, when I was on the verge of suicide, when Jennifer was dealing with her abuse, nobody ever thought to bring the three of us under supervision in a therapeutic session."

"It allowed Mom to disappear even more," I said.

"Yes!" He clapped his hands together as if trapping the realization in midair.

"Because she's nowhere here," I said.

"Nowhere!" He sighed. "My god. This makes me angry."

I studied his face. He looked more sad than angry.

"Basically if I had agreed to Jennifer's terms, if I had not fought it, I would have probably had the initial visitation schedule. The outcome would have been the same but without destroying your mental health." He banged the table hard. "Fucking idiot I am," he said in a violent whisper. I saw him see his past, remote and yet so close. I felt sorry for him. He seemed smaller and weaker than I remembered. I thought of Diane's dim room, where I told her that bodyguards would need to tie him to a chair for me to be able to confront him. But now, as we sat across from each other, I didn't feel threatened.

We broke for the day, and I went to the kitchen to pour another cup of coffee.

"More coffee? After so much coffee?" my father exclaimed.

"It's half decaf," I said.

I opened a kitchen cabinet and took out a rose-flavored loukoum candy, the size of a die, I had bought earlier and bit into it.

"You're eating that already? In the middle of the day?" he asked, a disproportionate disgust fattening his words.

"Yes," I said, suddenly unsure of myself.

"Let's go for a walk," Gregory suggested.

We decided to walk to Montmartre, a two-hour trek. I got some roasted red peppers and couscous from the refrigerator.

"You're eating now?" my father asked.

"Yes, we're going on a four-hour walk," I said.

"Yes, because people eat before a four-hour walk," he said, an ugly glaze of sarcasm stippling his words.

"Yes, they do," I said.

I mentioned to Gregory I wanted to buy a mille-feuille at the bakery because it had been years since I'd had one and I wanted him to try it.

"Another pastry?" interrupted my father.

"I haven't had one in years," I said, my voice becoming high-pitched.

My father walked onto the terrace and lit a cigarette. Gregory followed him. I watched them from the dining table. Gregory told him I had grown a lot since he knew me a decade ago. He said I was healthier than either of them, that I was a kind and loving and caring person who was trying really hard. My father listened intently, nodding his head. Then he got up and left the apartment, striding by me in silence. Fifteen minutes later, as I was putting on my shoes in the bedroom, the top of his head appeared near the bottom of the bedroom doorway. Then the rest of his prostrate body emerged. He was crawling on his hands and knees with a pink box held aloft with one hand.

"Mea culpa, mea culpa," he chanted.

He had bought me three pastries from the bakery across the street.

"You should be able to eat whatever you want. I'm sorry."

I laughed. This was an apology true to who he was—the funny, creative, intense man who had always been able to make life so colorful and so confusing. The swiftness with which he had heard and processed information, decided he was wrong, thought of a creative way to demonstrate his fault, and executed it with such panache moved me.

The next day we reconvened at the table with our notebooks.

"I'm not just here to talk about the allegations from the trial," I said, pretending to write something down so I didn't have to look him in the eye. "You did and said things that had lasting effects on me. That made me feel violated. I have them written down here."

I turned to a bookmarked page in my notebook. I read the list to him. I watched him as he heard me describe licking the tears from his eyes, hearing compliments about my ass or tales of my mother's cunt, being appraised by a pimp, being cast as lovers in incest cinema. He stared into the distance. I didn't know how he would react. I didn't know if he would be angry, if he would simply deny that any of this had happened, if he would call me crazy and accuse me of inventing things. His face flickered with clarity and, I thought, pain, like the sun slipping in and out from behind fast-moving clouds.

"Do you remember any of this?" I asked.

"Some of them I have a vague memory of. Some of them I don't," he said.

"Do you remember telling me I had a great ass? That was your favorite compliment for me."

"No, it was probably the most inappropriate compliment but I made many compliments about you," he said. He paused for a moment. "It was the way I inappropriately joked with you. I think it was also a way of starting to distance myself from you, to let you have distance and see you more as an adult. I don't know, I'm just thinking."

"Your attempt to see me more as an adult? Do you equate adultness with sexuality?" I asked.

"With, with words which, well . . ." He fell silent again. "It was not sexually connotated. It was as if I said, 'You have a nice nose.'"

"There's a difference between a nose and an ass," I said.

"Freud would say not," he said. "It was a comment. You have a great ass, Alice." He shook his head. His voice dropped lower and quieter. "You don't say that to your daughter, absolutely true."

He read the next incident from my notebook.

"'Lick the tears from my eyes,'" he read. "My god, I have a vague memory now that you mention that. Wait—" he started flipping through the stack of notebooks, dating back to the eighties. "Yes," he said, and read an excerpt from his notes: "'Alice licked my face on the way back from Lübeck. Then she licks my face while I'm napping and says, 'That's my way of kissing.' If you said that when you were four, right, July 10, 1989, maybe it was one of these rituals between us." Watching him comb through his stockpile of stories, I felt outmatched. He had written, dated proof of who little Alice had been and what she had done and said. I reminded myself that he did not own little Alice, she lived in me too.

"I don't remember that," I said. "But you asked me to lick the tears from your eyes. It doesn't matter if I licked your face three years before."

"You were also in a situation where you saw your father crying," he said. "You were probably doing it out of concern and compassion for me at that moment. I really tried to hide my despair from you, I really did. I had nowhere to turn with my despair and my helplessness. I felt existentially threatened. I had to let go constantly when I was going away. When we were together, I was very interactive with you. We did many things together. And I loved it, and you were very responsive because you were very precocious. I became a child myself in a way. I might have considered you my partner more than is appropriate. The connotations were not sexual. I never ever, ever, ever had any erotic fantasies concerning you. I made you my accomplice. It was a little transgressive probably, doing that with your child."

"To what end?" I asked.

"To be your pal. You were my only friend. It also had to do with the fact that I was losing your mother. I was losing Jennifer in two senses—because of my affair with the Spanish actress and because Jennifer was losing herself after she discovered she had been abused. And that's when all her fears started that I would abuse you. She would come into the room totally drunk when I was telling you a good-night story and try to drag me out of the room. My family was breaking up. Jennifer's fear that I would molest you was a driving element."

"But it wasn't just Mom's fears. You actually said and did things that were damaging. You told me you stuck your toe up Mom's cunt, you told me fathers secretly want to sleep with their daughters, you told me we should do an onscreen sex scene," I said.

"I think I said that every daughter secretly wants to sleep with her father, which is the Electra Complex," he said.

"Is that any better?" I asked.

"I never had any erotic fantasies about you. Never. Never. Never."
He sighed. "Verbally, I'm very inappropriate. I totally agree. I'm just
trying to understand how I felt when I said these things. I always had
problems with limits. Right before I met your mother, I had spent ten
years as the protégé of Gilles Deleuze. I was an anarchist. We were all
for revolution. It was a revolution that included sexuality. I was a
revolutionary in my fucking stupid young mind and I was in love with
Deleuze because he took me into his group. We saw ourselves as a
team of secret provocateurs, which is maybe how I treated you too. It
was my desire to be different with my children, a childish revolt
against the way I perceived America's puritanism. The way I treated
you didn't have to do with sexuality, it had to do with affirming my
special kind of being different." His last sentence rang in me like a
tuning fork. I had been trying to lilt myself into that lofty register of
specialness my whole life. I had used my brokenness as a way of setting
myself apart. I knew what it meant to scramble to fill gaps in a self. I
had done it with cuts and burns, with medications, with diagnoses,
and finally, with words. He had done it with me. I was torn between
recognition and repulsion.

"I understand that need for uniqueness," I said. "But the way you
were different with me had to do with sex, or was at least very sexual.
And it wasn't just words. You arranged naked photos of me to be
taken while I was, as you said, 'still a Lolita.'"

"Did I really use the word 'Lolita'?" he asked. "I don't remember
that."

"I remember it very clearly because I was about to turn eighteen."

"The big scandal of *Lolita*," he said, "was not that an older man fell
in love with a young girl, it was the idea that the young girl seduced
him. That it was sexually exciting for her, too." I noticed a change in
his voice, a tone suited for arguing a dissertation. We had entered into
abstraction; this was not about me anymore.

"Can a thirteen-year-old girl seduce an older man? Does she have enough agency in that context?" I asked.

"That was the revolutionary, scandalous idea of the book," he said. "Have you read Freud's theories on infantile sexuality? In those essays he describes babies masturbating, the idea that children can have sexual fantasies and sexualized behavior. That book almost got him shot when it came out, but it was a great discovery, which still today in America is not accepted because they have taught a very puritanical version of Freud. You must not forget, I might have enhanced your own Oedipal fantasies. I remember a conversation we had when you were sixteen where I said, 'Alice, I'm not attracted to you,' and you were very insulted."

I felt a rush of anger. It sounded too generic, placing the blame on the latent or overt sexual fantasies of a girl. I was offended and unnerved by the cliché. I didn't remember this conversation but I could easily imagine it.

"That may very well be true," I said, my words flinty and sharp. "But they were enhanced because of how you behaved. If your daughter asks you to take naked photos of her, you say no. It was up to you to say no."

"I'm not defending my behavior," he said. "I'm just trying to explain. You could be very persuasive, very demanding. I don't remember the term 'Lolita' and if I said it, it was not because I as an older man wanted to see my seventeen-year-old daughter naked; it was because you insisted that before your eighteenth birthday you wanted to do something transgressive. And I think that gave me the idea, which was based on Kleist's play *Penthesilea*, about the queen of the Amazons. She was always the woman I was most fascinated with. Not because she was sixteen but because she was the first successful woman warrior. We both developed the screenplay together. You were not a passive participant in this and in my point of view not a victim either.

It clearly went too far. And I was shocked myself when I saw the photographs. I was shocked about the scandalous aspect of it. And at the same time I found them great."

"This was my life," I said. "Not a play or a psychoanalytical theory or philosophical treatise. My life." I was angry and in my anger I felt clearer, more solid.

He was silent. He lit another cigarette and rubbed his brow. He read the lines of my list over and over again. I watched his eyes move back and forth across the page, the muscles of his face contract and release.

"That photographer who did the Lolita photos was one of your many friends who came onto me when I was a teenager. Do you remember all your friends we hung out with at bars and clubs? The ones who were always kissing and groping me? Tim and Karl and Johann?"

"I had no idea they were kissing and groping you," he said, his face twisted with disgust.

"It felt to me like you were encouraging those relationships," I said.

"No. I was not encouraging them," he said. "I was proud of you and I wanted to show you off. You had grown to be a radiant, intelligent, beautiful, articulate teenager, and I was proud of you. I tried so hard to pull you out of those nightclubs."

"But you brought me there in the first place," I said.

"I thought, okay, she's seventeen. Fuck it, she's old enough to take care of herself. And you wanted to go there!" He raised his voice. "We had been to clubs before. We had been going out. You were a wild young adult." This was true. I had been wild. That summer was just the beginning of the reckless choices I would make. Where did my recklessness begin and his transgression end? At what age did the mantle of accountability fall across my shoulders? I struggled to hold on to the mass of my convictions, the dimensions of my lived experience. I focused on the anger that was rising inside me, hot and bright.

"That wild young adult was your child! Not your girlfriend, not your wingman," I yelled.

"I tried to drag you out of there by your hair. You laughed at me and hid under a table!"

"Of course I didn't want to leave! I was a teenager! You can't obliterate all the rules and then expect me to follow them when it suits you."

The room echoed with my words. I braced myself for his retaliation, but there was only silence. My father looked down at his hands. Gregory appeared in the doorway. I waved him away, and he backed out of the room.

My father, his voice soft and low, said, "I was a mess. Bettina had left me and taken Elena to Venice. I had lost my second child. I was hundreds of thousands of dollars in debt. I was drinking. I was a total fucking mess for years. And I had no one. I had no one to turn to."

He put his hand on my list, as if suddenly aware of how real it was.

"I shouldn't have said or done any of these things period, period, period. There's no excuse," he said. "I'm totally shocked and ashamed."

Silence collected around us. He offered no more excuses, no more justifications. He let his shame rest between us, an offering.

"The big tragedy about all this is that I was in a desperate symbiosis with you and I let things happen," he said. "It was—I wouldn't say sick—but it's making your daughter share your own intimacy. That is crossing a line. It was out of pure desperation. I didn't have anybody else to share my despair with. That was . . . I don't like the word *inappropriate*. It was inconsiderate and selfish because I thought more of my own pain, of my own despair, than I thought of the effect it had on you."

I wasn't sure how to proceed. His vulnerability was so appealing, so comforting. But I also wanted to challenge it.

"It did have a huge effect. Why didn't you help me when I got sick? I remember thinking you were interested in the drama of it, and I remember your anger when you came to my apartment when I was first going manic," I said.

"I was unstable myself, and it took me time to realize you weren't well," he said. "You were always exuberant and hyper and then when I realized this was something more, I tried to accompany you. To accompany you and to find solutions for your manic and paranoid demands. I had no experience in this and you had screamed at me to get out. That was the third time someone I loved was yelling at me to get the fuck out. I was scared and overwhelmed and I acted not like I should have."

"You did have experience . . . with Till," I said.

"I should have brought him to a hospital," he said, and repeated it twice. "But you can't force another person." There existed in him pain of which I was not the center, pain that wasn't about me.

"And when I saw you suffering in the same way as my brother," he continued, "I thought, what can I do? What can I do? I saw my child going crazy. And what do you do? Sit down and say, 'Let's have a cup of tea'? No idea. No idea. No idea."

It had not occurred to me that he had come not to gawk at my despair, but because I had needed him, that it would have been difficult for him to come all the way to New York, in the middle of a desperately needed job.

"I was constantly afraid that you would kill yourself," he said. "I was, for eight years, waking up every morning at four o'clock, afraid I would get the phone call telling me you were dead. I didn't know who would call me. I was even afraid no one would call me."

"That must have been awful," I said. As I watched those years play out on my father's face, I felt a breathless, terrifying awareness. I imagined him in this apartment, wondering if his child was alive or dead, wondering if the woman he had loved would even acknowledge him enough to let him know. I saw the ways he had been inflated and shrunk down, at once too huge to be human and too insignificant to inspire compassion. Now, our exchange was rescaling him, changing his dimensions until we both fit inside the same story.

We decided to take a break and Gregory, my father, and I went to Montparnasse Cemetery, where Jean-Paul Sartre and Simone de Beauvoir were buried. My father kept asking strangers where Sartre's grave was. His words were apologetic and conciliatory but his body, tall and thin and vibrating, communicated a frenzied urgency that caused the strangers to take a step back. This intensity was so familiar; I recognized myself in it. Like he had always done since I was little, he walked far, far ahead, unaware of the distance accumulating between us. I remembered, as a child, watching his back as he left me a block and a half behind. But this time, I was not alone. I held hands with Gregory. I watched as my father got smaller and smaller, and I laughed.

When we arrived home, my father ran into the other room and then called for me. On the floor were two large portraits, drawings done by my father decades ago, one of my mother and one of him. They were beautiful. He had captured my mother as she put on makeup, making the exact same face I had seen her make my entire life when I watched her getting ready to go out—her eyes wide and her mouth open and round as if she were saying 'oh.' The drawing was dominated by rich reds punctuated by the intense turquoise of her wide eyes. This was an intimate, vulnerable moment. I felt joined to my father, realizing that we both housed the same memory of my mother. In his self-portrait, rendered only in grays and blacks, he stood staring at the viewer with a cigarette burning in his hand. His eyes were penetrating yet detached. This moment was intimate, but it was not vulnerable.

As we looked down at the portraits, I said, "The story I came to believe after trauma group was that the abuse was more physical when

I was little and then you were strategically changing your approach the older I got and the more aware I became. To me it was like you were the most intelligent predator I had ever seen."

"Oh my God. Can you say that again?" He ran across the room to get his notebook. I followed him and sat down next to him, repeating what I had said as he wrote.

"That's what they taught me in trauma group," I said. "The early years were more physical, and then, as I got older, it got dangerous for you to say words to me or do things to me, because you'd get caught, so you started living vicariously through your friends." He wrote furiously in his notebook. "That's what I thought until recently. Until this trip. Does that make sense?"

"It makes . . ." He paused and stared down at what he had written. "Horrifying sense. Because if any of that were true then I would really have to kill myself." He fell silent.

"I've had nightmares for years where you are raping me in a hotel room," I said, scraping the last, most secret dregs of his influence out of me. "I'll have a nightmare about a sexual encounter with you and wake up orgasming. I have deep shame because of that."

He put his face in his hands, trying to contain the tears that had come. I had never seen him cry like this. An intimate, discreet cry that was not meant to be seen by others.

"I'm so sorry," he said through his hands. "I'm terribly sorry. Can you forgive me?"

"I'm sorry it took this long for us to . . ."

"Talk about it," he said. "Thank you for having the courage to come here. Thank you."

He stared at his notebook, his shoulders shaking.

I felt my own body letting go, the fear and suspicion I had harbored for so long falling from me. I was proud of us. The way we exchanged words had been partially responsible for all the bad, but it had made

up the good as well. It was only because we were willing to say anything to each other that we could say everything we needed to.

"'To me you were the most intelligent predator I had ever seen,'"
he read aloud, my words echoing back to me.

"Are you flattered?" I asked, the teasing tone an offering, the
beginnings of forgiveness.

"At least it's a superlative," he said weakly. We laughed and closed
our notebooks.

3.

"Oh FUCK!" my father said, standing in the middle of the airport. "I forgot my passport and my credit card and my identification."

Gregory, my father, and I were flying from Paris to Hamburg. It was the first time I had traveled with my father in twelve years. Airports were a nexus of all the things that set him off: lines, rules, waiting. Going to a supermarket with him was like walking a tightrope between two buildings. Being at an airport was like defusing a bomb. He patted himself down muttering, "Fuck, fuck, fuck," and unzipped the little pouch strapped around his waist. He swung into action, finding the very first person in a uniform and telling them the unfortunate turn of events. The uniformed man had his bland work-patience face on, but when he understood what my father was saying—that he did not have the one essential thing needed to travel and wanted to travel anyway—his eyes sharpened and his mouth went rigid. He could not help him. There was nothing he could do.

We speed-walked to the information desk and my father explained the situation. No ID. No credit card. No passport.

"I'm sorry, sir, you will not be able to travel without identification," said the man behind the counter.

"Can't you just google me?" my father asked.

When they told him, like speaking to a child, that one could not fly on an airplane without identification, it simply couldn't happen, his remaining composure unraveled. He threw his arms around a large column near the counter and thrust himself backwards and forwards on it. His trench coat flapped behind his body as he threw himself around. From far away, it would have looked like the climax of a dance performance. I kept repeating his name, but he didn't hear me. He was not allowed to fly.

He was distraught, his rage and desperation giving way to sorrow. He apologized to us over and over.

We decided that Gregory and I would take our scheduled flight and he would take a later one. I tried to comfort him.

"This is how it's meant to be," I said. "Just think, now you'll be able to arrive home to *both* your daughters for the first time in twelve years."

His face brightened.

"I love that," he said. "You're absolutely right."

It felt good being able to comfort him.

Gregory and I flew to Hamburg, leaving my father behind.

When we pulled up to my father's apartment in the taxi, Elena was waiting for us, leaning her tall body against the building. When she noticed the taxi she ran to open the door for me, and we shared a hug that rocked us back and forth. Her excitement was pure and conspicuous and it felt good. I had not seen her in twelve years. Three years ago, at nineteen, she had been runner-up on the reality TV show *Germany's Next Topmodel* and had parlayed that exposure into a success-ful career as a model and Instagram influencer. I was unsure where I stood with her. She had told me once that I was her role model. At fourteen she had gotten some shady guy to give her a tattoo on the inside of her lower lip and she had chosen the letter "A" for "Alice." I had been both worried and touched. I had tried, as best I could, to nurture our relationship, despite the distance and my struggles. But it was difficult to keep in touch. We Skyped maybe once a year. She was traveling the world modeling and influencing, and I was going through things I didn't think she could understand.

We entered the Hamburg apartment where I had spent so much of my youth. The walls were covered in sentences and phrases and drawings and quotes and newspaper clippings that residents and visitors had scrawled or glued over the years, cave paintings that told the history of this place and its people. There was a framed black-and-white photo of an advertisement my father had done for VH1. He was shirtless, holding a burning newspaper. There was a quote above his head that read, "NO MORE I LOVE YOU'S—A RESOLUTION I'VE BROKEN AGAIN AND AGAIN," a reference to the Annie Lennox song. I used to read it over and over, thinking the quote the most beautiful sentence I had ever read. There was a newspaper clipping about my father kicking his girlfriend Sonia out, and replacing her with a pet rat. I located my contributions. There was a clay rendering of my father's head that I had made in middle school hanging on the wall. There was a transcription of a children's song about spiders in bathtubs my father, my toddler sister, and I would sing together loudly through the streets. There was a quote about hating George W. Bush. I still existed here, even though I had been away for so long. I felt a shudder of grief, reading these epitaphs of the person I had been, then a surge of warmth, that my traces on these walls, these lives, persisted and were valued.

Other people had added their marks to the walls, and I saw how much time, how much shared experience, had passed me by. An enormous poster of my sister hung on the living room wall. Envy growled inside me as I calculated the wall space we each occupied, the success she had encountered being the daughter of my father, the darkness and the failures I had gleaned from that parentage. I thought of the decade I had stayed away. In 2013, two years after I had gotten out of the treatment center, I received an email from my father. When I saw his name in my inbox, I stiffened. What trick was he trying to pull now? I opened it and read that Oma, after having suffered two strokes, "adamantly wanted to die" and that my father would help her. It had always been Oma's wish to die in my father's arms, and he was tasked with preparing the lethal medications. My aunt Mareike, my father, and Opa would be gathering the next evening to say goodbye as my father helped her pass. I called my grandparent's number at 6 a.m. the next morning. It was the first time I had dialed the number in years. Should I explain my absence? Should I apologize? Opa picked up. Should I tell him how much I'd missed him? Should I tell him how sorry I was, for his wife who was about to die, for staying away?

"You sound much younger," I said.

He didn't say anything and passed the phone to my father who put the phone to Oma's ear. I hadn't spoken German in twelve years, and I struggled with my words as I shared memories of my time in Lübeck with her. I paused and then told her I was engaged. I assumed my father was listening, and had hesitated to share the news because I was trying to follow Diane's rules and keep him from me, but I wanted to let Oma know that I was loved. I told her I loved her and said goodbye. Two years later, Mareike developed bladder cancer and asked my father to help her die too. I never went to see her. I was too angry, too afraid to risk exposure to my father's malignancy. Opa got more decrepit and eventually asked my father to help him die as well. I never spoke to him before he died. The last thing I ever said to him was that he sounded younger.

I stayed away until it was too late, until there was almost no one left. And I had not for one moment considered my father's pain. It had fallen to him to lovingly help end the lives of his entire remaining original family, and I had thought only of how this might be an attempt to manipulate me, a "game," as Diane had put it.

I had never explained to my sister why I hadn't come. I kept track of her life and her life with my father via the Internet. A simple scroll revealed how well she had turned out, successful and autonomous and liked at the age when I was accelerating my deterioration, and the pure-love connection she got to enjoy with a mother who had always focused all attention and energy on her and a father who had not said and become too many things to her. They were profiled in a magazine article that had the line "Between us there are no secrets" emblazoned above their laughing heads. I took a screenshot of that article and sneaked looks at it, fuming. I hated them in those moments. I felt used and left behind. In my silence and absence, I was protecting him, and being left with nothing. I felt jealous of what they had, and sometimes I made myself feel better by imagining that my father had not found her as irresistible as me. He had not chosen to recruit her as a partner so I must be the special one. I saw these ruminations for the petty, confused distortions they were but they still felt real. I was angry. I was angry at Diane for her stories, angry at my sister for not needing me in hers, angry at myself for needing to believe in one so badly. But really, I was heartbroken.

My father texted that he was in a taxi on the way to the apartment. We went outside to greet him when his taxi arrived.

Gregory, my father, Elena, and I all sat in the living room. After a few minutes of pleasantries, my father described what we had been doing for the past week.

"The reason Alice didn't come for all those years was because she thought I was a pedophile," he said to my sister.

I watched my sister's face. It was still and serious. She started to say something about how these were just rumors, stories Jennifer had invented.

"No," said my father. "I'm not a pedophile but I behaved very badly."

Elena was silent. She nodded her head. "It's good that you're both doing this," she said.

As I heard my father make this naked admission and my sister receive it without resistance, I felt held. My father had stuck up for me, confirmed my reality, invited my sister into it too, and she had accepted the invitation. I saw clearly the traces of the live-wire luck that had been sparking through my entire life, that had led me to the love hidden in the heart of our failings and misfortunes.

We walked to a nearby restaurant. I walked arm in arm with my father, and Elena walked with Gregory a few steps behind.

She confided in him that she had been nervous about this reunion.

"We were scared to come here, too," said Gregory. "But you should know that what happened between them was the beginning of something really special. A lot of healing has taken place."

"That makes me really happy," she said.

As I talked to Elena, my father and Gregory talked. My father asked him about our lives together, about his continued recovery. He asked his advice about how he could get along better with me.

"You don't always need to respond," I overheard Gregory say. "Sometimes silence is the best response."

The next day, Gregory, my father, and I rented a car to go to Lübeck to visit the cemetery where my grandparents and Till were buried. My father brought a bucket and brushes to clean the graves, just as Oma had done years ago. After an hour of scrubbing at the gravestones and pulling weeds, we got back in the car and drove to my favorite places in Lübeck. We ate potato pancakes at the Kartoffel

Keller, where everything on the menu was made out of potatoes. We posed in front of the stained-glass windows of the Marienkirche, which depicted the Totentanz, where people danced in a line as Death summoned them to their demise. We walked through rows and rows of marzipan pigs and marzipan potatoes and whole marzipan towns at the Niederegger, the large stone building where marzipan had been invented. At the end of the day, we visited my favorite building in Lübeck—the Holstentor, with its torture chamber. I remembered feeling, as a child, that this was a room that could hold the volume of my roiling imagination, even the murkiest, most disgusting sediment that bubbled up. Now in my thirties, I ran my hands over the spiked roller that was part of the machine that stretched the victim's body, and peered inside the torture barrel at the spikes that would pierce a man's torso as he was enclosed in it. It felt much smaller, much less menacing. I noticed that there were no spikes inside the barrel. My young imagination had filled them in. The thumbscrews were behind glass and looked tiny and innocuous. The chastity belt looked like it could easily be broken out of. A harmless crudeness had replaced the powerful sense of barbarity and transgression.

I bought a mug in the gift shop and we left. Outside the Holstentor, a man approached my father for an autograph. "Bitte, bitte," he pleaded as my father loped away.

"Nein, nein," said my father.

At first I chided him. "Why not just give him an autograph?" Because he didn't want to, because it was his time, because they always wanted to talk, because he didn't want to. I saw my father's own struggle to free himself of his story, distance himself from the person other people thought he was—a celebrity or a pedophile. I watched the fan pursue my father and saw a tired man who wanted to get away from his past. And I understood. I had the choice to leave behind the things that had pursued and defined me for so long. I could choose to stop defining my father, too.

WE FLEW BACK TO PARIS, and Gregory left for Nashville. I stayed behind to spend more time with my father and my sister, who had come to Paris to spend a few days with me. Elena and I went to the Palais de Tokyo. I took her to a drag show, and we marveled at the muscular drag queens singing Serge Gainsbourg through cigarette-plugged mouths, drifting en pointe across the stage.

As we walked through Paris, I stole glances at her profile. When I saw her face, a face I had known so well from infancy to middle school, I saw a record of the time I had been away, a record of my failings as a sister. I had been a regular presence in her life until she turned twelve and then I had vanished. Any pain she might have experienced on the other side of these years had never occurred to me until now. I had left her, a little girl who loved her sister, and disappeared with no explanation. I wanted to know this human being who had gone on without me, had accumulated her own hurts and disappointments, one of which might be me.

"I'm sorry I wasn't there for you," I said. "I'm sorry I didn't tell you what was happening. I wanted to protect Dad for you. I wanted to protect the image you had of him, to make sure I didn't project all my stuff onto your relationship with him."

"That's very brave and kind," she said.

To my surprise, I started to cry. Elena put her arm around me.

"I'm sorry we lost so much time," I said.

We continued to walk, my body wedged into hers, maneuvering through the streets, dodging passersby.

"I'm sorry I wasn't there," I said again. "Can you forgive me?"

"I think you need to forgive yourself," Elena said. "I'm not angry. When I was little I saw Dad suffering because of everything that was going on with you, and I was maybe angry at you for making him feel bad because I associated you with his suffering. But I'm not angry now."

She caressed my arm with one finger, and that small gesture felt like an agreement, a reassurance that I hadn't lost her.

The next day, Elena left for Hamburg and my father and I were alone together. Those last days in Paris we laughed a lot. We walked to the Musée D'Orsay and my father told me stories about Paris, its buildings and history. At dinner he had me write down all the German verbs I could think of that started with "ver" and pointed out the ones with multiple meanings. It reminded me of the stories and word games of my childhood. We watched one of his favorite movies, *Lawrence of Arabia*, on a daybed mattress on the floor. We sat close, watching the epic tale unfold on the tiny screen of his laptop, straining to hear the dialogue through the crappy speakers. I was aware of how neutered the space between us had become. It no longer coursed with nauseating electricity. When our shoulders accidentally touched, or when he squeezed my arm to indicate the imminence of a really good scene, I didn't shrink from the contact. I invited it. At thirty-four, I experienced for the first time his uncovetous touch—a hand that demanded nothing of my body, my personhood. Whenever I had watched my sister casually brush the hair away from my father's face, or walk arm in arm with him down the street, I felt I was watching something impossible and unattainable. And now I could access it too.

I was learning things about my father. I had forgotten he was a good cook. I had forgotten how funny he could be. I watched him tend to his plants on the terrace and saw in him a tenderness I had overlooked. I found myself tabulating all the signs of his aging. He was losing his hearing in one ear. I counted the dark spots that had formed on his arms, watched him as he changed shirts, as if I could fortify his rail-thin body with my gaze. I felt my heart unfolding, a novel hurt that

I finally understood as love deferred. One afternoon, I spontaneously patted his head while we were watching TV. I smiled to myself as I felt the temperature inside me fail to rise, as the cadence inside my chest chugged out an unremarkable ode, as my body told me there was finally nothing more to this story.

4.

My mother's disembodied voice came from the other room. She wanted a cigarette and she wanted to tell me that the local news anchor was wearing too much makeup. My mother was dying but didn't know it.

Two years after the trip to Europe, my father had been diagnosed with cancer. I told him I'd come look after him as he underwent radiation, and Gregory and I booked a flight to Paris. One month after that, shortly before we were scheduled to leave for Europe, my mother was diagnosed with acute myeloid leukemia and given two weeks to live. Gregory and I flew to New York and took the bus out to Amagansett.

We brought my mother to a hematologist to confirm the diagnosis. He was late in seeing us, and Gregory and I did our best to keep her distracted. I played her Rufus Wainwright's "Poses," and Gregory showed her funny animal videos. I paced the exam room and read strange Yahoo questions aloud to her (*How do you unbake a cake? Why does my arm shake and turn bright red when I'm eating dirt?*).

The doctor examined her and then spoke to us privately, without her in the room. He confirmed the diagnosis and told us to ask the receptionist for information about hospice care.

I approached the reception desk.

"I need the number for hospice," I said, my voice breaking.

"So she won't be coming to her appointment on August ninth?" she asked.

"No, she's dying. I need the number for hospice," I said.

"So you need to cancel the appointment?"

"I guess, yeah."

The receptionist wrote a number on a piece of paper and I folded it and refolded it before putting it in my pocket. On the way back home, my mother lay across the backseat with her head in my lap. In a small voice, she asked if she could hold my hand. I felt fear and awe at this gentleness. I opened my hand to receive hers. Her hand felt like silverware wrapped in a warm silk napkin, her bones slippery under her thin, hot skin.

"Am I squeezing you too hard?" she asked.

"You can squeeze me as hard as you want," I said.

I turned my face toward the window and felt the feelings crowd my throat until it throbbed, tears bottlenecking behind my eyeballs. I could not cry right now, in front of my mother. Gregory, who was driving, snaked his left hand between the door and the seat to hold my free hand.

Rufus Wainwright's "Poses" played again.

"Now who is this?" my mother asked, though I'd answered the same question just before.

"Rufus Wainwright," I said.

"He's sort of fabulous, isn't he?" she'd say.

There was a pause and we listened to the song.

"Now what does he look like?" she asked.

I pulled up a photo of him as a young man, as he was when he'd recorded the album.

"Hideous brooch," she said.

We arrived home and while my mother slept, I broke the news to my aunt and uncle and the two caregivers. When she woke up, I was relieved to hear her ask for a cigarette, but she didn't want to eat. I tried to tempt her with potato chips, bacon, Chinese food. All her favorites. Finally I bought six pints of fancy ice cream at the farmer's market. I stood over her bed and spooned ice cream into her mouth, reading aloud the copy on the back of the container that described how the Earl Grey ice cream was made.

Gregory came in to give her the pills she had been taking for years.

"What are these?" she asked.

"They're the medication to turn you into a mermaid," he said.

"Again?" she quipped.

I lay in bed next to her and showed her the photograph my editor had sent me of the book jacket. I'd finished my book months earlier and had sold it to a publisher. I had only told a handful of people. I told my mother the good news over and over. She was in ecstatic disbelief every time. I angled my iPad toward her and zoomed in on the book jacket.

"Fabulous," she said.

I told her about my impostor syndrome, about my fears for the future.

"I'm so scared," I said.

"Don't be scared."

"Why not?"

"Because what's the point?"

I realized I would not only miss my mother, I would miss Jennifer Bartlett. All I'd ever wanted was to sit with the great artist and brilliant thinker and discuss my work, but that was no longer who she was. I would not be her peer, but I could be the daughter whose hand she wanted to hold.

A few days later, hospice came to have me sign paperwork and give us the medications my mother would need. They presented me with a box of morphine and a box of lorazepam, and syringes to squirt the medications under her tongue. They gave me a pamphlet that described exactly what dying would look and sound like. I slipped it into a folder without looking at it.

I had ordered her a hospital bed and we moved her into the living room while the bed was being set up. She moaned and yelled. To distract her I googled Marlon Brando photos on my phone and showed her the one with the most bulging biceps. Every so often I'd put the photo in front of her face and she'd stop moaning.

"He's fabulous," she'd say.

"What do you like about him?" I'd ask.

"Everything," she'd say.

Soon she'd begin to moan again.

"Why am I sitting here?" she'd ask.

"Want to see a photo of Marlon Brando?"

"Sure," she'd say, her voice weak.

I'd show her the picture on my phone.

"Oh, he's fabulous," she'd say, her voice stronger.

"What do you like about him?"

"His lips. His hair. His eyes. His neck."

It went on like this until the bed was finished.

We moved her back into her room, and I sat next to her, writing as she dozed.

"What are you doing?" she asked.

"I'm writing," I said.

"Oh, good."

My aunt Julie arrived later that day. I was in my mother's room reading *David Copperfield* aloud to her. I left the room so they could be alone. I heard them laughing. My mother had a good day, asking for cigarettes, listening to music, drinking a smoothie, laughing. That night, things turned quickly. She moaned and asked what was wrong with her.

"You have a fever," I told her.

I stood to re-wet the compress I was holding to her forehead.

"Don't leave," she said.

I lay down next to her.

I wanted to hold her, to take her in my arms and squeeze her tightly. But I didn't move.

"Do you want to hold my hand?" I asked.

"Yes," she said.

I held her hand.

I couldn't help myself. "I love you very much," I said.

She scrunched up her face and in a voice gravelly with contempt said, "Why?"

I didn't know what to say. I had thought I could sneak in, get at the soft place, but it was still bulwarked.

She squirmed in the bed.

"Is there somewhere I can go?" she asked.

I could sense her panic.

"Do you want to go to the beach?" I asked.

"Yes," she said, her eyes closed.

"Do you want to go swimming in the ocean?"

She had always loved the ocean.

"Yes," she said.

"Is the water calm or wavy?"

"Calm," she responded.

"Is it dark blue or can you see to the bottom?"

"I can see to the bottom."

I asked her how far out she was going to swim.

"As far as I can go," she said.

"Do you want someone to swim with you?"

"No," she said.

"You like being alone, don't you?" I said.

"Yes."

"Are you going to swim back to shore?"

"No," she said.

"What are you going to do out there alone in the ocean?"

"Stay there and have a really nice time," she said.

Two days later she died.

AFTER THE HOSPICE NURSE ARRIVED and made the pronouncement, my aunt and I washed my mother's body. We put her in a hot-pink Shamask dress, and I doused her in the requisite high dose of Fracas perfume. I lifted her cooling wrist to my nose and smelled the fragrance on her skin one last time.

The weather forecast that day had been for an isolated tornado, which was the best description of Jennifer Bartlett I'd ever heard. The meteorological isolated tornado never happened, I could only assume because the departure of my mother, my very own isolated tornado, left no air for it.

All day the next day, I kept thinking I heard my mother calling me. I kept hearing "Alice" from the other room. Or maybe it was "Alice!" Or maybe it was "Alice?"

A disembodied voice that was now only in my head.

A week later, we spread her ashes in the ocean. I chartered a sailboat and my aunt, uncle, twin cousins, Gregory, and I boarded the water taxi to bring us to *The Starlight*. The weather was gray and rainy, but the captain and crew were kind and we shared our food with them. When we reached a nature preserve, we dropped anchor. Miles Davis's *Sketches of Spain* played through a Bluetooth speaker as we poured a bottle of white wine into the sea. The moment the booze hit the water, the clouds split open, the gaudy guts of a shamelessly showy sunset spilling across the horizon. A thick, golden light spread over our faces, which were all turned toward the sun's extravagant sinking. It looked exactly like an endless, excessive oil painting. It looked, in its extreme, bragging beauty, almost insolent. I recognized it. Gregory, tears and light in his eyes, said: "Jennifer looks good up there." We laughed. I stripped down to my swimsuit and I lowered myself into the Atlantic. I swam out, holding my mother's ashes aloft. We were as far out as we could go. I didn't want to leave her, but she needed to be alone.

Acknowledgments

Thank you to Vincent Katz and Bob Holman, whose temperatures rose from the long-form fever dream this book originally was and who believed in its communicability. Thank you to Jan Hashey, Peter Schlesinger, and Eric Boman, who were, one after the other, the critical components in the Rube Goldberg machine that slingshotted this book from that land of dreams and sickness into reality. Thank you to David Plante for your early guidance and enthusiasm. Thank you to Jane Rosenman for the gift of "warm and direct" and of chronology. Thank you to Julian Lethbridge for your support and friendship. Thank you to my chosen family, who have stuck with me through everything written here and more: Leah Aron, Oliver Barry, Kate Biggart, Jacob Bills, Erica Blinn, Bracket the Cat, Nancy Brooks Brody, Paula Cooper, Madison Cox, Jessica Craig-Martin, Thelma Denyer, Jamie Diamond, Amelia Edelman, Sophie Ellsberg, Caitlin Evanson, Ilian Georgiev, Daisy Holman, Trinity James, Adèle Jancovici, Molly Josephs, Effie Kammer, Joan LiPuma, Jessica Losch, Julie Manheimer, Ricky Manne, Julián Mesri, Kristine Michelsen-Correa, Rachel Eve Moulton, J.P. Nocera, Gavin O'Neill, Jessica Pearson, Eduard Riddle, Ivy Shapiro, Kevin

Smith, Amanda Stone, Anna Della Subin, Tiffany Taalman, Aaron Lee Tasjan, and Emily West.

Thank you to Nicole Dewey, Cindy Spiegel, Andy Tan-Delli Cicchi, Nora Tomas, Liza Wachter, and Alexis Hurley.

Thank you to Strick & Williams for the impossibly perfect cover.

Thank you to Kimberly Witherspoon and Maria Whelan at Inkwell Management for seeing what you saw and seeing it through. I adore you both.

Thank you to my publisher, Spiegel & Grau, for giving me a professional and creative home.

Thank you to my editor and friend, Julie Grau. You put my life between two glossy covers and my dream into my hands. To steal your words (after you've made mine so much better): Some people just feel necessary.

Thank you to Colombe Pringle for your steadfast care of the Carrières.

Thank you to my in-laws, Gary and Patricia Lattimer, for defying every in-law cliché and for believing in me and offering so much support.

Thank you to Julie, Takaaki, Max, and Julia Matsumoto for being the family I would also choose and for all the laughter.

Thank you to my sister, Elena Carrière, for your open mind and open heart.

Thank you to Eileen Denys Maynard, "Nanny," for your love, sacrifice, and diligent note-taking.

Thank you to my mother and father. Thank you for everything you did right and everything you did wrong.

And finally, thank you to Gregory Lattimer, who healed me and who knew all along.

Reading Group Guide

1. As the daughter of conceptual artist Jennifer Bartlett and European actor Mathieu Carrière, Alice is raised in a glamorous environment of fame, privilege, and upper-class luxury. But there are other aspects to her upbringing—loneliness, danger, negligence. How did this background shape Alice as a person? Consider other examples of children of celebrity parents. To what extent are these trappings of fame and wealth a blessing for them? And in what ways might they be a curse?

2. Alice spends her childhood at 134 Charles Street, a sprawling multifloor mansion in New York City's West Village, with bespoke furnishings and a constantly revolving carousel of assistants, celebrities, and parties. Alice describes growing up in this "irresistible nexus of strangeness, luxury, and niche functionality" as if she were living "inside [her] mother's mind." In what ways is 134 Charles Street a metaphor for Alice's relationship with her mother? How did your own childhood home reflect the personalities or psychologies of your parents?

3. Alice's mother, Jennifer, recalls horrific incidents of Satanic ritual abuse that took place during her childhood—memories that traumatized her and influenced her work. Eventually, Alice learns that these incidents may never have occurred, that these "recovered memories" may have been a product of a vogue in psychotherapy in the 1980s, now known as the Satanic Panic. Real or unreal, how do the stories and mythology around Jennifer's recovered memories affect Alice? Discuss the similarities and differences between both of their experiences in therapy, and the relationship between trauma, truth, and self-mythology.

4. Growing up, Alice spends almost all her time with Nanny, the woman her parents hire to take care of her. "Nanny was family but she was also not family," Alice writes. "To me, she was a mother, but one who could be fired and disappear at any moment." Over time, Nanny becomes an integral fixture of her world, a protector and a constant parental presence, more than Alice's own parents were. Are there people in your life that you consider family, even if they are not related to you by blood? How do you view the durability and permanence of such relationships?

5. Alice's father, Mathieu, champions an anarchic theory of desire, informed by the French philosopher Gilles Deleuze, that attempts to dissolve certain boundaries and social norms. His relationship with Alice frequently veers into uncomfortable territory—choreographing a nude, horseback photoshoot for his teenage daughter; leaving her in dangerous situations with older men; asking her, as a child, to administer his injections or lick his tears. How did you respond to him as a character? Did your view of him change when you learned about his own childhood? And by the end of the memoir, when Alice confronted her father, did his response to her accusations force a reconsideration? Do you think Alice is right to forgive him?

6. Alice's doctors prescribe a slew of medications that warp her sense of reality and ultimately trigger a harrowing psychotic episode. Jennifer doesn't question the doctors and the growing roster of pills that Alice takes every day, even when it brings about radical and terrifying changes in her daughter's behavior and appearance. We also learn that Jennifer's own psychiatrist was notorious for conducting unethical human experiments on her patients (as depicted in the documentary *Three Identical Strangers*). What does this book bring to your view of—and experiences with—what Alice calls the "American psychiatric complex"?

7. The book has many vivid sensory descriptions of Alice's dissociation, as she drifts away from herself, her body, and her mind. She describes feeling her "I" slipping through her fingers like a "heavy, slick rope"; feeling as if "each moment was the first moment in the history of the universe, when things were just taking shape, though never forming something solid"; holding a cup of water and feeling like "there was nothing separating the water from me"; looking in the mirror and being unable to "unlock or lock into place that it was me, my face." Which descriptions or moments struck you most powerfully, and why? What do you understand about the visceral experience of dissociation and how it relates to self-harm?

8. Moving between centers and therapists in Massachusetts, Florida, New York, and elsewhere, Alice encounters a variety of approaches to treatment and therapy. Which of these were most effective and ineffective? By the end of the book, Alice is highly critical of the antagonistic process of the trauma group, which positions her childhood as the "story of the molested girl who had overcome her monster." What are the shortcomings Alice sees in this model, and do you agree or disagree with her assessment?

For Alice, the act of writing becomes a salve against dissociative spirals. She realizes, "Words were the only thing that tethered me to some splinter of myself." How does the act of writing help Alice? Do you have a regular writing practice, and if so, how does it help you? There is a variety of source material quoted in the memoir— journals, letters, case reports, ephemera. What did you think about the interplay between these original texts and Alice's own writing? How do these other writings factor into the stories we tell about ourselves—and into Alice's understanding of herself, both at the time and later, when she gained perspective? What does it mean for Alice's story, finally, to belong wholly to herself?

10. In an interview, Alice says that she thinks of *Everything/Nothing/Someone* as a love story. How do you understand this book as a love story? Does the trajectory of Alice and Gregory's relationship fit (or resist) the tropes of other love stories you've read? What other kinds of love do you see in the book?

11. Toward the end of the book, Alice and her parents have come almost full circle: Alice takes care of her mother after she is diagnosed with dementia, and confronts her father for his transgressions. What was the turning point in both of these relationships? Do you think they were able to achieve reconciliation, or at least resolution, by the book's conclusion? Why or why not?

12. Discuss the title and how it relates to Alice's experiences in each section. What is Alice's journey from "everything" to "nothing"? How does she finally become "someone"?

About the Author

Alice Carrière is a graduate of Columbia University. Her work has appeared in the *New York Times*, in *New York* magazine, and on Oprah Daily. She lives in Nashville, Tennessee, and Amagansett, New York. This is her first book.